NOVELIST TO A GENERATION

NOVELIST TO A GENERATION:
THE LIFE AND THOUGHT OF WINSTON CHURCHILL

by

Robert W. Schneider

Bowling Green University Popular Press
Bowling Green, Ohio 43403

Cover design by Gregg Swope.

For

Anne

Rick

Ron

and

Lynne

CONTENTS

Foreword

I would like to express my appreciation for financial assistance to the College of Wooster for a summer grant, to the American Philosophical Society for two research grants, and to Northern Illinois University for several grants from the Deans' Fund as well as a summer research grant.

The manuscript for this book was read and criticized by my colleagues Carl Parrini, Alfred Young, and my former colleague Paul Carter of the University of Arizona. Portions of the manuscript dealing with New Hampshire politics were read by Richard Sewell of the University of Wisconsin. Robert Gale of the University of Pittsburgh and the late Ray Ginger both helped me reduce a manuscript of unmanageable length to publishable size, and David Noble of the University of Minnesota was helpful to me in many ways. Creighton Churchill, Mrs. Mabel Butler, and Dr. Allan Butler were more than helpful in supplying personal details that only members of the immediate family could provide. Finally, I want to acknowledge the constant assistance and unwavering support of Anne S. Schneider who has been an indispensible part of this project from beginning to end.

The following have kindly given permission to quote from material in their possession or over which they control the literary rights:

Creighton Churchill and Mrs. Allan Butler for all of Churchill's letters, manuscripts, notebooks, and other unpublished material.

Houghton Library, Harvard University for Churchill letters.

Yale University Library for Churchill letters.

New Hampshire Historical Society for Senator Chandler letters.

Hope Harding Davis Kehrig for Richard Harding Davis letters.

Franklin Hollis for Henry Hollis letters.

Franklin Delano Roosevelt Library for Roosevelt-Churchill letters.

Mrs. Isabel Garland Lord and the University of Southern California Library for Garland-Churchill correspondence.

C. W. Barrett and the University of Virginia Library for Churchill letters.

Robert P. Bass and Baker Library, Dartmouth College for Robert Bass letters.

Jonathan Daniels for Josephus Daniels letters.

Norris Darrell for Learned Hand letter.

Upton Sinclair and Lilly Library, University of Indiana for Sinclair-Churchill correspondence.

American Academy of Arts and Letters for Churchill letter.

Albert Shaw, Jr. and the New York Public Library for Shaw-Churchill correspondence.

The Macmillan Company and the New York Public Library for Macmillan records and Churchill-Brett correspondence.

Warren I. Titus, "Winston Churchill, American: A Critical Biography."

Collins-Knowlton-Wing, Inc., Ernest Poole, THE GREAT WHITE HILLS OF NEW HAMPSHIRE.

Upton Sinclair, MONEY WRITES.

John Chamberlain, FAREWELL TO REFORM.

Oxford University Press, Morris E. Speare, THE POLITICAL NOVEL.

The SATURDAY REVIEW and Upton Sinclair, "The American Churchill."

Dorrance and Company, Winston Churchill, THE UNCHARTED WAY.

Charles Scribner's Sons, Winston S. Churchill, MY EARLY YEARS, A ROVING COMMISSION.

Pattee Library, Pennsylvania State University, Fred Lewis Pattee, PENN STATE YANKEE.

Ginn and Company, Percy H. Boynton, LITERATURE AND AMERICAN LIFE.

Frederic B. Irvin, "The Didacticism of Winston Churchill."

Dodd, Mead and Company, Leon B. Richardson, WILLIAM E. CHANDLER: REPUBLICAN.

Appleton-Century-Crofts, Fred Lewis Pattee, THE NEW AMERICAN LITERATURE, 1890-1930.

Boston Public Library, Lloyd W. Griffin, "Winston Churchill: American Novelist," MORE BOOKS.

Meredith Press, Elliott Roosevelt, ed., FDR HIS PERSONAL LETTERS.

Holt, Rinehart and Winston, Frederic Taber Cooper, SOME AMERICAN STORY TELLERS.

MISSOURI HISTORICAL REVIEW, J. Breckenridge Ellis, "Missourians Abroad No. 11: Winston Churchill."

THE YALE REVIEW, Winston Churchill, "An Uncharted Way."

Scholastic Magazines, Inc., Henry Steele Commager, "Creating a New Nation: Based on THE CROSSING," SENIOR SCHOLASTIC.

Yale University Press, Henry Steele Commager, THE AMERICAN MIND.

Preface:
Spring, 1940

The bombs fell in mounting numbers on an embattled England as she faced the greatest test in her long history. But the island empire had found a war leader who would inspire a sustained effort to resist the formidable power of the Third Reich. That man was Winston Churchill. During the same months, on the other side of the Atlantic, a religious philosopher was putting the final touches on a treatise espousing a doctrine of noncontention. The book, entitled *The Uncharted Way*, was a product of twenty years of thought and reflection. The author of this book had also been christened with the name Winston Churchill. In the 1930's, while the nations of Europe blundered their way toward world holocaust, this man had worked out an interpretation of the Hebrew prophets and of Jesus and Paul which proclaimed that the religion called Christianity had grossly misinterpreted the ideas of the leaders of the Judeo-Christian tradition.

News of the book's publication and review headlines told the public about "The Two Winston Churchills," or "America's Winston Churchill," while the Manchester *Guardian* chuckled that they had known it all the time. Readers were informed that a quarter century earlier the American Churchill was considerably more eminent than his British namesake. He had written ten popular novels; as an enthusiastic supporter of Theodore Roosevelt he had run as the Progressive Party's candidate for Governor of New Hampshire; and for three years his palatial house had served as Woodrow Wilson's summer White House.

Those whose memories were jogged by these facts remained puzzled. The Winston Churchill of a quarter century before had attacked the trusts, the political bosses, and orthodox Christianity. He had thundered loudly that the individual who would find personal fulfillment must submerge himself in service to society and he confidently proclaimed that World War I would bring about the socialized state and eternal peace. At the same time he had lived the life of a socially respectable young aristocrat, dined with the wealthy and politically powerful, and maintained his family in luxurious quarters. Yet in 1940, he lived in a modest way, caring little or nothing for the world, shunning society, and ignoring political controversy.

That he no longer occupied a position of power and influence did not bother him at all. Those who met him at a time when Europe was tearing itself apart saw a man at peace with himself and with the world. A Boston reporter who went to interview him found the author seated along the main street of a small New Hampshire town doing a water color sketch, constantly filling and lighting, refilling and relighting a pipe which he never seemed to smoke. Churchill had made the interview contingent upon two conditions — the reporter must read *The Uncharted Way*, and he must promise not to talk about the British Prime Minister. The reporter, who had some misgivings about interviewing the author of a book on religious philosophy, found Churchill "a thoroughly delightful and jolly person when he isn't discussing philosophy — and even when he does there is a friendly twinkle in his brown eyes."[1]

The Boston journalist also discovered that Churchill accepted the mass horror of World War II as he did all human tribulations. "Wars," he declared, "solve nothing, but if one party doesn't realize that then the other party, in self-defense, must resort to war." Contrary to Churchill's earlier pronouncements that World War I would witness the advent of international cooperation, he told the reporter that while World War II must be fought

as a matter of duty, its termination "will bring no final solution —
unless the idea that wars solve nothing is instilled in the minds of
all people."

How did this pleasant, peaceable man, who faced the world
with humor, courage, and resignation, evolve from the active,
sometimes brash young writer who had flashed into the forefront
of American letters at the turn of the century? Certainly those
who were familiar with Churchill as the most popular novelist
of the Progressive generation would not have recognized the
man whom the Boston reporter interviewed in 1940. Nor would
they have understood his retirement from active involvement
with politics and literature, at the height of his popularity, over
twenty years before. Yet there are few ideas in *The Uncharted
Way* which were not nascent in the novels, and his retirement
was a logical outcome of changes in his outlook on life that
began as early as 1910.

When I began to study Churchill's writings several years
ago, I saw him as a counterbalance to the more critically ac-
claimed but less popular novelist such as Stephen Crane, Frank
Norris, and Theodore Dreiser. The latter group constituted the
"Big Three" of the Progressive era in the minds of the more
sophisticated, less optimistic critics of the post-Versailles world.
Crane, Norris, and Dreiser were the creative artists, I suggested,
the men who correctly interpreted the frustrations and shattered
dreams of a people raised to believe that the world was getting
perpetually better. Churchill, in contrast, was hopelessly mired
down in the traditional view of life as a morality play in which
the leaders and heroes triumphed over the forces of evil and, by
virtue of their individual goodness and leadership abilities, saved
the Republic.

When I worked on Churchill's novels and other writings,
however, I discovered that after about 1910, the novelist had
changed his outlook. No longer was he writing as a popularizer
of romantic history designed to entertain overstuffed matrons
who wanted to hear about the daring do of dashing heroes and
dazzling heroines; instead he would be a hero himself. Along
with Washington, Lincoln, and his own fictional heroes, he would
enter into the political arena and defeat those who would enslave
the people. Through his popularity as a story teller and his com-

mitment to "Progressive" politics, he would lead the people out of bondage to the mistaken institutions and traditions of the past and into the bright new world of a scientifically sanctioned co-operative commonwealth where human beings realized that their salvation as individuals was achieved through service to humanity. Individualism and socialism (in the true scientific form) were, he contended, not only compatible but one and the same thing.

Historians have contended that it was the shattering of this optimistic dream by the war and the botched peace that destroyed the faith of many Progressives. If Churchill was to continue to be the popularizer of middle class intellectual liberalism in the post-Versailles world that I felt he had been in 1916, he too should have followed the path to disillusionment paved by his intellectual mentors in the social sciences. I decided to document this logical pattern by writing a biography of the man whom I viewed as the maincurrent within the mainstream of American thought.

As I began to dig into the material for the biography, much of it consisting of documents that had never been examined before, I was reluctantly forced to alter my plan. Churchill was indeed a good example of the changes in respectable middle class thought until about 1910, and he was a prime choice to portray the rapid evolution of intellectual Progressivism until the end of World War I. After that, however, my model disintegrated. He simply did not quit publishing novels because he was disillusioned by the prospects of social reform or because his brand of fiction went out of style. His retirement was the result of personal convictions that had evolved slowly, painfully, and (sometimes) aimlessly during the preceding two decades. It was Churchill's own perception of his role in history that finally provided the key to understanding the various dramatic changes in his life. The following pages will attempt to demonstrate this interpretation of Churchill's life.

PART I THE DEVELOPMENT OF A POPULAR NOVELIST

CHAPTER I

From St. Louis to Annapolis

One of the most important influences upon Churchill's life style was his enduring interest in the history of his family. This arose, in part, from his love of history and proved invaluable to him when he was writing historical novels. In addition to scholarly material on the historical background of the period in which the stories took place, he could call upon family letters and diaries, as well as family legends and traditions, to add the small detail here and there which brought the tales to life.

Winston's earliest American ancestor was John Churchill, who first appears on the records of Plymouth Colony in 1643.[1] The Churchills continued to live in Massachusetts until about 1759, when John's great-grandson Thomas moved his large family to Newmarket Plains, New Hampshire. It was James Creighton Churchill (Thomas' grandson and Winston's great-grandfather) who made the Churchill name a prominent one in New England. Born in Newmarket in 1787, he became a ship builder in Portland, Maine, until the War of 1812, when he served in the United States Infantry. After the war James returned to Portland and his former occupation, but within a few years he became interested in the West Indies. With several associates, he bought some sugar plantations in Cuba and established a trading firm, which soon was

1

among the most prominent in Portland. Before his death in 1865, he was also associated with a firm that manufactured railroad locomotives and cars, and with the Casco Iron Works, at the same time maintaining an extensive insurance business.

In addition to his business activities, James Creighton Churchill was also actively involved in politics. He became known as "the star of the East" when he cast the only New England electoral vote for Jackson in 1828. A few years later he changed his political affiliation and conducted an unsuccessful campaign as a Whig candidate for Congress. In 1844 he was elected Mayor of Portland. It seems likely that the image of James Creighton Churchill loomed large in the mind of his great-grandson. A successful businessman, a respected politician, a man who stood firm for what he believed and won the respect of his city – he represented all the things young Winston was taught to admire.

James' son Edwin was associated with his father's firm of Churchill and Carter, and for a number of years lived in Cuba. When he returned to Portland, Edwin became head of the new firm of E. Churchill and Company. According to James Spaulding (a Portland doctor who knew the family well), Edwin's family lived in a fine three story brick house, kept a pair of good horses, "lived in style and entertained widely. People thought them extravagant."[2]

This taste for the good life was passed on to his youngest child, Edward Spaulding Churchill, Winston's father. Little is known about Edward's adult years, but he appears to have been tenuously connected with the family firm as its New York representative. Tradition has it that he was a charming young man although spoiled, allergic to work, and a heavy drinker.

His good looks and engaging manner did win the heart of Emma Bell Blaine of St. Louis, and they were married in January of 1871. Her American ancestry also extended back to the early colonial period. In his maternal line Winston was descended from New Amsterdam Dutch settlers through the Van Hornes and DeWitts, and through the Dwight family from the great theologian, Jonathan Edwards. In this maternal ancestral line the New England branch crossed with settlers who migrated from Virginia to Kentucky when his great-grandmother, Margaret Van Horne Dwight (a niece of Yale President Timothy Dwight), journeyed to Ohio in 1810 for a visit and married William Bell of Pittsburgh.[3] Their daughter, Margaret DeWitt Bell, married John Logan Blaine whose family had participated in the emigration from Virginia to Kentucky. John Logan Blaine (Churchill's grandfather) went to St. Louis from Kentucky about 1845 and engaged in business as a commission merchant. In the middle 1850's he was a bagging and rope manufacturer and carried on his business until the start of the Civil War. When the secession movement in Missouri failed, he left his family and went to Texas, where he worked for the Southern cause until his death in 1865. According to a family friend, John Blaine had been a Kentucky planter and slave owner before the move to St. Louis, and was the prototype for the distinguished Colonel Comyn Carvel in Churchill's novel, *The Crisis.*[4]

Soon after Edward Churchill married, his uncle (James Morrell Churchill) started to build the young couple a house in Portland, but it was a house they would never occupy. In order that her own doctors could deliver her first child, Mrs. Churchill decided to return to St. Louis. She died there two weeks after her son was born on November 10, 1871.[5] The infant was left in the care of Emma's mother until her death two years later. Winston was then taken in by James Braiding Gazzam and his wife Louisa Blaine Gazzam, Emma's half sister. From that time on the Gazzam house at 2810 Pine Street became Winston's home.

Until recently little was known of Churchill's childhood. He was interviewed hundreds of times during the years that he was a public figure but little was ever printed about his childhood or his family life. In 1965, however, two autobiographical manuscripts were discovered that deal at some length with his early years. One of these, the Gideon manuscript, he wrote in 1924; the other, the Jonathan manuscript, was written about 1932. Of course it is impossible for a man of fifty or sixty to remember every detail of his childhood, but these manuscripts do reveal those things that remained with him, and they supplement or substantiate the other materials. They clearly demonstrate the great influence that his upbringing had on his entire life and the extent to which he relied on his own experiences in writing certain of his novels. The early years in the lives of Honora Leffingwell in *A Modern Chronicle* and Hugh Paret in *A Far Country*, for example, are both fictionalized accounts of Churchill's own child-hood. The attitudes and problems of both Honora and Hugh are identical to those that Churchill attributes to himself in both manuscripts.

The most complete account of the Gazzams is that presented in the characters of Uncle Tom and Aunt Mary Leffingwell in *A Modern Chronicle*, but the fictionalized version is substantiated by the manuscripts. The Gazzam family lived in what might be called genteel poverty, reduced in worldly possessions but still held in high regard by their friends and neighbors. Churchill describes his uncle as having "the attributes of a saint, utterly unworldly and uncomplaining. Helpless relatives were thrust on him, and often he did not know what way to turn, yet his patience and kindness were unfailing."[6] In *A Modern Chronicle*, he pictures Uncle Tom as about forty-eight at the time Honora, his niece, came to live with them. Constitutionally incapable of par-ticipating in the rat race of modern business, Uncle Tom "lived enveloped in a peace which has since struck wonder to Honora's soul."[7]

Mrs. Gazzam was the strongest influence in forming Church-ill's personality. He portrays her in *A Modern Chronicle*, as a kindly, self-sacrificing woman who was incapable of under-standing her imaginative young charge. She is described as a Puritan of Southern ancestry, a woman almost totally without personal vanity. She thought of the world as a place of trial and sorrow, and believed that the highest form of greatness was to accept life's burdens cheerfully. She tried very hard to implant these ideas of self-sacrifice and hard work in young Churchill. Feeling that his guardians' love for him was constant and perfect, Winston was troubled that his own emotions were not so. "Gideon loved his father and mother at times, but often, as he grew older, he was indifferent to them, and occasionally he hated them."[8] He further claimed that in later years he suffered from a certain incapacity for deep, emotional love, a situation which he says arose from the fact that "the springs of emotion were choked in childhood, all unwittingly, by those who tried to give him all they had."

All of the common Victorian ideas of the day were drummed into the head of the young boy. The Gazzams "wanted him to study and to gain character for his own sake, because they could not bear to think of him growing up to be a worthless, selfish, and perhaps unscrupulous man." They also instilled in him a fear of failure that was to have a marked influence on his life.

> The prospect of growing up a nobody, an unsuccessful man whom nobody thought much of, alarmed him. An unsuccessful man meant a poor man. Now his mother was far from a snob; her ambition was not that he should make a large fortune. She wanted to give him culture, and he inevitably connected culture with work; and work was doing something you didn't want to do, in order to be somebody you didn't want to be.[9]

Life meant hard work, doing a lot of things one did not want to do, self-sacrifice, personal integrity, and self-control. And all of this seems to have been taught in an absolute way; either one was a good man or one was not. There was no margin for error, or even for discussion.

It was this absolute standard that gave Churchill a lifelong feeling of guilt and inadequacy. Honora lied to Aunt Mary once, and her uncle looked at her in such a way that she never forgot it. "The anger of such a man had indeed some element in it of the divine; terrible, not in volume, but in righteous intensity. And when it had passed there was no occasion for future warning. The memory of it lingered."[10] The Gideon manuscript contains several similar instances of childhood misconduct — spending streetcar ticket money for candy or playing sick to escape going to school — and the same disproportionately deep guilt feelings. This tendency to exaggerate his transgressions out of all proportion tortured Churchill throughout his lifetime. As a child and an adult he was convinced that those people who had the admiration and respect of the world were perfect; he could not believe that the world, or the friends whose affection he so desired, would forgive him for falling off a pedestal that in reality did not exist. This conviction is one of the most important clues to understanding Churchill's private life.

In retrospect, Churchill's childhood seemed to him a series of failures. This was in part a conflict between his romantic nature and the Gazzams' efforts to prepare him for life. He liked to plan houses and ships, using tools to build models of them.

This was fine. At some sacrifice his aunt and uncle bought him a tool box and sent him to a carpentry class, but their purpose was not his. They thought that learning to use his hands would make him a better professional or business man; it would equip him for life. His purpose was the joy of creating something that had thrilled him when he saw it in his own imagination. He tried to make a four-foot ship, constructed along the lines of a real ship. He spent weeks studying ship construction and drawing designs to scale. In the process he learned a lot about ship-building, but the end product would not materialize. Time and again he showed the unfinished product to others, tried to give them some notion of the perfect shape it took on in his mind, but he could not get them to share his vision. The ship was never built.[11]

Naturally it was young Winston's father whom the Gazzams viewed as a perfect example of the idle dreamer they feared Winston might become. While Churchill painted an accurate picture of his own childhood in the life of Honora Leffingwell, there is one very important difference. Honora grew up thinking her father had been a prince among men and that it was only his accidental death that separated her from the world of beauty, wealth, and adventure she longed to inhabit. Churchill had no such illusions about his own father. In the Gideon manuscript he said:

> There were worthless persons in the family connection. There was Cousin James, who believed it incumbent upon the world to support him as a gentleman; who was always seeking short cuts to wealth, who demanded to live in luxury and self gratification. One could not respect him. Such an example, when Gideon heard him talked about, often struck the chill of fear to Gideon's heart.[12]

There can be little doubt that Cousin James was his own father. Elsewhere Churchill wrote about a highly respectable and respected family with whom he had associated from early youth and of his relationship with them.

> He was of their kind, and he wasn't. He had known them from infancy, and we think now that they had suspected him from infancy. As a boy he had been good to look at, perhaps, and charming in a degree, but facile and not dependable. His ancestry was much the same as theirs, but there were streaks in

it at which they looked askance, though they never
said so to him. They must have thought that he inherited these streaks.[13]

People frequently commented that Winston had the same
good looks and personal charm that his father possessed. How
often in those early years must friends and relatives have reminded
him of that fact? And the obvious corollary to this inheritance of
looks and charm was that Winston also inherited what the good
people of St. Louis considered his father's less desirable characteristics. In *A Modern Chronicle*, Aunt Mary becomes worried
about Honora's refusal to accept the stolid outlook of the older
woman, and remarks to her husband, "I'm afraid it's inheritance,
Tom. And if so, it ought to be counteracted. We've seen other
signs of it."[14] It would be surprising indeed if young Winston
escaped overhearing similar comments.

These childhood experiences probably explain the rather
peculiar fact that when he became famous Churchill never
mentioned in public interviews that his father was alive. Most
biographical accounts, in interviews and elsewhere, simply state
that his mother died shortly after his birth and that he was
raised by his aunt and uncle. The actual contact between Winston
and his father was in fact minimal. As far as can be ascertained
from the documents they did not see each other from the time
Mrs. Churchill died until Winston was almost twelve years old.
Although the elder Churchill apparently contributed nothing to
his son's support, the Gazzams kept Edward informed about
Winston and made the boy write letters to him.[15] There is no
indication that Edward answered any of his son's letters until
the spring of 1883 when he wrote to tell Winston that he had
remarried and that it had been arranged for the boy to spend his
summer vacation with Edward and his new bride.

That summer was the first time Winston had been away from
his St. Louis home, but after an initial bout with homesickness,
Winston adjusted to the situation and had a good time. This
was the first time in his life that he had lived in a household
with other children of his own age (Edward's second wife apparently had four children when he married her). The Gazzams
had a son of their own named Joe, and the two boys seem to
have been fond of each other, but Joe was about ten years older

than Winston and they were not particularly close during their childhood years.

The visit did bring out some fatherly concern in Edward, at least briefly. The following summer he wrote Mrs. Gazzam that he feared Winston would come to feel closer to the Gazzams than to his own father and Mrs. Churchill. This, of course, had happened long before. He said that in allowing Winston to stay with them, "we have thought only of your feelings and the love and care that you have shown him."[16] This letter, and some of the others, suggest that Edward felt his son was not quite so manly as he should be, and that he was too sheltered. In the same letter Edward indicated his disappointment that Winston was not coming East again that summer and inquired whether his winter vacation was long enough for him to make the trip. It is difficult to say who decided that he would not spend a second summer with his father. Perhaps he did not want to. It was undoubtedly flattering to a sensitive twelve-year-old to have two groups vying for his affection, but it must also have been confusing and disturbing. Certainly the Gazzams did not want him exposed to his father's influence, and they were convinced that his father did not really want him. Whoever was responsible for the decision that Winston should not visit his father that summer, the break was clean. There is nothing to indicate that Churchill ever saw his father again.

According to Churchill's daughter, "His father was never mentioned in our family and we children thought him dead though we often saw his sisters, our great aunts."[17] Churchill's sense of family responsibility (which was very strong) would not, however, allow him totally to dismiss his father. From at least 1907 (and probably earlier) until Edward's death in 1919, Churchill sent him money through a lawyer, who handled all of the transactions. The letters imply that Edward was not to reveal the source of the money or to make any attempt to contact Churchill or his family.[18]

Since Churchill remained with the Gazzams in St. Louis after the summer of 1883, there are no letters and little other information about his next few years. His aunt and uncle did send him to Smith Academy, a local private school, beginning in 1879, and he graduated with honors in 1888. Some ten years later, when Churchill was first emerging as a prominent author, Principal Charles P. Curd recalled the boy's career at Smith Academy. Everyone, according to the principal, liked Winston because "he was such a polite and elegant little fellow." Every morning Winston left his house and met a group of girls (one of whom he would later marry), and walked them to school. James E. Yeatman, a famous St. Louis philanthropist, frequently joined them. Churchill had no particular fondness for books, Curd recalls, and while he liked athletics he did not take an active part in them. The boy's grades were good, and the principal began to notice his talent for literature, especially for Latin. Yeatman, on the other hand, was not impressed with Churchill's talents at the time. "Winston," the philanthropist contended, "was a bright boy, a good boy and a frank, manly little fellow." "He was not precocious and gave no sign of possessing the talent which he has developed since he grew up."[19] The evidence suggests that young Winston was a well-mannered boy, of above-average intelligence, who took life a bit more seriously than the average child. Certainly he showed few signs of having the drive, ambition, and ability that he would demonstrate in succeeding years.

The fact that Churchill went to a local private school is symbolic of the ambivalent position in which the gap between the Gazzam's traditional affiliations and their financial status placed him. It would not have been considered proper for him to attend public schools, but neither could he "go away" to school as many of his friends did. This was another circumstance that made the boy feel he was not quite as good as his friends and associates, and when his own children were born they would be enrolled in the best private schools on the day of their birth. The Gazzams gave him all they could, but it was not enough to satisfy a youth who saw the worldly possessions and advantages of the moneyed gentry and the newly rich around him.

The most serious gap between Churchill and his richer friends came after he had graduated from Smith Academy. His associates packed their bags in the fall and headed for Harvard and Yale — leaving him behind in St. Louis. This phase of his life was rarely mentioned in later years. Churchill made no real secret of the fact that he had not gone directly from the Academy to college, but he seldom discussed the intervening period and it was commonly assumed that his schooling was uninterrupted.[20] Yet it was a time of considerable importance, for it gave him his first taste of business life — and one taste was enough to last him a lifetime.

In later years Churchill wrote about this period of his life on two occasions — in fictionalized form in *A Far Country* (1915), and in the third-person autobiography of Gideon. The facts are fairly simple. Churchill had not been an enthusiastic student in school and had not seriously considered what he would do when he graduated. In addition the Gazzams simply could not afford to send him to college. They could, however, use their influence in St. Louis to get him started in the business world. The starting position was a modest one, as a clerk in a wholesale paper store, and from his first day to the last he hated it.

The life of Hugh Paret in *A Far Country* is closely patterned on Churchill's own feelings and experiences during these years. The question of college does not occur to Hugh until he is almost ready to graduate from the academy and he has not discussed it with his father, the final voice on such matters in the family.[21] Hugh was afraid to ask his father about what future was planned for him, but Mr. Paret's manner led Hugh to suspect

> that I had been judged and found wanting, and doomed to "business": Galley slavery, I deemed it, humdrum, prosaic, degrading! When I thought of it at night I experienced almost a frenzy of self-pity. My father couldn't intend to do that, just because my monthly reports hadn't always been what he thought they ought to be! Gene Hollister's were no better, if as good, and he was going to Princeton. Was I, Hugh Paret, to be denied the distinction of being a college man, the delights of university existence, cruelly separated and set apart from my friends whom I loved! Held up to the world and especially to Nancy Willett as good for nothing else! The thought was unbearable. Characteristically, I hoped against hope.[22]

Hugh thought of himself as a child of hope, and he determined to show everybody that he was as good as the rest of them; there is every reason to believe that this same youthful determination fired Churchill's ambitions.

Hugh's experiences and feelings as a clerk also were essentially those of his creator. He was torn between two worlds. He could not identify himself with the other clerks around him; yet when his friends returned from their colleges for the Christmas holidays he saw that he was no longer a part of their world either. Although Churchill himself went to work in a wholesale paper store (not a grocery business), his reactions were identical. The memories of those miserable days remained so vividly with him that he could describe his thoughts and feelings years later. In the Gideon manuscript he wrote:

> He thought himself better than the other clerks and the porter with whom he was obliged to associate. His friends, with whom he had been brought up, went off to college. He pictured them in a new and bright and larger world, with other fortunate boys, while he had to go to the store at eight every morning, into that detested business district, and wait on people whom he was really ashamed to wait on, and make out bills and lick stamps.[23]

Winston did his job, but had no desire to excel at it or to rise in the firm. The paper stock, he says, was a nightmare to him. He simply could not learn to tell one kind of paper from another because he had no interest in learning. He just wanted out. "Sometimes Gideon would sit down beside the grimy windows of the third floor wareroom, and wish, and wish and wish. How could he get away?"[24]

How indeed could one get to college without the encouragement and financial support of his family? Hugh Paret convinced his father that he was sincere in his desire by studying at night and, since Mr. Paret had the money, he sent his son to Harvard. The Gazzams did not have the money. Even if Churchill could have convinced them that he could succeed at Yale with his friend Arthur Shepley and the others, they could not have sent him. Harvard, Yale, and the other prestige schools were beyond reach, but there was one way to get to college and ingeniously Winston found it in the Naval Academy. His decision to go to Annapolis was made on the spur of the moment and on his own initiative. One Sunday at church he saw a boy who had been appointed to Annapolis. After the services he waited for the boy and discovered that he had had to give up his appointment to the Naval Academy because of poor health. The next day Winston called at the St. Louis office of the local Congressman, worked his way through the offices of various functionaries, and after a wait of several hours obtained an interview with Congressman F. G. Niedringhaus. His patience and youthful powers of persuasion were rewarded when the Congressman agreed on the spot to propose Winston for candidacy.[25]

There is no reason to suppose that Churchill's actions were anything more than the response of a bored but intelligent and resourceful young clerk who saw an opportunity to escape his overly protective environment and seek his fortune in the world beyond St. Louis. It is possible, of course, that he responded more quickly and eagerly because the opening was at the Naval Academy. He was descended from a seafaring family and the romance of the sea attracted him. He could remain loyal to the Gazzams and still regain a part of his family's tradition, a sense of belonging, by returning to the sea — not as a trader or businessman but as a naval officer. His continuing interest in ships, sailing, and navigation could also be put to practical use.

The Gazzams were unenthusiastic about his impetuous actions. "My uncle and aunt were skeptical when I went home and told them what I had done. I hadn't been a shining mark at school, as they well knew. Moreover, they had started me in business, and that was to have been my career."[26] But if he disappointed his family by throwing over his business opportunities and fleeing from St. Louis, they could rest assured that they had done their job. An orthodox upbringing, in a household that seemed to hold conventional behavior as the greatest good, had been deeply instilled in him. The young man who departed for Annapolis believed firmly in all the traditional middle class attitudes — self respect, independence, hard work, religiosity, and all the rest. These values and beliefs were to guide him — and to frustrate him — for the next thirty years.

In March of 1890 Congressman Niedringhaus wrote to Secretary of the Navy Benjamin F. Tracy, recommending Churchill for the vacancy that existed for his district.[27] Winston signed a form expressing his willingness to report to Annapolis on May 15 for an examination of his qualifications for appointment as a cadet, and the Gazzams gave their permission for him to sign up for the required eight years of service. After passing the physical he signed his official acceptance on May 27.

The boy from St. Louis seems to have attained instant popularity with his classmates, for he participated, usually as a leader, in many activities. The Gazzams sent him his homemade banjo, and he related, with some pride, that the other cadets made him bring it out every evening and play for them. And, although he had not been particularly active in sports before this, he became deeply involved with them at Annapolis. That first summer he rowed stroke in the class crew and when football season came he played center rush on the class team. All of this activity, on top of the required drills and workouts, gave the boys an appetite that navy food did not satisfy. Churchill mentions one occasion when eight of them, with Winston as captain, marched out to a farm where they ate four watermelons. On the way back they raided a cantaloupe patch, and finished off with two plates of ice cream for each man, a snack that "did not interfere with my supper in the least." His increase in appetite overshadowed the stepped-up activity, however, and he put on weight in a hurry. The other cadets nicknamed him "House" and predicted a brilliant future for him on the football team.[28] This reputation as a great eater remained with him during the Annapolis years; in his senior year *The Lucky Bag* devoted a full page to a caricature of a mythical two-member organization called the Eating Club, of which Churchill was named President and Commissary. It was the only period in his life when he was overweight in the least.

During the years he attended the Academy Winston's relationship with the Gazzams underwent a subtle change. He continued to address them in his letters as Aunty and Uncle, as he always had, but the signature changes from "your loving nephew" to "your affectionate son." This change implies that he had accepted the Gazzams as his only family. There is no doubt that, at least during the first two years, he was anxious to impress them with how hard he was working and with the undoubted success he was making of his self-chosen venture. When he was made adjutant of his group, and then first sergeant, he reported these facts to the Gazzams with obvious delight. And this was in spite of the fact that he despised having to report the misdeeds of his fellows — a trait which would get him into difficulty more than once during his Academy career.[29]

For a youth who disliked the classroom there were more important things to think about at that moment anyway. In October the drills and the physical activities of the summer months faded into the background as Churchill turned, with considerable misgivings, to the more formal, academic side of his training. The first results were discouraging. He spent too much time on English, and in the first set of examinations his mathematics grade was low. "Don't tell anyone about the Math in St. Louis," he wrote. "I am so ashamed of it and know I can do better."[30] He was concerned about his performance and went to great lengths to convince his aunt and uncle that he was working hard. Much more importantly, he understood what had to be done and he set about doing it with determination. Mathematics was his weak point, so from then on mathematics would come first. Since it was too expensive to go to St. Louis over the short vacation at Christmas, Churchill had intended to go to Norristown, Pennsylvania, with his roommate, Roscoe Spear. The mathematics grade changed this plan; he stayed in Annapolis and pounded the elusive subject into his brain. By the time of the mid-year examination in February he had cleared the first hurdle. Not only was his grade in math considerably improved, but, to his surprise, he also did well in other subjects.[31]

The official record shows that the Academy was never successful in teaching young Churchill to follow the dictates of its iron discipline. While he never received any "Days on Santee," the Station Ship used as a place of detention for refractory cadets, he did pile up a respectable number of demerits for some 120 violations of minor rules during his four years there. These ranged from sending unmarked items to the laundry, to going back to bed after reveille. There are enough reports of such things as "skylarking on the stairway" to show that he had the usual exuberant spirits of a college boy.[32] His Academy record indicates that Churchill was an above-average student who took his education seriously, worked hard in his classes, respected the overall disciplinary training, and yet had a healthy disregard for the minor rules of the regimented life.

Other activities did not prevent the young cadet from pursuing the collegiates' traditionally favored subject — the opposite sex. His letters home contain accounts of numerous hops in Baltimore and names of enough different girls to indicate that he was spreading his attentions as far over the field as possible. Despite the Gazzams' Victorianism, he made no attempt to disguise his interest in the local feminine population. In one letter he mentions that he was having a good time touring a Baltimore museum until he met two girls, "and then I didn't see much more of it." While his family apparently did not disapprove of his participation in the social whirl, they did object to his continuing problem with discipline. Churchill continually apologized for the demerits and tried to show them how much luck was involved in who got them and who did not, but the preparation for life theme is seldom absent. "Indeed I do realize the importance of preparing for life," he wrote to his aunt, "but demerits seem to be my worst stumbling block."[33]

During the spring and early summer of his second year, Churchill did accomplish two things of which he was very proud. The cadet was made crew captain in June of that year and was instrumental in reviving crew as an intercollegiate sport at the Academy. According to a book by two Academy crew coaches of a later period, the boat houses and shells had been carried away by a storm in 1870, and this "put a damper" on intercollegiate rowing activities at the Academy until the spring of 1892, "when interest was revived through the efforts of Winston Churchill . . . . " He spent all his spare time learning the sport and developing a crew. The following year, the cadets themselves raised between eight and nine hundred dollars for the purchase of a boat and Churchill managed to secure a coach from Columbia. He captained the team, himself, and rowed in the number seven position. Some of the cadets considered Winston a fanatic on the subject. The captain of the 1895 team said that "Winston Churchill was called a crank on the subject of rowing, but it was greatly due to his efforts that a new boat house, two new shells and a float were procured . . . . "[34]

Both Churchill and his family were equally proud when he finished his second year as an honors man in his class. This was an unexpected victory. He had written in May that, although his grades were good enough, he feared he would not "star" because of his numerous demerits. But he rose from his previous ranking of seventeenth in a class of seventy-two, to a position of ninth in a reduced class of sixty. For the first and only time, he was allowed to wear the stars of honor on his uniform at the June ball.[35]

It is perhaps more than coincidental that achievement of academic honors and his first mention of quitting the navy at the conclusion of his training came simultaneously. In 1890 becoming a naval officer had seemed like a tremendous improvement over being a clerk; by the summer of 1892, he had proved that he could accomplish this goal, and his ambitions soared beyond the immediate prospects. The rest of the classes had gone on cruise, and Winston had some leisure time. He put this to use by turning to non-academic reading for the first time. "I am trying to read a great deal this summer," he wrote, "as I may never have another such chance." Part of his time, however, was occupied with brooding about his future and he broached the matter with his uncle for the first time.

> Do you know I have been thinking ever since January, that if I could graduate high, and there seems some chance of it now, that I will not go in the Navy or on the year cruise if I can get a good position with a future outside. I realize more and more that the Navy is no place for a man who has the smallest ambition, and there never has been the slightest trouble experienced by our graduates in getting good positions. The education is I think the best in the country. Of course the training is almost perfect. I think so far it has been the making of me. I thought it best to tell you now as it is never too early to look around and moreover if it were generally known that I intended resigning in two years a position might be got. I feel no compunctions as my resignation would only let in a man below who has probably set his heart on it. Write me what you think of this.[36]

There is no record of his uncle's reply, but it is not difficult to imagine his reaction. It was not part of the Gazzam's philosophy of life to prepare for one profession, then throw it over — especially when no definite alternative was in sight.

During the last year Churchill was at Annapolis his thoughts followed an increasingly serious path. He had fallen in love with

Mabel Harlakenden Hall, later to become his wife, and was giving serious thought to his future. In his notebooks for various classes he began to copy quotations from things he was reading and to write resolutions about his own life and conduct. In one of these he wrote:

> To Practice —
>
> I   Repose of manner.
>
> II   Speaking and enunciating slowly and clearly —
>
> III Nothing in your conversation to be said for effect, everything to be true, however small —
>
> IV   Extreme self reserve

The same notebook contains a number of quotations from Lord Chesterfield's advice to his son, though Churchill indicated he felt there was a certain superficiality of manner and a moral laxity in some of these. He also quoted and referred to the writing of Swift, Pope, Hugo, and especially Emerson. He firmly agreed with Emerson's belief that each man is in charge of his own destiny, and, with the arrogance of the young, he was confident that his own life was completely in his keeping. The notes also indicate that he was going to keep a record of facts and examples from the lives of great men, and that he was going to stay away from modern politics since the two parties, ceasing to have distinctive principles, had become mere factions. But the resolution he mentioned most frequently was the admonition to himself to be reserved at all times and never to give vent to emotions of any kind.[37]

All of this, of course, is the first conscious effort of a young man to understand the world in which he lives and his place in it. Perhaps the thoughts were a bit more serious, the admonitions urging a life of gentlemanly restraint more extreme than most, but the overall temper is not different from that of any moderately serious college senior of the day. He gave his political party as Republican in *The Lucky Bag* sketch of each senior, but probably with the same automatic response that he listed his religion as Episcopalian. Neither religion nor politics had entered his thoughts seriously at this time. He had, however, begun to write, and his notebooks are filled with stories, some of them more than a hundred pages in length.

Churchill's letters to his family during his last year at the

Academy dwell on his future possibilities. He still hoped that he might find a satisfactory position in St. Louis, but he was making serious efforts elsewhere as well. There was a good chance that he could get a position with Westinghouse in Pittsburgh, and he went so far as to take a special course in electricity to help him in this. He was unenthusiastic about this job (which paid twelve cents an hour to start), but it was better than nothing. "I have made up my mind that I would rather shovel coal than go in the navy," he wrote, "and will gladly go to Pittsburgh for 12 cents an hour rather than go in." Then — perhaps to convince the Gazzams that his past decisions had been sound ones — he added, "I shall never regret my education and training here however."[38]

At the time of his graduation from the Academy, success must have seemed a long way off to the young cadet. On June 2, 1894, General Lew Wallace, a Civil War soldier and author of the novel *Ben Hur*, gave the commencement speech to the graduating class, and Winston Churchill, a dark, trim, handsome young man of twenty-two (*The Lucky Bag* lists him as 5'11, 173 pounds) was confidently expected by many to pursue a promising career in the United States Navy. He graduated thirteenth in a much-reduced class of forty-seven, but his overall grade point for the four years was 3.325, about a B plus.[39] The faith which the Academy placed in his ability to command is perhaps better indicated by the fact that throughout the four years he was consistently given responsible positions of leadership and that he was named one of four Cadet Lieutenants at the time of graduation, outranked by only one man in his class.

When the festivities of June Week were over, Churchill had not yet secured a civilian position. He was still a naval officer and he was assigned to the USS SAN FRANCISCO for a two-week cruise with the Naval Reserves in the coastal waters. During the cruise Churchill served as aide to the Admiral. His big break came suddenly and from an unexpected quarter. On August 2 he informed his uncle that he had taken the long contemplated step of resigning. This news could not have come as a surprise to the Gazzams, but the nature of his employment probably did. Although he had been writing stories for some time, it was not until his letter of August 2 that he told his guardians about his new interests. According to this letter he had been trying for some time to "get a place in the literary line" in New York. There he ran into Colonel Church, editor of the *Army and Navy Journal*, whom he apparently knew. The Colonel took him to dinner at the Century Club and offered him the naval editorship of the *Journal*. He was to begin in September with the somewhat less than lavish salary of ten dollars a week. Admitting that the salary was not impressive, Churchill contended that there were other attractions. The Colonel did not expect the job to occupy all of Churchill's time, so the young editor would have the opportunity to write things on his own. In fact, he had already written a short article on the naval militia which the Colonel had purchased for the *Journal*. Another advantage was that Colonel Church had a large number of acquaintances among literary men and journalists in New York, "and of course," Churchill wrote, "you can see what an opening this is for me."[40]

Although he had been contemplating this step for some time, Churchill gave no definite explanation as to why he wanted out of the navy so badly — why he would prefer a poorly paid position on a minor journal in preference to a career of almost certain success as a naval officer. His later statements on the matter are vague and sometimes contradictory. In the introspective Gideon manuscript, he states that "he had discovered that he did not want to be a naval officer; he hated discipline, and he had no aptitude for mathematics, mechanics, seamanship or fighting. Learning all these had been work indeed."[41] In 1940 he told a young graduate student, "I had no interest in the Navy: was likely to wreck several ships if I stayed in."[42] He expressed similar sentiments in an interview with Peter Macfarlane in 1913. According to Macfarlane, Churchill did not enjoy the work at the Academy and used every opportunity to steal away to the library (where he steeped himself in American history) and to walk through the streets of the historic town itself, looking at the old houses and absorbing the tradition.[43] These sentiments, however, are at odds with what is known of his life at Annapolis, and his letters give little indication of real dissatisfaction with the naval way of life as he experienced it at the Academy. It seems more likely that the prospect of a life in the peacetime navy simply was not very exciting. Promotions would be slow in coming and much of his life in the immediately succeeding years would have had to be spent outside the country. To a young man deeply in love, this prospect was not very inviting. Then, too, there was the more obvious matter of his growing desire to write. Churchill himself offered this explanation in an interview in 1899.

> So certain was I that literature was my vocation that before I graduated I had decided that I would resign at the end of the course, and try my fortune at literary ventures. While I was at Annapolis I wrote lots of stories, but none of them ever saw the light of day, and it is just as well that they did not.[44]

Most of these early efforts concerned dashing young naval officers and beautiful girls; the stories themselves were trivial, turning on some vague point of honor that could seem important only to a very young man at the end of the Nineteenth Century. They do indicate, by their very existence, that Churchill's interests were moving in a new direction. Throughout his life he intensely concentrated on those things that seemed most important at the time. When they no longer interested him, he quickly dropped them. Such was probably the case with his naval career. According to young Churchill and his idol, Emerson, a man's life is in his own keeping. Why then should not he change the course of his life as he saw fit?

CHAPTER II

Launching A Career

The early months of Churchill's literary career were discouraging ones. He faced solid opposition from his family and friends at a time when he most needed their support. The pain which this caused him left scars on his relationship with most of them that never completely disappeared. In 1908, at the height of his fame, he spoke jovially of their reaction.

> The editor of the Army and Navy Journal offered me $10 a week. Although my friends tried to dissuade me, I took the place, sacrificing my commission and considerable salary. But I . . . thought I should like literature, as I called it, better than anything else. All prophecy was against me. Another idiot had taken the wrong train at the junction.[1]

Only years later, in the Gideon manuscript, did the scars reopen completely.

> In launching himself as an author he felt alienated from them. He had lost much of their esteem. When he sat down to write he heard them saying, "We predicted that Gideon would never amount to much. This business of being a writer is only a scheme of his to evade reality, to get out of work."
> Not only when he was alone, writing and rewriting those drafts which no publisher would accept,

> but when he met the friends of his childhood he felt
> that this was their attitude. The boys with whom he
> had grown up were all getting established in life, in a
> profession or a business. They were justifying them-
> selves. They had the good-will of their families and
> of the community.[2]

Those months were dreary indeed, and Churchill's dissatisfaction with his job increased steadily. He was grateful to Colonel
Church for having saved him from the navy but did not feel that
he was being treated properly. Then, suddenly, the breaks came
his way. *Century Magazine* accepted one of his short stories for
publication, and J. B. Walker offered him a position with
Cosmopolitan Magazine.

"I am so delighted at getting off a paper with a limited
scope to one like the Cosmopolitan that I can scarcely realize
it," Churchill effused, and he accepted the varied duties of the
job with enthusiasm.[3] Most of his time was spent in rewriting
articles and in helping with the general composition of the
magazine. Walker was more than satisfied with the young editor's
efforts and gave particularly high praise to Churchill's own writings. In fact, almost from the beginning, Walker appears to have
been grooming Churchill to be managing editor of the magazine.
The offer was made in late April of 1895, and the rising young
editor was delighted. It gave him a chance to point out to his
family how well he was doing.

> I have just time to tell you that Mr. Walker has
> offered me the position of managing Editor of the
> Cosmopolitan. I am very much dazed and do not
> know what to think of it. I was recommended by
> both his sons and Hart, the present managing editor,
> but Mr. Walker made the proposition himself. I do
> not know what my salary will be yet but I shall have
> to be content to start low. Mr. Hart is over 30, and
> it is really phenomenal that I should get the position.
> . . . Mr. Walker laughed when I told him my age [23],
> but he thinks I can do it. I have had the good luck
> to please him. He asked me frankly first what my
> ambitions were — editor or writer. I chose Editor.
> He seemed to take it for granted I could do either.[4]

The new editor was naturally proud of the magazine itself

and of his part in its success. In July he claimed that they were going to make it "the best in the country."[5] The joint success of magazine and editor was doubly welcome because Winston intended to be married in the fall of 1895. Walker had agreed to raise his salary from $100 a month to $150 after the marriage, and there is every indication that Churchill fully intended to stay on with the magazine. He told his future bride that they would have to be married early in October so that he could be back at his desk in time to put together the elaborate Christmas issue.

His editorial duties took time which he would have preferred to devote to his own writings, but he continued to work on his stories whenever he could. Every morning he arose early to write before he left for the office, returning in the evening to take up where he had left off. Sometimes he even wrote a page while he was at lunch. He was aware, however, that his assiduous labor was not producing literary masterpieces. In April of 1895, he wrote his fiancee:

> I have almost finished the story. I am going to offer it to Mr. Walker because I think I ought to, although if I gave it to the Century I have a chance of having both it and the one I read to you accepted. But the faults of the latter are so obvious to me that I am going to take some of it and throw the rest away, and write another. Of course I do not know whether the present story is good enough, I have my grave doubts in spite of favorable criticism and can only hope.[6]

None of these stories are of any particular importance. They are pleasant little excursions into a land of noble men and Gibson girls that were so popular with both authors and readers at the time. The settings, however, demonstrate Churchill's ability to describe scenery, always his best literary achievement. Many of the descriptions draw on scenes he had recorded in his student notebook and journals. From the beginning he wrote fiction by putting imagined characters into settings taken from his own experience — and the settings were always more credible than the characters.

But Churchill's mind was occupied primarily with neither short stories nor editorial duties during these months. His first concern was his courtship of Mabel Harlakenden Hall. Her father had made a small fortune as a businessman in St. Louis, but she, too, had lost her parents and was under the guardianship of an aunt.

In later years some newspaper stories implied that Churchill married Mabel for her money (a charge which many writers have continued to make), but their letters seem to indicate that this was an affair of the heart, not of the pocketbook. The following outpouring of emotion is one example among many in their correspondence.

> To begin by telling you that I miss you, and miss you dreadfully, would be quite as useless and unnecessary as to tell you that I love you — you know both with a comprehension far beyond the power of words. So I have set about, with all the philosophy in my power, to put a bright face upon the matter. And the matter has a very bright face indeed — a long life, God willing, for us both and such happiness as rarely comes to man and woman and only to those whose qualities, like the colors of a master painting, are blended under the painter's hand into a perfect picture.
>
> . . . . . .
>
> I had never hoped that any betrothal could be so perfect and sweet as ours had been. I thought it would be much more matter of fact. We are both naturally so reserved that when we revealed to each other our true natures we both looked with wonder at what we saw, and experienced that rapture which is alone called forth by things sacredly beautiful.[7]

It could be argued, of course, that such statements are simply typical of the absurd effusions that young lovers write to each other. In light of Churchill's later statements that another woman was the true love of his life, it also could be argued, conversely, that he was trying to overcome his own lukewarm feelings about Mabel. These arguments, however, are not supported by the cumulative evidence in the love letters, nor by the extended campaign which he launched to convince Mabel's family that he was a suitable match for her.

In any case, the long-awaited ceremony took place on

October 22, 1895, in the home of Mrs. Beverley Allen, Mabel's grandmother. This event was to be one of the most decisive in Churchill's career. The new Mrs. Churchill's wit, charm, and drive were continuing assets to her husband; her determination was a spur to his own ambition. Of more immediate importance in the initial year or two of the marriage, however, was Mabel's trust fund inheritance from her father. It is unlikely that Churchill thought much about this when he proposed marriage — he was too determined to make his own way, too much in love to give much weight to such rational considerations. Shortly after the marriage, however, he left *The Cosmopolitan* because of difficulties with his employer. At this point Mabel's determination and trust fund both came into play; she seems to have convinced him that he should turn all his time and energy to creative writing, rather than look for another job. While he was getting started on still another career, they could live on her modest income.

Given their backgrounds, this was a bold step for the young couple to take. The acceptable path for the offspring of a respectable "mugwump" family in the late nineteenth century was clearly marked. A young man was expected to prepare himself for one of the respectable professions, enter that profession and pursue it diligently for the rest of his life. Winston had chosen the only profession open to him, the navy; it was not the most prestigious, but it would do. He had prepared himself for a naval career in the accepted way but when the time came for him to actually enter upon that profession, he jumped ship. This in itself had been a shock to the Victorian sensibilities of his family and friends. Still, he did have a job; he could support himself and his wife. Now he had compounded his offense by deserting the acceptable path entirely, by giving up his job as well as the profession for which he had been trained. And as if this were not bad enough, he further disgraced himself by living off his wife's income while wasting his time writing stories. This was not a unique arrangement, even in the late nineteenth century, but it was quite outside the frame of reference of either the Gazzams or Mabel's family. Mabel's willingness to support her husband in this difficult situation is an expression of her confidence that he would one day achieve fame as a writer, the same confidence that led her to save every letter he ever wrote to her. Her confidence did not lessen Churchill's sensitivity about the situation, either then or later. At the time he made his decision the most serious objection was raised by one of Mabel's brothers. Churchill's reply to him not only defends his honor but also states what he believed the profession of literature was. Some people, he observed, "do not recognize the profession of letters until after it has been made a success," and do not consider that, like law and medicine, it has its period of conscientious labor and meagre return.

> These people have no means of knowing, and do not care to know, that day after day I sit in my office writing from early morning until late at night, with only a few hours intermission for a walk and reading; and if by chance some of my work gets into print it is put down as the result of a few hours of pastime, because perhaps the phrases flow easily and are read smoothly . . . .
>
> I am not now, and have never been, the stamp of man who shirks work, and I would rather die today than have my wife support me the rest of my life. No one is more keenly sensitive of my position than am I, and believe me it would be much pleasanter, as far as my pride goes, to be studying law in a downtown office for a pittance, or with a father's support. I had to shift for myself from the time I was eighteen, when I obtained my appointment by my own endeavor, until I was married, and I am quite capable of money-getting now. I had no advantages, no opportunity to follow my own bent, until an unfortunate temper drove me from the magazine and Mabel urged me to go into writing.

Here one can see the pride, the concern for his honor (along with the consequent defensiveness and guilt), that were an important part of Churchill's character from his earliest days.

Churchill had made the crucial decision to rise or fall on his ability as a man of letters and never again would draw a paycheck as an employee. He had put security and the respect of his elders, at least for a time, behind him; ahead lay the uncertain future of a literary career. He approached it with the enthusiasm, determination, and confidence of youth. Up to that time he had written nothing but short stories, and the only one of these that had been accepted was still unpublished. So it was without ever having seen a line of his own in print that he set forth to conquer the literary world.

During the first few months of his marriage, Churchill conceived the basic outline for his first novel *The Celebrity*, and he had written about half of it by the time the young couple left for a trip to Europe (paid for by one of Churchill's relatives) in April of 1896. By this time Winston had also made one of the most important acquaintances of his career in Dr. Albert Shaw of the *Review of Reviews*, a prominent political and literary journal. Shaw was some fifteen years older than Churchill when the two men became friends. He had studied history and politics at the famous Johns Hopkins graduate school at the same time Woodrow Wilson was a student there and had received a Ph.D. from that institution in 1884. Declining the offer of the chair of International and Political Institutions at Cornell, he chose instead to found and edit the *Review of Reviews*. The correspondence between Shaw and Churchill during the years after 1895 reveals that Churchill relied on Shaw for both personal and professional advice, and that the older man served as almost a substitute father. When the Churchills sailed for Europe, Winston left the unfinished manuscript of his book with Shaw for safekeeping. But after he embarked the aspiring author received Shaw's announcement that George P. Brett of the Macmillan Company was interested in the book.

Brett, who was already started on an illustrious career as one of the foremost publishers in America, liked Churchill's tale about the tribulations of a pompous literary figure, and he asked to see the rest of the manuscript. Churchill later recalled, "I was busy running around at that time studying old castles and abbeys, and, as you can imagine, not at all in sympathy with a flippant American story such as 'The Celebrity'. However, I decided to stop everything else, and sat down in Edinburgh and finished it and sent it off, but with the lurking feeling that it would not answer."[10]

When Churchill returned to America in late September he had lost interest in the story but he went to see Brett, who urged him to continue working on it. He followed Brett's advice, but that fall he also wrote two more naval stories, which he submitted to the *Century*, and began work on an historical novel dealing with the Revolution in Maryland. First at Dobbs Ferry, and then at Bolton on Lake George, he worked on the two books alternately. Nearly a year later, in September, 1897, he finally submitted the completed manuscript of *The Celebrity*.[11] Along with the completed manuscript went the first seven chapters of the historical novel, with the understanding that Brett's acceptance of *The Celebrity* would depend on how well he liked the historical novel. This time Brett was satisfied; a contract was signed for *The Celebrity*, Macmillan was given the right of first refusal on the historical novel, and a publisher-author relationship was formed that was to grow more intimate over the years.

With considerable hesitation over associating the name of an important man with his light comedy, Churchill acknowledged Shaw's role in the publication of his first novel by dedicating it to his patron. The book was released in November of 1897, and Churchill confessed to Shaw, "I find that I have a most shameful curiosity to read any reviews that may appear, and am going to ask you to get one of your boys to subscribe for me to a clipping service."[12]

The story of the novel was typical of its genre in the dependence of its plot on the rather superficial code of polite society. The narrator is a young lawyer named Crocker who has set up practice in a thriving town near one of the Great Lakes. Through the good offices of his friend Farrar, a professional forester, Crocker is engaged by Mr. Cooke, an eastern businessman, to represent him in a dispute over land ownership. Their victory in the case brings Crocker the office of District Attorney and enables Cooke to go ahead with plans for the construction of his summer estate, Mohair.[13] Near the site of Mohair is the small, sedate summer resort of Asquith, frequented by summer residents from mid-western cities. A quiet, clannish set, these residents resent the intrusion of a nouveau riche like Cooke.

One day Crocker reads in the newspaper that the Celebrity, an extremely popular novelist whom he had known in his youth, is leaving for Europe. When the Celebrity subsequently arrives at Asquith — traveling under a false name — he immediately monopolizes all the young ladies, and the very proper Crocker finds the whole situation distasteful. What follows is a series of adventures that lead to the Celebrity's exposure and humiliation.

The Celebrity was a pleasant example of a common genre, and was accepted as such by the critics. Some of them pointed out that the plot was trite and contrived, but the majority were kind to the young author. Churchill looked upon the novel as a light, maiden effort and was not particularly proud of it, although in later years (after he had stopped writing fiction and had abandoned reform causes) he contended that it was a more natural expression of himself than any of his later novels.[14] The first part of the book, in which he introduces the characters and describes the social scene at Asquith and at Mohair, is quite good. He uses an appropriately light touch; his humor is subtle and effective. But the characters are stock types, and from this point on the plot becomes contrived, as improbability is piled upon improbability.

Churchill exhibits in his first novel, however, the first signs of his later disapproval of certain aspects of American society. This disapproval is most evident in his characterizations of Mr. Cooke and of "The Ten." Cooke is certainly the most viable portrayal in the novel, and although Churchill expresses his dislike for the nouveau riche and their false standards in his discussion of the Philadelphia merchant, he sees good qualities in him as well. Crocker disapproved of Cooke's unrestrained manner, including the way he stopped to chat with strangers on the street (some of whom smelled); this, of course, says at least as much about Churchill's stuffed shirt heroes as it does about Cooke. But if he was crude, if he personified the distasteful side of the new barons of wealth, Cooke also had some admirable qualities. "I am convinced," Crocker observes, "that Mr. Cooke possessed at least some of the qualities of a great general." Nor was he totally lacking in morality. Pondering Cooke's willingness to pay for the Celebrity's defense on the grounds of insanity, Crocker thought, "This was downright generous of Mr. Cooke. We have all, no doubt, drawn our line between what is right and what is wrong, but I have often wondered how many of us with the world's indorsement across our backs trespass as little on the other side of the line as he."[15]

So, despite his crudeness, Churchill's first captain of industry and finance was not to be utterly condemned. He had a good heart and generous instincts. Not so the hangers-on in this new sphere of society. The pretentiousness, the indolence, the uselessness of these people was exemplified in "The Ten" (a group of young men), of whom Churchill wrote:

> I shall treat the Ten as a whole because they did not
> materially differ from one another in dress or habits
> or ambition or general usefulness on this earth . . . .
> Likewise the life of any one of the Ten was the life
> of all, and might be truthfully represented by a single
> year, since each year was exactly like the preceding.
> The ordinary year, as is well-known, begins of the
> first of January . . . . Theirs began in the Fall with
> the New York Horse Show. And I am of the opinion,
> though open to correction, that they dated from the
> first Horse Show instead of from the birth of Christ.[16]

The unusual amount of attention which *The Celebrity* attracted was not, however, the result of Churchill's remarks about the indolent class in American society; it was due to the fact that the book was widely interpreted as an attack on the literary darling of the age, Richard Harding Davis. Critic Alfred Kazin has described the dashing, handsome Davis as "the golden boy of the nineties, the man who personified the union of literature and life."[17] He was the most famous war correspondent the country had ever produced; in between wars he entertained the public with his romantic, Graustarkian "Van Bibber" stories.

A letter written to Shaw at the time suggests that Churchill did have Davis, among others, in mind when he wrote the book. In later years, however, and in all of his other comments on this question, Churchill categorically denied that Davis was the model for his title character. Asked by an interviewer for the *New York Times* in 1901 if Davis and the Celebrity were one and the same, Churchill replied, "No, indeed. At the time I was living a very retired life. I had never met Mr. Davis and knew nothing about him. So that I was thunderstruck when the reviewers all came out and charged me with caricaturing him."[18] Although it is true that the two men had never met, it is hard to believe that any writer lived so retiring and secluded a life that he knew nothing about the most widely publicized literary figure of the decade.

CHAPTER III

A Crisis of Conscience
and Professional Success

Even before *The Celebrity* was published (in November, 1897), Churchill was absorbed in more serious work. Leaving the residence on Lake George in the summer of 1897, the Churchills and a new baby daughter established housekeeping on the second floor of a house in Baltimore, where the author could soak himself in local color for his historical novel. For him it was a return to a city which he had loved as a cadet, but for Mrs. Churchill — weakened by the birth of her first child and depressed by the strange city — it was decidedly unpleasant. So in October of 1897 they moved to St. Louis. Mrs. Churchill was put under a doctor's care, and Winston, looking forward to an undisturbed winter of work, took an office across the hall from his uncle in the Security Building. He could leave home in the morning (like a doctor or lawyer), secure in the knowledge that his wife and child would be watchfully tended, and spend the day conjuring up daring deeds to be performed by his fictional hero, Richard Carvel.[1]

Despite this freedom to work, the novel progressed slowly and by the following spring Churchill was ready to return to the East. The family spent some time in Clifton Springs, New York, moving on to Nyack in May, 1898, where they remained for nearly a year. But this geographic stability did not bring the young author emotional peace of mind. In the spring of 1898 a complex combination of spread-eagle nationalism, economic imperialism, and humanitarian concern for the people of Cuba brought the United States into its comic opera war with Spain.

The war placed the young ex-cadet in a difficult position. On the one hand was his duty to the nation and the service which had taken him out of a paper warehouse and given him an education. On the other was his duty to support his family, an obligation which called for the early completion of his novel. "Yesterday the strain became unbearable," he told Shaw, "and I wired to the Navy Department that I offered my services for the war in case Naval Academy graduates were needed."[2] As it turned out, his decision made no difference. The navy acknowledged receipt of his application for appointment with assurances that it would be placed on file and given consideration when the next appointments were made. Before they got around to this the war was over.

Churchill did contribute two patriotic articles about the navy. The first of these, entitled "Admiral Dewey: A Character Sketch" shows the author's admiration for his subject and respect for the admiral's accomplishments. It also gives a glimpse of the Anglo-Saxon racism which Churchill shared with most of his contemporaries.

> It may be well to mention here that Admiral Dewey is the logical result of a system which produces the best naval officers in the world. The reason of this is not far to seek. We have not only the very finest of material to choose from, for the American officer combines valuable qualities of his own with the necessary traits which are found in the English and other northern races, but also because the whole result of the Annapolis training may be summed up in the phrase "the survival of the fittest."[3]

The other article, "The Battle with Cervera's Fleet Off Santiago," is a song of praise to the gallant American Navy, but again the main theme is that the outcome of the war was a foregone conclusion, since the Spaniards had made the mistake of challenging a nation of Anglo-Saxons.[4]

It was the American Revolution, rather than the Spanish-American War that was giving the young author headaches as he attempted to move from the comedy-of-manners genre to that of historical romance. Various reasons have been offered as to why he made this change. His critics have contended that his interest in the historical novel, like his previous work in the field of light comedy, was an example of his ability to read the public mind. Historical novels were extremely popular in the 1890's, and Churchill is said to have simply exploited this popularity. But it was quite logical for Churchill to turn to the historical novel as a means of expression. He was a serious young man and a highly patriotic one. What better topic for his pen than the nation's past glories? Here he could put to work his knowledge of the sea and use his strongest points as a writer — his powers of description and his ability as a story-teller. He could be creative without depending upon great flights of imagination; the basic raw material was there.

It was natural also for him to choose the area around Annapolis and Baltimore as the setting for his first historical novel and, if the events were to take place in Maryland, the logical time period was the American Revolution. So Churchill immersed himself in the historical literature, both American and English, to prepare for this task. His letters to Shaw and Brett contain constant requests for this book or that which happened to be unavailable to him in St. Louis. When he encountered a problem of historical fact that was important to his story he sought advice from experts.[5] Indeed, his desire for accuracy sometimes extended to the point of pedantry. Writing to Brett as the publisher was about to sail for Europe, Churchill said, "When you go to England I wish you would do me the favor of looking at the shores of Ireland as you pass, or else make inquiries whether or not they are green the middle of March. I have been able to get no precise information on this point . . . . "[6] These details he kept in a working notebook which contains long lists of miscellaneous information regarding the historical characters, along with descriptions of places and accounts of events.

Richard Carvel (released in May of 1899) centers upon the southern phase of the American Revolution and is presented through the eyes of the title character — a descendant of a wealthy Maryland family, who is brought up by his grandfather. Richard's adventures take him to England as well as the colonies, allowing

Churchill to introduce many historical figures from both areas. Interwoven with the historical events is the love story of Richard and Dorothy Manners, and an extended series of crises in which the youth does battle with his evil Uncle Grafton. All ends happily as the victory of the revolutionaries is capped by the wedding of Richard and his childhood sweetheart in Carvel Hall.

The Celebrity had been a happy little literary exercise to which neither Churchill nor the critics attached much importance. *Richard Carvel* was quite another matter. In the context of the time, this was serious literary business. Letters of congratulations poured in from friends and well-wishers across the country and from other parts of the world. But the person Churchill was most anxious to please was Albert Shaw, and he succeeded admirably. Shaw wrote that he was glad Churchill had put in so much history, biography, local color, and contemporary flavor, and though some critics suggested that this interrupted the movement of the story, "It is exactly this remarkably faithful grasp you have shown of the spirit of the times you have chosen to write about that will give your book its permanent value . . . . 'The Celebrity' was a very appetizing dessert, and 'Richard Carvel' is good Yorkshire roast beef."[7]

Certainly the popular success of the book was beyond question, and the author was elated. "Sales to date 70,000, printing 100,000," he wrote. "Is it not the millenium?"[8] Women's clubs had special programs on the book; teen-age girls wrote him letters that were almost idolatrous. Newspapers across the country printed biographical sketches of the new literary success and Churchill suddenly found himself a celebrity in his own right.

The critics' reaction to *Richard Carvel* was also enthusiastic. Some of the more aesthetically oriented critics pointed out that the style was cumbersome, that the fictional characters were cast from a worn-out mold, that the hero was impossibly heroic and the situations contrived. Others criticized what they felt was a rather blind imitation of Thackeray. But even those who found fault with the artistic side of the novel, felt that Churchill projected excellent portraits of the historical personages whom he employed and of the epoch under consideration.

Many later critics have pondered over the success which *Richard Carvel* attained with the reading public, and there is no simple answer. The popular success of any novel is difficult to analyze; the public acceptance of an historical novel almost defies analysis. One historical novel differs from another basically in time setting, and in the skill with which the author handles his characters and places them in the given historical epoch. Churchill's choice of the Revolutionary War period was fortunate. America in the 1890's was concentrating its attention on healing the breach of the 1850's and the 1860's by emphasizing its national past. An intense nationalism, which found expression in the Spanish-American War, was spreading over the country just at the time *Richard Carvel* was published. And the war, which was fought in large part on the seas, awakened public interest in the navy. Churchill's training in naval warfare and his decision to bring the maritime side of the war for independence into the foreground were undoubtedly factors in the success of his novel. His use of a Southern setting for the novel was also a wise move. Americans were inclined to think of the Revolution as a Northern war; Churchill reminded them it was not.

Still, none of this is unique. What basically lay at the core of Churchill's success, both in *Richard Carvel* and in the later historical novels, was his skill as a story teller. The strictly fictional characters were wooden paragons of virtue or the epitome of evil, but the historical characters — John Paul Jones, Charles Fox, Washington and others — had the breath of life within them and Churchill moved them skillfully through the novel. Although the plot of the book was somewhat contrived, Churchill managed to combine Richard's adventures with the greater events of the revolution in such a way that the reader was willing to follow him. At the same time the story was sufficiently balanced in its treatment of the British so that English readers a century after the events found little to complain about. Actually the book was extremely popular in England and the English critics were, if anything, more favorable in their comments than were their American counterparts. As in his later historical novels, Churchill's emphasis was on the greatness of the Anglo-Saxon, rather than being narrowly nationalistic.

Indeed, the treatment of the British was so fair that many of the English readers, and several of the reviewers, credited the novel to a young Britisher named Winston Churchill. Many of the newspapers in both the United States and England printed pictures of the two Winston Churchills along with biographies of each, but there are indications that the publishers did little to disabuse the English public of the idea that Churchill's novels were written by one of their own. The feeling seems to have been that more copies of the novels could be sold in England if the English continued to believe the author was a young member of Parliament. Be that as it may, the two young men were quite anxious to set the record straight. Both were barely started on their careers (the Englishman was just three years younger than his American namesake), and neither of them were anxious to share their laurels.

It was the Britisher who first expressed concern about the confusion which had arisen. According to his own account, it was in the spring of 1899 that he first learned "there was another Winston Churchill who also wrote books . . . . "[9] This was called to his attention by a sudden burst of letters congratulating him on his skill as a novelist. At first he hoped that this was a belated discovery of the merits of his own venture into the world of fiction, *Savarola*. When this happy illusion was destroyed, he initiated what became a rather delicate correspondence and relationship. In June of 1899 the British Churchill wrote a letter to the American stating that, in order to avoid further confusion between their writings, he would sign all of his works as Winston Spencer Churchill. Churchill expressed his appreciation that his new acquaintance would use his middle name (he, himself, did not have one) and raised the possibility — later vetoed by Brett — that he might add "The American" to the title pages of future novels.

Evidence indicates that a personal meeting was not the fondest wish of either Churchill; it was an event, however, that was planted firmly in the mind of an enterprising entrepreneur named Major J. B. Pond. The Major entered Churchill's life in January of 1900 when Brett suggested that a series of lectures by the author of *Richard Carvel* on the subject of the American Revolution would be a good addition to Pond's lecture series. The Major thought this a fine idea, but Churchill was horrified. "I have no intention of committing that particular form of suicide," he wrote.[10] By June, Pond had arranged an American tour for Winston Spencer Churchill and was inspired to suggest that the two Churchills should appear on the same platform, the American to introduce the Englishman. "I can see nothing undignified or showmanlike about it," Pond insisted plaintively. "It will be a magnificent and unique occasion."[11] Soon thereafter Pond convinced Mark Twain to appear on the program with the Englishman. He wrote Churchill that he had talked it over with "Mr. Clemens" and the humorist had agreed that it would be a fine idea to have him introduce both of the Churchills and then have the American introduce the visitor. Churchill again refused. Persistent to the end, the Major invited Churchill to a farewell dinner for his lecturer at the conclusion of the tour in February. Mark Twain and several other "good men" were to be there and Churchill's presence was much to be desired.[12] He did not go.

He did give a private dinner for Winston Spencer Churchill in December while the Britisher was lecturing in Boston. It is impossible to tell whether or not Pond had informed his lecturer of the novelist's repeated refusals to appear on the platform with him, but his reply to Churchill's invitation to dinner indicates no hard feelings on his part. According to one source, the two men first met in a Boston hotel room where Winston Spencer Churchill received the novelist in bed. They exchanged greetings and compliments, during the course of which the Britisher is supposed to have stated, "I was interested when I read your first book. Didn't think a great deal of that book; but the other one, 'Richard Carvel,' I was willing to become responsible for that."[13] Churchill was not attracted to the Britisher before they met; it is unlikely that this encounter increased his affection. In any case the two Churchills had finally met, the dinner took place, and a relationship of quiet hostility was established — a relationship that never changed.[14]

CHAPTER IV

A Famous House and an All-Time Best Seller

Soon after the publication of *Richard Carvel*, the Churchills left for New England to supervise the construction of their new home. In the fall of 1898, Churchill had gone to Cornish, New Hampshire, to get construction under way on a piece of land which he had recently purchased; by June of 1899 the foundations were in and the carpenters were at work. Meanwhile the Churchills were living in a small farmhouse on the property and, according to the author, "are suddenly become very gay and dine out and go to evening entertainment galore."[1] It was not until early in November that they were able to move into a part of their new house, which even then was far from complete. The process of getting settled was interrupted in December when Churchill decided to go to St. Louis to do research for his new novel. He moved into the old office where he had written much of *Richard Carvel* and, with his usual diligence, began searching out information about St. Louis during the Civil War — the scene of his projected novel. They returned to Cornish in March, and in April they completed the move into their new home. The novelist worked there until November of 1900 when they left for a house which they had rented at 181 Beacon Street in Boston. This move began a pattern of dual residence that they were to follow for a number of years. New Hampshire was attractive, but the Churchills found the winters there entirely too cold.

Some of the state officials in New Hampshire realized the commercial value of Churchill's residency there and asked him for a statement relating why he had chosen the area for his home, what it had cost, and other information that would help them in persuading others to follow his example. Churchill's reply contains the best description of his holdings and the reasons he chose to settle in New Hampshire.

> I had been searching for some years for a country in which to build a home, and a stay of two days in the townships of Plainfield and Cornish decided me to go no farther. In the autumn of 1898 I bought one hundred of the acres which I now possess on the Connecticut River, in view of Mt. Ascutney. They are perhaps, one-third very good second growth woodland, mostly oaks and pines and hemlocks, with a scattering of birches and beeches .... The price paid was $2600 . . . . . I have since bought about twenty acres of cleared land on the River for $450. My land is very sandy, and I do not attempt to farm it, although I have perhaps thirty or forty acres at the extremities of the farm, on Blowmedown Brook at one end and on the Connecticut at the other, that is considered fairly good land and with renewal would make first rate farming land . . . .
>
> Since the spring of '99 I have built a residence on a wooded eminence two hundred feet above the Connecticut, and overlooking that river. I have had to thin out a forest, chiefly of oaks, in order to do this . . . . The house is brick, and probably cost with furnishings, between $35,000 and $40,000. I have since rebuilt the barns and stables, and have probably expenses of $2,000 on them. There is an excellent spring on the place and I have put in an engine that pumps water to all the buildings. This water plant probably cost $1,500. The continual work on the place, tennis courts, grading, road building, and clearing out has probably cost between $3,000 and $4,000 . . . . My house contains three furnaces, and is a winter house as well as a summer house. Personally, I am a resident of New Hampshire, and regard this place as my home . . . .
>
> You ask me why I like New Hampshire. It seems to me that the townships of Cornish and Plainfield

> merely have to be seen to answer that question. The
> hills are high and the valleys deep, and the scenery has
> all the ruggedness necessary to great beauty, while
> it remains pastoral . . . . [2]

Churchill had hopes that his royalties would pay for his new house. "Your prophecy that 'Carvel' might pay for my place here seems destined to come true," he wrote Shaw. To Brett, he said, "I should like to be able to look at my house and say that 'Carvel' built it for me."[3] "Carvel" did not sell enough copies to pay for such a luxurious house, however, and it looked for awhile as if Churchill would have to turn once again to his wife's inheritance. By the terms of her trust, Mabel could have the executors sell up to ten thousand dollars in property or stocks to build a home. This would mean, however, that the house would have to be in her name and the trust company would hold the mortgage — a situation which appealed to neither of the Churchills. In this instance Churchill showed more business acumen than he usually displayed in his relationship with his publisher. The precise terms for his next novel had not yet been agreed upon, and Churchill humorously indicated that this time he was going to hold out for all he could get. Shortly after this he asked for a substantial advance against his royalties on the next novel, pointing out that he would be sacrificing some lucrative offers for short stories if he concentrated solely on his long novel at that time. The implication was that he would take time out to write the short stories if Brett did not meet his terms. The publisher did accept them, however, and Churchill agreed to go ahead with the novel.[4] As construction of the house progressed it became clear that the builders had underestimated the cost and for another year the house absorbed every cent that Churchill, with Brett's continuing aid, could raise.

In form, as well as in title, the novelist attempted to keep the house as his own. He carried on an extensive correspondence with Charles A. Platt, who was the architect for the house, going into detail about every aspect of the design and construction. The same kind of correspondence with his cabinetmaker indicates that the house was almost as much a product of Churchill's suggestions as it was of Platt's skill as an architect.

Their combined efforts produced notable results. Harlakenden House, named in honor of Mrs. Churchill, became famous over the years and was the center of national attention when it was chosen by President Wilson for his summer White House. The house stood about two-thirds of the way up a long hill which rose from the covered bridge connecting New Hampshire with Windsor, Vermont. Of pure Georgian design, the house was a two and a half story building of plum-colored brick built around three sides of a court. In the center of the house was a large living room with heavy oak beams and dark oak wainscoting. This also served as the front hall. On one side of the living room was a square hall with a curved staircase and a balcony around the top, leading to the upper halls. A small library (largely planned by Mrs. Churchill) opened off the hall and one complete side of this room was a huge plain glass window which looked down on the river and the green hills of Vermont beyond. Down a few steps from the hall and in the wing opposite the kitchen wing were a music room, billiard room, and Churchill's study, located at the far end where he would not be disturbed. At the rear of the house was a semi-circular terrace which provided a view of the river, the hills, and Ascutney Mountain. The hill on which Harlakenden House stood was covered with pines and very tall white oak which were thinned out in places to perfect the view.

Churchill added to the estate in later years, ultimately owning some five hundred acres which were equipped with a tennis court, a swimming pool, a stable for his horses and supplementary farm houses. Churchill kept a close eye on the operation of the estate and when he was not there to oversee matters personally he sent long, detailed letters of instruction to his various farm hands.

Keenly sensitive about any invasion of his home and hearth, Churchill was particularly sensitive about having pictures of either his family or his house appear in print. One woman drove a considerable distance for the specific purpose of taking photographs of the house, only to be turned away by one of Churchill's men who told her it was against the rules. She also discovered that she could not even buy pictures from the local photographer without the novelist's consent. Churchill was extremely irritated when a photo of Mrs. Churchill and one of himself did get into general circulation, and he commissioned lawyers to get the pictures back. References to his family in the newspapers disturbed him even more. After one such comment in a letter that appeared in the *New York Times*, he wrote to the editor: "I take the greatest interest in your paper and it occurs to me to write to you privately, and in a perfectly friendly way, and ask that you cut out of any letter that you may henceforth receive anything which refers to my family."[5]

The valley in which Churchill built his house and secreted his family was known as the Cornish Colony. During the last half of the nineteenth century, New Hampshire had experienced the flight of the small farmer. Although the total population of the state did not decline, it did drop significantly in proportion to that of the nation as a whole. Those who remained in the state participated in the surge to the city that the entire nation experienced when post-Civil War industrialization swept the country. The agricultural township of Cornish reflected this trend as its population declined from 1726 residents in 1840 to 962 in 1900. Six hours by train from Boston and nine hours from New York, Cornish was too far away from the industrial centers to attract large numbers of people who wanted to build houses for weekends in the country. Nor did it ever become a haven for rich people. What it did attract was an interesting assortment of artists, lawyers, and literary people. According to Homer St. Gaudens, "the peace and dream-like ripeness of the hills, with their dark clumps of trees and their river winding south before the mountain, called strongly to these artists who desired simple living."[6] These people built homes on both sides of what was generously referred to as a highway which ran along the New Hampshire side of the Connecticut River in the area of Mt. Ascutney.

Although the settlement has frequently been referred to as an artists' colony, this is a misleading description. It had its beginnings in 1884 when a rising young New York attorney named Charles C. Beaman married the daughter of a retired Senator from New York, William Evarts, and bought land for a permanent country home across the river from Evarts' home in Windsor, Vermont. Beaman rented (and later sold) land to his friend, Augustus Saint-Gaudens, the nation's most famous sculptor. These two men were responsible for attracting those who came in the late 1880's and early 1890's. By 1895 the group was composed of about eighteen families including such artists as George deForest

Brush, Thomas Dewing, Henry Oliver Walker and Stephen Parrish, along with the landscape artist and etcher turned architect, Charles A. Platt. It was Platt and Kenyon Cox, according to the colony's historian, who brought in the literary contingent during the next decade. In addition to Churchill, these included the dramatist Louis Evan Shipman; Herbert Croly, whose occupation would be hard to define at that point in his career; Norman Hapgood, a writer and later editor of *Colliers Weekly*; poet-dramatist Percy MacKaye, and dramatists Langdon Mitchell and Philip Littell. Scattered among the literary and artistic people were a physician, a couple of businessmen, and two famous attorneys — George Rublee and Learned Hand. The local people lumped them all together as "City Folks" and referred to the area as "Little New York," but the group really had little cohesion and each resident lived his life in his own way.

Churchill quickly became acquainted with most of the members of the so-called colony. He was known for his grace and dignity, his fashionable dress, and his handsome equipages — complete with footman and coachman. The courtly hospitality of his lovely wife and his equally lovely house was known throughout the area. Churchill, however, was a reserved man both by nature and acquired habit. His relationship with most people, including many who were closely associated with him, remained on a relatively formal level. He had what was perhaps an ingrained suspicion of "arty" people; the friends of his childhood in St. Louis and of his days at Annapolis remained his most intimate friends. Over the years, however, he did maintain either a professional or personal relationship with many of his neighbors — even the enigmatic Herbert Croly. In later years Churchill liked to describe his relationship with Croly by telling the story of how he and the future founder of *The New Republic*, finding themselves thrust together at a party, both escaped to the front porch. There, having nothing in particular to discuss, they sat for two hours in silence.[7]

Shortly after the Churchills moved into Harlakenden House, a journalist arrived from Boston to interview the author of *Richard Carvel*. The two men got on well, even though the interviewer once referred to Churchill as Mr. Carvel, and Churchill gave him a long interview and even a picture of the house. The journalist was impressed by Harlakenden House and even more impressed by the man he found inside.

> With the grace and dignity of his great characterization, Winston Churchill welcomed me to his new home. He appeared a fashionably attired young man of twenty-eight, displaying a most fastidious taste in every detail of his costume, combined with the courtly grace and dignity of colonial times. A typical college man, smooth-shaven with heavy black eyebrows that join above dancing and gentle brown eyes; with a manner that inspires good nature and good cheer, and a suggestion of a thorough course in athletics; there you have the author of "Richard Carvel." A solid, rugged type of genuine American manhood, with that love of dash and spirit which means "go!" in our national life.[8]

His reference to Churchill as Mr. Carvel, along with the above description, indicates that he went to visit not a man, but the author of a best-seller. Even so, there is probably some truth in his confusion between the author and the hero of the Revolution. A young man of twenty-eight who had achieved fame on the basis of one novel may well have assumed some of the characteristics of his own creation.

It would also seem logical for such an author quickly to produce another novel in the same genre; but Churchill had no such intention at that time. Brett had suggested another course of action even before *Richard Carvel* appeared. His thinking on the matter is fairly obvious. As a publisher he wanted to take advantage of the publicity which the historical novel received, to get something out in a hurry; he knew Churchill spent months doing research when he wrote an historical novel, months more in working and reworking his material. So the logical step was to encourage him to do a book that would not have to be researched. Something along the lines of his earliest work — a series of short stories with a naval setting — was the obvious choice. Churchill described the project to Shaw.

> I have mapped out my naval stories. The same characters are to run through nearly all, and they are to have few or no women in them. I have taken types of all the naval officers which have come under my observation, from the gruff admiral and silent, bull-

> dog captain to the dashing young Ensign — nor have
> I left the mechanical element out . . . . This inventive
> genius of the Yankee sailor coupled with his Anglo-
> Saxon fighting qualities, seems to me an invincible
> combination.[9]

In April, 1899, he asked Richard Watson Gilder of the *Century* if he would be interested in publishing the stories. His intention was to have them appear in a magazine as soon after the publication of *Richard Carvel* as possible and then to publish them in book form in the spring of 1900. Several stories dealing with the adventures of a Mr. Keegan do exist in manuscript form, but they were never to see the light of day. Early in June, 1899, Churchill indicated their fate. "Alas! for the Naval Academy stories. My brain has been seething with the novel I wish to write, and a prospectus whereof I hand you."[10]

As with *Richard Carvel*, the exact nature of the new novel evolved slowly. The original title was to be *The Third Generation* and it was intended to be "of the present day with the roots of it, so to speak, running back to the Civil War." These ideas changed rapidly. In June he said, "I forgot to say that this story is scarcely more of a romance than Mr. Howells' 'Rise of Silas Lapham'. It might be called 'realism', in a sense. It will, I think, lend itself largely to satirical treatment." His intention apparently was to combine the satirical technique of *The Celebrity* with the panoramic canvas of *Richard Carvel*. About six weeks later he told Brett, "The 'Third Generation' will make its bid for greatness as a novel of manners and customs . . . . "[11]

It was the publisher who, either purposely or accidentally, planted the idea of restricting the novel to the Civil War itself. When Churchill sent him the synopsis of the novel, Brett replied that he was happy to hear that Churchill was writing a book in the period of the Civil War. "This," the novelist wrote, "started me to thinking that I would better write the book entirely in that period, and reserve the present-day novel for another book."[12] This decision also meant altering the storyline of the novel. Churchill had intended to concentrate on the adventures of the third generation of the Carvel family, and to follow their fortunes from the Civil War to the turn of the century. As he worked with the material his concentration centered more and more on the origin and events of the war itself; the Carvel descendants still figured prominently in the story, but the center of the stage was taken over by the actual historical events. The title of the novel remained unchanged until some months later when Churchill discovered that Stephen Crane had just published a book called *A Second Generation*. Not wishing to lay himself open to a charge of plagiarism, Churchill changed the title of his novel to one which more accurately indicated the nature of the book — *The Crisis*.

To an even greater degree than for his first historical novel, Churchill mastered the scholarly literature on the period. Shaw sent him a set of James Schouler's *History of the United States* and recommended the relevant volumes in the American Statesman Series. The novelist also poured over the writings of James Ford Rhodes, read biographies of the major historical figures, leaned heavily on Nicolay and Hay's multivolume edition of the writings of Lincoln, and consulted — without accepting the ideas of — *Uncle Tom's Cabin*. One of his characters was an exile from the German revolutions of 1848; so he asked Shaw to recommend the best book on the subject. The editor, a trained historian in his own right, came up with the most perceptive study of the subject that was then available, *The Revolution and Counter-Revolution In Germany* by Frederick Engels.[13]

Beyond the scholarly sources and the sage advice of Shaw, Churchill had the additional advantage of first-hand reports from friends and acquaintances in St. Louis. There were many people still living in 1900 who had vivid recollections of the Civil War period, and Churchill used them to full advantage. Some of these people entrusted him with both their memories and their valued letters and scrapbooks of the period. Isaac H. Sturgeon wrote him about the beginnings of the war in St. Louis, with which he was intimately associated, and sent him his scrapbooks. Churchill's old friend James Yeatman wrote letters relating many stories and events of the Civil War days, and George Leighton gave him information on the important German element in the city. He also had discussions and correspondence with Congressman R. R. Hitt, who was present at the Lincoln-Douglas debates; from him Churchill picked up the little details that give life to his account of that historic encounter. When the standard histories and the eye-witnesses both failed him, Churchill wrote to authorities on the particular subject.[14]

This historical information Churchill transferred to working notebooks where he also wrote down ideas, character sketches, and bits of conversation that he might be able to use. The notebooks show the infinite number of details about the life and times which the author studied before composing the novel. Even more interesting are the large number of historical questions which he posed for himself. Did the slaves go to church in St. Louis in the 1850's? Was the war looked upon from the beginning as a war to free the slaves? What were the implications for the South of Lincoln's election? Some of his questions were quite astute and indicate an historical sophistication equal to that of many professional historians of his own day.

The story in *The Crisis* is essentially that of the coming of the Civil War and the ways in which these events influenced the lives of the people in St. Louis. The hero, Stephen Brice, is a young New Englander who goes to St. Louis with his mother to study law with an ardent abolitionist named Silas Whipple. Judge Whipple had been a friend of Stephen's dead father in the days before Mr. Brice lost the family fortune. In St. Louis Stephen meets Colonel Carvel, a noble Southern aristocrat; his lovely daughter, Virginia; Eliphalet Hopper, the Colonel's wily New England clerk; and a host of historical characters who pass in and out of St. Louis. Churchill traces Stephen's evolution from a good New England conservative to a staunch supporter of Lincoln, and finally his career as a Union Army officer. At the conclusion of the novel the North and South are reconciled as the Union officer and his Confederate lady, Virginia Carvel, proclaim their love for each other in President Lincoln's office.

The public response to *The Crisis* was immediate, enthusiastic, and enduring. The book was reviewed in journals and newspapers throughout the English-speaking world, and the reaction of the reviewers was overwhelmingly favorable. In general they felt that *The Crisis* was a better novel than *Richard Carvel*. Reviews were copied in whole or in part from one newspaper to another, and Walter Littlefield's comment in *Book Reviews* was one of the most frequently repeated. He wrote, "To borrow a Hindu idea, just as *Richard Carvel* is the work of a literary artificer who builds like a giant, so *The Crisis* reveals the fact that this same artificer is capable of finishing like a jeweler."[15] While some critics had extravagant praise for his fictional characters, most recognized that they were not particularly well drawn. Cornelia Atwood Pratt, among a host of others, excused this on the grounds that Churchill — quite rightly — had subordinated the individuals to the force of the events themselves.[16] The historical characters were again recognized as considerably better than the fictional ones, particularly Churchill's portrait of Lincoln.

One of the problems which had given the author most concern when he was writing *The Crisis* was walking the tightrope of sectional objectivity, and the reception of his novel in the South must have been gratifying. The book was written from a Northern point of view, but most of the reviews in Southern papers indicated they felt he had been fair to the South. A typical reaction was that of the Savannah *Press*. This review praised Churchill's portrayal of Virginia Carvel (it would be hard for a Southerner to object to such a glorification of Southern womanhood), but did not approve of his much more realistic picture of Clarence Colfax. The real Southerner of his class, according to the reviewer, "was a natural parliamentarian and leader. He had the manners of a knight, the soul of a Templar, and the dash of a Crusader. And, more than that, he had the highest ideals and was a natural lover of liberty. Winston Churchill did not understand this, evidently . . . . "[17] The reviewer did accept the laudatory portrait of Lincoln — whose merits most Southerners were willing to admit by 1900 — but suggested that Churchill's presentation of Sherman, whom the South would never forgive, was much too full of praise.

The book went into a large number of editions and was translated into several foreign languages. Churchill received requests to name both a waltz and a march after the novel. Charles Williams based a highly successful series of reading recitals on excerpts and scenes from it, and the publishers of Webster's International Dictionary wrote the author about word etymologies. Professor Henry van Dyke of Princeton, who felt that Churchill's treatment of Lincoln was the best in fiction, asked permission to include scenes from *The Crisis* in a volume called Historical Scenes from Fiction that was to be part of a series under the general editorship of Thomas Bailey Aldrich. In many ways *The Crisis* was Churchill's most significant historical novel, and it is the only one to continue to sell in the present day. For these reasons, and because he revealed so many of his own attitudes in the novel, several facets of this work need to be examined in detail.

Churchill's choice of St. Louis as the center of action for his novel was neither accidental nor a simple matter of pride in his birthplace. In part the choice was dictated by his own knowledge of the area and the availability of material, but it was also a matter of dramatic situation. It was in St. Louis, in Churchill's view, that the two strains of Puritan and Cavalier were to meet.

> . . . two currents flowed across the Atlantic to the New World. Then the Stern men found the stern climate, and the Gay found the smiling climate.
>
> After many years the streams began to move again, — westward, ever westward. Over the ever blue mountains from the wonderland of Virginia into the greater wonderland of Kentucky. And through the marvels of the Inland Seas, and by white conestogas threading flat forests and floating over wide prairies, until the two tides met in a maelstorm as fierce as any in the great tawny torrent of the strange Father of Waters. A city founded by Pierre Lacleada, a certain adventurous subject of Louis who dealt in furs, and who knew not Marly or Versailles, was to be the place of the mingling of the tides. After cycles of separation, Puritan and Cavalier united on this clay-bank in the Louisiana Purchase, and swept westward together. Like the struggle of two great rivers when they meet, the waters for a time were dangerous.[18]

This is Churchill's real historical error in *The Crisis*. The South was, of course, not settled by English gentlemen but by the same middle class groups that peopled the North. The Civil War was not, as he sometimes implies, a continuation of the English Civil Wars, an inevitable conflict between two cultures or two ways of life. Yet it would be unfair to blame the novelist for this misinterpretation; the same one was being put forward by most of the professional historians of the day, and it is a myth to which professional Southerners still adhere.

But what in Churchill's mind was the nature of the two societies and of the people who were the products of these societies? Here (as in *Richard Carvel*) it is obvious that Churchill

believed that heredity is the most important element in the formation of character, but, at the same time, each individual is held
responsible for his own life. Discussing Stephen's meeting with
Lincoln, Churchill writes, "It is sometimes instructive to look
back and see how Destiny gave us a kick here, and Fate a shove
there, that sent us in the right direction at the proper time." But
he adds, "And when Stephen Brice looks backward now, he
laughs to think that he did not suspect the Judge of being an ally
of the two who are mentioned above."[19] Fate and Destiny, in
fact, had almost nothing to do with the meeting or with most of
the other situations in the book. And while Churchill makes some
mention of universal human characteristics, it would be hard to
contend that there was much similarity between Eliphalet Hopper
and Stephen Brice; nor were their differences simply a matter of
free choice. Churchill first introduced into this novel a concept
that was to be of tremendous importance to him some years later
in a quite different context. This was the idea of rebirth. Judge
Whipple, on his deathbed, says to Stephen:

> I was harsh with you at first, my son . . . . I wished to
> try you. And when I tried you I wished your mind to
> open, to keep pace with the growth of this nation. I
> sent you to see Abraham Lincoln — that you might
> be born again — in the West. You were born again. I
> saw it when you came back.[20]

But this rebirth of a more democratic Stephen through a contact
with the West was simply the development of an already noble
character; heredity was more important than experience, though
good character was brought out by experience.

With this emphasis on heredity, it is obvious that the
descendants of the two distinct strains of Englishmen will be
almost as unlike as their forebears. His general picture of the
Puritan or Yankee strain tends to be less complimentary than that
of the Cavalier. Indeed he suggests that the villain, Hopper, is a
typical New Englander; from the very beginning Eliphalet is presented as ambitious, shrewd, and hard working. "He had no time
for skylarking, the heat of the day meant nothing to him, and he
was never sleepy." "While Kansas was furnishing excitement free
of charge to any citizen who loved sport, Mr. Eliphalet Hopper
was at work like the industrious mole, underground."[21] At the

same time, he was a devout member of the Congregational Church and his one friend was its minister. Naturally Eliphalet was not impressed with the Brices. "He had ascertained that the golden charm which made the Brices worthy of tribute had been lost. Commercial supremacy, — that was Mr. Hopper's creed. Family is a good thing, but of what use is a crest without the panels on which to paint it?"[22] He sees the war simply as an opportunity to make money in the black market and to take advantage of Colonel Carvel's precarious financial position. Hopper's highest goal would have been marriage to the symbol of those who had ignored him, Virginia Carvel. The fact that this unprincipled upstart would dare covet the hand of the noble Virginia was, in Churchill's eyes and probably in the eyes of his readers as well, the height of his villainy. It was almost miscegenation.

The other self-made Northerner in the novel is the volatile Judge Silas Whipple. Like Hopper, the Judge is proud of being a self-made man and, though he had been a close friend of Stephen's father, is full of scorn for the pusillanimous attitude of the rich toward slavery. When Stephen remarks that the conservative classes in the North are not abolitionists, the Judge explodes. "Why not come out with it, sir, and say the moneyed classes, who would rather see souls held in bondage than risk their wordly goods in an attempt to liberate them."[23] This is about as critical a remark about the old aristocracy as ever found expression in a Churchill novel, but there is no indication that Churchill shared this unflattering view; although the Judge is presented as a good man, he is also presented as a rather eccentric radical. So, while the self-made man need not be a conniving rascal like Hopper, he still lacks the moderating influence that comes from an aristocratic background.

The Northern aristocrat is exemplified by the hero, whose grandfather had made his money in the India trade and served as Minister to France. Although Stephen did not inherit the family fortune, he did inherit the conservative outlook of the old aristocracy and the air of the college bred. Churchill wrote, "It would be so easy to paint Stephen in shining colors, and to make him a first-class prig (the horror of all novelists), that we must begin with the drawbacks." But the worst thing that he could think of to say about Stephen was that he had "what has been called 'the Boston manner'."[24] What he needed was to get out and rub shoulders with the plain men who were building the West.

Throughout the novel, Churchill refers to Stephen's Puritan background as an important factor in his stiff, formal, somber outlook on life. This quality, however, did not prevent either Stephen or his mother from understanding and liking the "Gay" people of "the smiling climate." Mrs. Brice observed of the Southern upper classes: "They are very proud. A wonderful people, — born aristocrats."[25]

Churchill's own admiration for these born aristocrats was unbounded. After the surrender of a Southern company in St. Louis he exclaimed:

> How those thoroughbreds of the Cavaliers showed it! Pain they took lightly. The fire of humiliation burned, but could not destroy their indomitable spirit. They were the first of their people in the field, and the last to leave it. Historians may say that the classes of the South caused the war; they cannot say that they did not take upon themselves the greatest burden of the suffering.[26]

The noblest product of this noble race was Colonel Carvel, a man of such impeccable honor that he once shot at a man who suggested that the Colonel might like to "buy his influence." Afraid of nothing, awed by no one, this luminary was a staunch supporter of the old order. To him the Negroes were "a low breed that ain't fit for freedom" and the German element were "Dutchmen, sir! Hessians! Foreign Republican hirelings, sir . . . . "[27] Unwavering in his loyalty to the South, he does not turn against Captain Brent — the man he himself would have chosen as his daughter's husband — even though he is broken-hearted when Brent remains loyal to the Union. So strong are his feelings that he sacrifices his business and later his life to the Southern cause, but he risks death as a spy to visit his dying Republican friend, Judge Whipple.

Yet the novelist was aware that the younger products of the slave system did not always measure up to the standards of Colonel Carvel, and it was his portrayal of the young aristocrat, Clarence Colfax, that drew the most fire from Southern extremists. Clarence spent much of his youth in drinking and listless indolence; still "his features were of the straight type which has been

called from time immemorial <u>patrician</u>."[28] Even the attitude of
Clarence's own kind toward him was not completely flattering.
Virginia said,

> I am fond of Clarence. But he isn't good for anything
> in the world except horse racing and — and fighting.
> He wanted to help drive the Black Republican
> emigrants out of Kansas, and his mother had to put
> a collar and chain on him. He wanted to go fili-
> bustering with Walker, and she had to get down on
> her knees. And yet . . . if you Yankees push us as
> far as war, Mr. Brice, just look out for him.[29]

This, of course, was the point. In time of crisis, according to the
myth, his dormant nobility and manliness were brought forth.
Although it was a desire to prove himself to Virginia that motivated his actions, it was the hereditary quality within him that enabled him to be a hero.

The association of strength of character with a distinguished
lineage is even more apparent in the treatment of Clarence's
mother. A beautiful woman of forty-three, she was of lower class
origins — the daughter of old Judge Colfax's overseer. She behaves
badly in all crisis situations, and her hysterical conduct stands in
stark contrast to Virginia's courage and calm. The reason for her
behavior is obviously to be found, not in her environment, which
was the same as Virginia's, but in her lowly origins.

Given Churchill's affection for the Anglo-Saxon race, it is
not surprising that he treated the Germans in St. Louis with considerably more respect than he was to treat the later immigrants
from Southern and Eastern Europe. Still he could not separate
himself completely from the Southern aristocratic attitude that
the Germans were vulgar scum. Of some of the German soldiers,
he wrote, "They searched the place more than once from garret to
cellar, muttered gutteral oaths, and smelled of beer and sauerkraut.
The haughty appearance of Miss Carvel did not awe them — they
were blind to all manly sensations."[30]

Nor, given the time and his own predilections, could Churchill be expected to present a flattering picture of the Blacks. These
were the very years during which the fight between the conservative Democratic leaders and their Populist opponents led to the
disenfranchisement and legal segregation of the Blacks in the
South. At the same time conservative Republicans in the North

were urging the nation to take up the White Man's Burden by imperialistic ventures in Latin America and the Pacific. Racist feelings were more widespread and more respectable in America during these years than at any time in history, and Churchill shared them.

The impression one gets is that Churchill's position was quite close to that of most Northerners in the years before the Civil War; he was completely opposed to the institution of slavery but at the same time he did not feel that Blacks were equal to white men. Although no Black people figure prominently in the story, those who do appear seem to be happy with their lot in life. On the other hand, Churchill does present a realistic picture of the slave auction and of the oily auctioneer who invites the buyers to pinch his wares. "Men came forward to feel the creatures and look into their mouths, and one brute, unshaven and with filthy linen, snatched a child from its mother's lap."[31]

Slavery as an institution was brutal and wrong, but when Churchill presented any discussion of the Blacks as human beings he tried to keep his personal views out of it. Most of the arguments on slavery are presented in the battles between Judge Whipple and Colonel Carvel. Whipple argues largely from a moral point of view, while Carvel presents most of his arguments in terms of the economic necessity of slavery to the South — a point which the Judge never really counters. More importantly, the Colonel contends that Blacks have no self-control and cannot be allowed to become enfranchised citizens. Nor is education the answer — as the Judge suggests — because education in self-government takes centuries. The Colonel also presents most of the other arguments used by the historical apologists for slavery, and in the debates he seems to have the better of it. The only interpolation the author makes is to say, "All honor to those old-time Negroes who are now memories, whose devotion to their masters was next to their love of God."[32]

A contemporary reviewer, who obviously disliked historical novels, wrote that he went out on the streets of New York City and asked people if they had read *The Crisis*. Most replied they had. When asked how they liked it they answered universally that they thought it was dull. Why then read it? Because everyone was doing it! The whole thing was mob psychology, the reviewer contended, mob psychology stimulated by half-educated critics who gave such books adulatory reviews. Although this is undoubtedly part of the explanation for the popularity of *The Crisis*, it is far from the whole story. Others remarked on the vast amount of publicity that preceded the publication of the novel; this too must have had some effect. But beyond these things is the obvious fact that Churchill had a live subject, especially in the wake of the Spanish-American War; he was a storyteller who did interest his readers in the historical narrative, and he wrote the book in such a way that it could be popular over the entire country. Jeannette Gilder called it "probably the best story of the Civil War that has been written." If one views Stephen Crane's *Red Badge of Courage* as a study of human beings in a crisis situation and not as a story about the Civil War, this statement was true in 1901. Perhaps it is still true. One modern critic has said:

> One of the best novels dealing with the struggle between North and South, *The Crisis* is memorable for its judicious handling of the issues involved, for the strategic placing of its main plot within a border state, and for its sympathetic portrait of Abraham Lincoln.[35]

With all of these things in its favor, the popularity of the novel is not such a mystery after all.

CHAPTER V

Life As A Popular Novelist

With proof that his first serious novel had not been a matter of chance, Churchill was now unquestionably in the first rank of America's popular authors. During the period that followed the publication of *The Crisis* he was showered with honors, offers, and requests of every variety.

Naturally the requests for articles and stories were numerous; the magazines for women were most anxious to obtain stories from him, and he was also asked to write some nonfiction articles.[1] Requests for interviews, information, and assistance of all kinds also came in a constant stream. Children were named after him, and he was asked to be an honored guest at more functions than he could possibly attend.

Perhaps it was the friendliness and hospitality of the Churchills that encouraged people to ask favors that went beyond normal bounds. Perhaps also it was Churchill's habit of answering even the most presumptuous or inconsequential of letters. The editor of the *Imperial and Colonial Magazine and Review* asked if he would like to become co-editor of this new weekly, which would be devoted to anti-imperialism. They had already approached the British Churchill and, not surprisingly, he had declined their offer. Therefore, since the Churchill name was a household word in England, they decided to turn to the American Churchill.

He would get twenty-five percent of the anticipated profits when the journal got underway; in the meantime what they really needed was cash. A similar though less presumptuous request came from the *Christian Century*. They wanted to obtain short articles by "the best writers in the English speaking world," and Churchill was included in the list of men to be so honored. They had hopes of paying liberally in the future, but at the moment did not have any money either. Occasionally there were open requests for money; more often people asked for his time and talent. An attorney in Dallas had collected a large amount of material for a story illustrating life in Tennessee around the time of the Civil War, but had no idea how to put it together. He wanted to know if "it is asking too much of you to map out for me how to proceed."[2] Churchill received numerous letters of this kind over the years, and he handled them with considerable kindness. Although once in a while he agreed to read and criticize someone's work, he usually just reiterated his belief that good writing is ninety percent hard work.

Churchill found life as a famous author somewhat hectic. In reply to one request for a short article he wrote:

> I cannot begin to tell you the exigencies and troubles and trials of this time that you have asked me to break into. I have not taken a day or an hour this summer that was not needed for exercise or necessary recreation. I have not contributed to any periodical, and I have put off a most remunerative article until after the book is finished . . . . It is on my mind night and day. I make it a rule never to appear in print unless I can do my very best work, and therefore I could not write you a thousand words under three days, which would mean a great loss to me, as it would take three more days at least to get into my stride again.[3]

Busy as he was, Churchill did find time to participate in local affairs. Among other things he was active in the local Episcopal Church, communicated with Senator Gallinger about RFD delivery for the colony, wrote many letters concerning local road repairs, worked to raise money for a monument to Colonel Putnam, and contributed half the money for library rooms in Cornish. He also took the time to receive an honorary M.A. from Dartmouth.

And he could now indulge his childhood fondness for horses. He kept his own stable and was frequently seen driving his four-in-hand about the country. This interest in horses did not prevent him from owning and driving one of the first automobiles in the area, an activity that brought him considerable trouble. A letter which he wrote to the editor of the *Vermont Journal* in Windsor indicates that the local press had some reservations about his driving habits.

> I hope you will give me an opportunity of answering the charge which appeared in your last issue against me, and which was evidently calculated to injure me in the eyes of my fellow townsmen and neighbors. I think that any fair-minded person in this neighborhood will be glad to bear witness that I have used people on the road with every consideration. I have always stopped, not only my car, but my engine, when I have seen teams approaching. And I always intend so to do. Anyone who is acquainted with a motor car will know that this is going to a great deal of trouble.[4]

Despite the fact that he was a hard worker and tried to avoid as many distractions as possible, Churchill did enjoy being with other people. His home was well equipped for entertaining the large number of guests that arrived and departed in a steady stream, and he was a member of numerous clubs. He particularly enjoyed playing squash at the Tennis and Racquet Club in Boston, and fly fishing in Canada where the Triton Club owned a wilderness of lakes and streams. A two-hour drive from his home took him to Corbin's Park (a well-stocked private game preserve of thirty square miles), known as the Blue Mountain Fish and Game Club. Harlakenden House held many trophies of these excursions, including a large stuffed rainbow trout and several wild boars' heads.[5]

Churchill's frequent companion on fishing trips was Senator Redfield Proctor of Vermont, and, through Proctor, the novelist met a number of political figures. Indeed Proctor seems to have used these men as a lure to tempt the author away from his literary labors. One such occasion was particularly important in Churchill's life, for it was the Vermont Senator who introduced him to Theodore Roosevelt. Churchill had accepted a request from the Vermont Fish and Game League to address their meeting at Isle La Motte, on Lake Champlain, September sixth. The special guest on this occasion was to be Vice-President Theodore Roosevelt. Although Churchill had received a letter from Roosevelt praising *The Crisis*, the two men had never met. Despite this fact there are some indications that Churchill was already involved in a movement to make the young political maverick the next President. This is suggested in the course of a letter from Churchill's close friend and attorney, Guy Murchie, in which the lawyer states:

> Roosevelt will be back in a few days now probably and later we can have crystallized our political boom scheme. General Wood thinks it a fine one and so does another confidential of mine. It remains to be discovered what the man himself will say! By the way has it occurred to you how we can keep the individual parts of the club focussed and together for three years?[6]

With this movement already underway, Churchill must have looked forward to the meeting with a good deal of interest.

Roosevelt, of course, became President sooner than was anticipated. In fact it was during this visit to Isle La Motte that the Vice-President was informed of McKinley's death and his own accession to power. Although newspaper reports at the time stated that Churchill was with Roosevelt when he was told of the assassination, this is unlikely. A newspaper reporter who was present records that he hurried out to find Churchill but was unable to locate him. So while the novelist was on the scene, he was not actually with Roosevelt when the next President received the news.[7]

In any case, the novelist and the new President enjoyed each other's company and when Roosevelt took office he asked Churchill to come to Washington with his wife and Guy Murchie, to dine with him and meet Mrs. Roosevelt. The President wrote again in November, and on November 10, the Churchills and Murchie were present at a White House dinner for members of the Cabinet. This event must have impressed the young novelist, who in seven years had progressed from sub-editor to successful novelist and at thirty years of age to a position of friendship with the President of the United States. And this friendship, or the inspiration which Churchill derived from it, was to have important consequences for his career. When Roosevelt again returned to Vermont and New Hampshire, Churchill also had entered into the political world and he was anxious to have the President as a guest at Harlakenden House. Although this did not come about, he did drive the President from Cornish Flats to Windsor — much to the consternation of Senator Proctor who was worried about Churchill's reputation as a wild man behind the reins.[9] The political side of this friendship is a story in itself, but the personal relationship continued through the years and endured the growing fame of both men.

Another of the interests which were to lead Churchill ultimately into politics was forestry. This concern developed early in his career; in *The Celebrity* he wrote: "Farrar likewise received an income from the state, whose legislature had at last opened its eyes to the timber depredations and had begun to buy up reserves."[10] When he moved to New Hampshire, where the timber lands were being plundered by the corporations, his interest increased and on the advice of the Society's president, Frank Rollins, he was appointed as a Vice-president of the Society for the Protection of New Hampshire Forests in his own county of Sullivan.[11] And he took this position seriously. He obtained pamphlets on forestry from the crusading Gifford Pinchot, contributed considerable amounts of money, distributed placards, wrote innumerable letters, and was at least partially responsible for the appointment by the Association of a professional salaried forester who traveled about the state giving free advice to anyone who requested it. He also made a number of speeches around the state supporting bills in the legislature which would establish a state nursery, exempt properly planted timber lands from taxation, and provide funds for a forest survey of the White Mountains. In addition to this, the Association and Churchill worked for the establishment of a national forest preserve in the White Mountains.[12]

The role of speech-maker was a new one for the novelist and one which he assumed reluctantly. In 1901 he was asked to speak at the dedication of the Louisiana Purchase Building at the Pan-American Exposition in Buffalo, and, after considerable hesitation, he decided to make his maiden effort. In this speech (on July 2, 1901) one can see glimpses of the reform ideas which Churchill was one day to embrace with enthusiasm. The logic of his remarks is sometimes hard to follow, however, and it is obvious that he was still wrestling with the problems in his own mind. What emerges is a combination of manifest destiny and moral decline. He contends that with Jefferson's purchase of the Louisiana Territory, Americans were faced with a continent that had to be controlled. The settlers who went to this new land thought in terms of "Land, Plenty and Freedom." Occupied with the conquest of a continent, Americans had no time for questions of ethics. But in 1901 the time had arrived for a return to the moral supremacy of the nation's founders. Now that the continent had been conquered and Americans had some leisure time, they must get to know themselves. "And let us hope that in the midst of our prosperity just a little shame will come to us, and so, after awhile, we may get back some of the old traditions which we have lost."[13] He never did state or define the basic problem, but the speech does foreshadow some of the ideas which he was to formulate in his novel *Coniston* five years later.

In December of 1901 the Churchills embarked on their second trip to Europe. They had intended to spend a month or so in England, then go on to Rome and ultimately to Egypt. In fact, however, they went to Italy first, touring Venice, Florence, and Rome. On leaving Venice in the middle of February, they proceeded to Munich and on to Berlin. As they progressed they broadened their acquaintance in diplomatic and governmental circles, dining in Germany with the American Ambassador and meeting a wide range of influential people. From Germany they went to Paris and on to England, arriving there early in May. They were widely entertained in England and Churchill was pleased with their reception.[14] The discordant note of the trip was Churchill's second meeting with his namesake.

The continued confusion of names had begun to gall the novelist even before he left the States. He wrote Brett that "if any Englishman is fool enough (and I suppose that there are a great many who are), to believe that Winston Spencer Churchill wrote *The Crisis*, he is perfectly welcome to do so. I am not writing for the English public and I am heartily sick and tired of them. I do not know whether I shall go to England or not."[15]

When Churchill arrived in England, the young M.P. sent a letter saying that he wanted to see his American "friend," but he was leaving for a holiday in the country. In the meantime he obtained a temporary honorary membership in the Pall Mall Club for the visitor and invited Churchill to dine with him at the House of Commons, where he said he would "make up a pleasant party for you of men who think." Apparently oblivious to the novelist's tender feelings about the matter, he closed by saying, "Your books are still praised here and I am loaded with spurious literary business." In another letter the Englishman compounded this by stating "I have added 'of America' to your address, for I am known at the Carlton [the hotel where Churchill was staying] and I fear my letter might come back to me."[16] The novelist's reaction to this whole affair can be seen in the following account which he wrote in a notebook.

> On Thursday, May 29, dined with my namesake Winston Churchill of House of Commons. Considering the fact that when he came to America I dropped my work and went to see him, and gave a supper in his honor, he has acted like a cad. He wrote me on my arrival that he was just leaving town for a parliamentary recess, and that he would be at home at such an such an hour. Needless to say I did not go. I heard nothing more from him until the day of the dinner when I got a telegram asking me to meet him in the lobby of the House of Commons at 7:55. I thought that it would be more dignified to go. I was not his guest, but one of the guests of a club called the Hooligans which meets on Thursday Evenings. Sir Henry Campbell-Bannerman sat on Churchill's right, I on his left.[17]

He went on to make some rather unflattering comments about how Campbell-Bannerman and a number of others "toadied" to the English Churchill and to the other sons of Lords who were present, concluding, "And so Charles Dickens wrote in vain."

It was evidently during this visit that Churchill became disenchanted with the British social system. He noted that his love for the "British race" had not been increased by the trip, adding that "it is hard to respect a nation which must have a class to worship, and which adds to an already inane body a still more inane set of toadies." Contact with the British aristocracy convinced him that just being a gentleman was not enough. In recording his impressions during the trip back to the States, he related an incident that occurred when he and his wife were having dinner with Lord Bryce and his wife. He and Bryce had been discussing Roosevelt, whom they both greatly admired, and the noted observer of the American scene commented that Roosevelt was the first gentleman to occupy the White House since the early days of the Republic. After a moment Bryce corrected himself. "Buchanan was a gentleman, I believe," he said, to which Churchill replied, "Yes, but he was nothing more."[18] Churchill's intense patriotism was always strengthened by his visits abroad. Although he enjoyed associating with the European upper classes, he preferred American society. Reporting to Shaw after his return in 1902, Churchill said he had had a good time, but "seven months in Europe is enough to give a man patriotism enough to last him the rest of his life."[19]

Despite the second meeting of the two Winston Churchills the confusion of names continued. When *The Crisis* was published the Chicago *Chronicle* wrote:

> The great American novel which has been asked for so often of late cannot be said to be here, but a prophecy of its coming is found — strange to say — in the work of the Englishman, Winston Churchill.[20]

Nor were American midwestern newspapers the only ones to continue in error; even the august and unfailing Manchester *Guardian* made the same mistake. And the confusion never ceased to annoy the American novelist. As late as 1906 he displayed his irritation in a letter to Richard Harding Davis.

> I read your article on the Baron and King of Trinidad with great interest, and I am looking forward with equal interest to that on my namesake. By the way, as a little bit of justice to me, would you mind calling him Winston Spencer Churchill. He has written me that he will be known by this name, and he signs all his books in this way. You are undoubtedly aware. that his name is legally Spencer-Churchill. When the male branch of the original Duke died out, they became Spencer, but petitioned the Crown to be called Spencer-Churchill.[21]

The Churchills arrived back in New York aboard the steamship *Teutonic* on June 13, 1902. After a short visit to St. Louis they returned to their home in New Hampshire. The novelist was undoubtedly glad to be back; he always was. He enjoyed travel, but was always happy to return to his own home, his stables, his friends, and his work.

That particular summer of 1902 was a busy one. Churchill had decided to run for the State Legislature, and during the months that followed he conducted a modest but successful campaign for the Republican nomination and then for election. During the same period he began to work in earnest on his next historical novel, which was to deal with the migration through Kentucky and the eventual acquisition of the Louisiana territory. The sources for this aspect of American history, in the days before Frederick Jackson Turner and his followers flooded the country with monographs on Western expansion and sectional history, were neither numerous nor reliable. Churchill seems to have relied heavily for the later sections of his novel on C.E.A. Gayarre's two-volume *Histoire de la Louisiane*, a work originally published in French in 1846. It was revised and translated in a four-volume edition in 1903, but this was probably too late to have been of much use to Churchill.

The historical sources may have been minimal, but the scenes of the great migration were still there, and in December, Churchill set out in Parkman-like fashion on a trip of several months duration to visit the sites that would occupy a place of prominence in his story. In St. Louis on the first leg of the journey he addressed a group of 160 New Englanders at a celebration of the 282nd anniversary of the Pilgrims' landing at Plymouth. During the course of his remarks on "New England Today" he stated:

> The largest part of New England, has resigned itself to its fate, not an unpleasant one, of becoming a park for the rest of the United States. All our legislation in New Hampshire is tending this way. We have a progressive party in our legislature, which is gradually gaining ground, and we hope soon to build roads in order that we may sell our abandoned farms and take advantage of the new class of citizens which this latest evolution has brought about.[22]

In speaking of a progressive party here he was referring simply to a group that was interested in such things as conservation and good roads, not to a political party. He was still enough of an innocent (politically and economically) to feel that good roads and conservation were all the state needed to make it prosperous, and also enough of an outsider to be unaware of how the above statement would appear in the eyes of the natives. His remarks were widely reported in the New England press and not with great enthusiasm; some, quite naturally, were openly resentful. His suggestion that New England was being turned into one big national park was made in all innocence but was not one to endear a neophyte politician to his constituents.

As a politician, Churchill had to interrupt his St. Louis visit to return to New Hampshire for the opening sessions of the legislature. He then returned to complete his investigations in St. Louis and proceeded on to New Orleans for a two-week visit. While in New Orleans, and throughout his research for *The Crossing*, Churchill's task was facilitated by his friendship with Pierre Chouteau, who was preparing a bibliography of materials on the Louisiana Territory. He worked closely with Churchill from the beginning, sending him papers and documents, and obtaining for him a copy of Gayarre's work, which had been out of print for years.[23]

Before the Churchills arrived in New Orleans, Chouteau had made arrangements for the novelist to meet the local authorities (both academic and amateur) on the history of the area. At least part of the visit was spent with Chouteau's brother-in-law, John Henshaw, and Churchill was fascinated by this glimpse of life in the deep South. "Here we are in a true Southern house," he wrote, "in the heart of the Acadian Country. You could go mad here — no clocks — no hours for meals, everything casual . . . . The house is a vast wooden structure, bare of furniture except in a few rooms, surrounded by the great live oaks and pecans of the primeval forest, hung with spanish moss. Behind is the famous Bayou Teche, lined by oak and cypress and magnolia." Churchill used the visit with Henshaw in New Iberia to collect facts for one of the detailed settings which were characteristic of his novels. "I spent yesterday trying to learn the flora. I have a list as long as this page. I bought a kodak in New Orleans and spent two entire days in the Vieux Carré (the old New Orleans) photographing old houses, doorways, etc."[24]

After this short but fruitful stay in New Orleans, the Churchills journeyed to Nashville, Tennessee, where they remained for several days in the middle of April as guest of Colonel Jere Baxter. Continuing to follow in reverse fashion one of the paths used by the pioneers in their trek to the west, they went into Kentucky and the Cumberland Gap area, returning home for the closing days of the legislative session. When that was over Churchill settled down to work. During the summer they took a house in Marion, Massachusetts, for a while, but it was too hot for Mrs. Churchill and they returned to Cornish, where they remained until the following winter, when they again established a residence in Boston during the cold winter months. Their son John was born there in December, 1903.

It was at this point in his career that Churchill made a statement in an interview which has served to damn him in the eyes of future critics and occupants of Axel's Castle. The article quotes him as saying:

> I have no patience with literary cant. Writing, it appears to me, is a business, and a direct means to the end. If people read, they want to read for their own entertainment or instruction and not to serve the author's pleasure or hobby. The lawyer prepares his brief to secure a verdict; so must the author. The judgment must be passed from a standpoint entirely apart from that of the author.
>
> I make a business of writing. Action and atmosphere, bone and blood are the things I try to put into books.[25]

These sentiments are nothing more than a continuation of the attitude with which Churchill entered the writing profession in the first place. The artist who lives in a garret and is willing to watch his wife and children go hungry while he slaves over a masterpiece that no one will buy, may be an appealing figure to the critic, but such conduct was quite outside of Churchill's frame of reference at this point in his career.

CHAPTER VI

The End of a Phase

As early as the fall of 1902 Brett was beginning to worry about Churchill's next novel. He wanted as much advance notice as possible because it was becoming harder than ever "to get a really great sale on a new novel, partly because so many are appearing and partly on account of differing trade conditions."[1] As with *The Crisis*, the basic theme of the new novel quickly took form in Churchill's mind, but the development of it evolved slowly. In the summer of 1901 Churchill told Shaw, "I was thinking just the other day that it was you who suggested to me long before I thought of doing it, the writing of a novel of the making of the West."[2] Quite possibly he originally intended to deal only with the settlement of Kentucky and Tennessee and with the fight for the Northwest Territory. If he planned to include the story of Louisiana, neither his publisher nor his friend, Pierre Chouteau, knew about it. One factor in the decision to include the Louisiana Territory in the novel may have been the forthcoming centennial celebration of the acquisition of the area by the United States. The commercial possibilities of this event surely did not escape the astute business eye of George Brett. In any case the decision to expand the coverage was made and somewhere in the process the title of the novel was changed from *The Conquest* to *The Crossing*.

By this time Brett had replaced Shaw as Churchill's principal counselor. From 1896 to the summer of 1899 Churchill had written to Shaw frequently, asking his advice on just about everything; by the fall of 1899 communications were less frequent and the letters gradually became more formal than before. Since there is no evidence of a disagreement between the two men, the probable explanation for the changing relationship is in the maturing of the younger author. He no longer felt the need for a substitute father. A more satisfactory relationship at this point in his career was the developing closeness of his association with Brett. The Bretts now visited the Churchills at least as often as the Shaws did, and from the tone of Churchill's letters to his publisher and the change in greeting from "Dear Mr. Brett," to "My dear Brett," it seems that their relationship became less formal and more intimate in the late spring of 1900. From then on Brett served as advisor, but an advisor who was more of an equal than a father. And it was a role to which the publisher was extremely well-suited. He had an uncanny knack for anticipating what people wanted to read, an understanding of the mood and temper of the reading public, and Churchill usually took his advice.

Churchill's research included most of the standard historical works pertaining to the time and territory under consideration. Although it is impossible to tell exactly what he read, his readings included at least the following: Theodore Roosevelt's *Winning of the West*; three biographies of Daniel Boone, including the current one by the scholarly R. G. Thwaites; a biography of George Rogers Clark; several biographies of Burr; the third volume of Henry Adams' *History of the United States*; David Clark's *Proofs of the Corruption of General James Wilkinson*; the Blennerhassett Papers; some edition of the Federalist Papers; Thomas Ashe's *Travels*; Mrs. Trollope's *Domestic Manners of Americans*; John Reynolds' old *Pioneer History of Illinois to 1818*; and Henry M. Breckenridge's *Views of Louisiana* — in addition to Gayarre's work. He also received large collections of papers and documents from Chouteau and from C. A. Billon, whose father had written a history of St. Louis to 1820.[3]

Churchill's third historical novel was the first one in which a major war was not the focal point, but the theme was certainly one of conquest. In the Afterword, the author states:

> This book has been named "The Crossing" because
> I have tried to express in it the beginnings of that
> great movement across the mountains which swept
> resistless over the Continent until at last it saw the
> Pacific itself. The Crossing was the first instinctive
> reaching out of an infant nation which was one day
> to become a giant. No annals in the world's history
> are more wonderful than the story of the conquest
> of Kentucky and Tennessee by the pioneers.[4]

The story of this migration across the mountains and rivers
to the plains beyond is told through the eyes and the adventures
of David Ritchie, who was born in the Blue Ridge Mountains of
North Carolina during the reign of King George III. When his
father is killed in the Revolution, Davy accompanies a young
pioneer couple to Kentucky and fights Indians in the Ohio country
with George Rogers Clark. In later years, as a lawyer in Louisville,
he helps to foil the Wilkinson conspiracy and the machinations of
Citizen Genet. These activities take him to New Orleans, where
he meets and falls in love with a lovely, aristocratic refugee from
the French Revolution.

Some commentators have contended that the era of the
historical novel was passing when *The Crossing* appeared, that this
novel was not the overwhelming success that the others were; they
have gone on to imply that such considerations caused Churchill
to change the genre of his stories.[5] It is true that this novel
received more unfavorable reviews than *The Crisis*. Many reviewers
felt that Churchill had chosen too large a canvas and crowded it
with too much detail; more than one remarked that while the
story had its lighter moments, Churchill's touch was not light
enough to produce good humor. Probably the majority saw that
the story line of the novel tended to be subsumed by the history.
These same critics pointed out, as they had before, that his
fictional characters were wooden; his heroes and heroines were
impossibly heroic. One writer, mentioning Davy's great accomplishments, commented, "The wisdom of Solomon, the craft of
Ulysses, the physical dexterity of Daniel Boone, when compounded in a stripling, produce, not a human being, but a phantasm
of the fancy."[6]

Actually, *The Crossing* has many of the same merits as

Churchill's other two historical novels — and nearly all of their faults. The best character portraits are again the historical characters or (more particularly in this novel) the minor characters. Churchill was rather skillful at sketching a character in a few incidents; it was in sustaining a believable character throughout the story that he had difficulty. The main characters are too much like robots and the reader has no trouble in predicting their actions and reactions once the scene has been established.

With regard to the construction and style of the novel, most of those who have studied Churchill's work feel that *The Crossing* is the best written of his historical romances. One critic has stated that Churchill's chapter on Davy's journey over the Wilderness Trail "is as good a description of a pioneer journey as one can find in fiction." Another student of Churchill's work feels that the first part of the novel, called "The Borderland," is the "best single part of any of his historical novels."[7] This part of the novel, through the Vincennes campaign, was separately printed and continued to be read (especially in schools) long after the novel itself had faded into oblivion.

So far as historical accuracy is concerned, Churchill's reputation as an historian was elevated by the novel. In addition to his excellent description of the trip across the Wilderness Trail, he gives a good picture of the separatist movement in Watauga or Franklin and his discussion of the conflicting land claims in Kentucky (with the resulting legal chaos) is accurate. Although he wrote from a definite Federalist point of view, he understood the dissatisfaction of the trans-Appalachian pioneer with the central government, and the fact that the basic reason for this dissatisfaction was not so much a matter of politics as of the simple inability of the government to control the only outlet to markets available to the frontiersmen — the Mississippi River. The historical characters are fairly accurately portrayed, though the frontier leaders like Daniel Boone and John Sevier are made larger than life. His brief sketch of Andrew Jackson is very realistic, including his picture of the future President's early life, his spree in Charleston, and the state of affairs when he arrived in Tennessee. Aside from more or less incidental details, the major distortion is in the person of George Rogers Clark. He, too, appears as a giant in the early section of the book, and in the later sections Churchill makes him fall lower than he really fell. Bitterness, dissatisfaction, and drunkenness were all facets of the real Clark but (probably to play up the lack of appreciation of republics for their heroes) Churchill exaggerated these qualities. And yet all things considered, including the state of historical scholarship on these matters at the time he wrote, Churchill again presented an accurate picture of a scene from the American drama.

All of these are qualities which *The Crossing* shared with Churchill's previous novels, but there are some ideas which he either introduced in a new way or amplified in this novel. One of these ideas involves the question of environment, heredity, and the nobility of character. In his earlier works, Churchill had dealt more or less unconsciously with this problem; in this novel and later works he would become increasingly aware of the force of the environment in forming character. In *The Crossing* the problem revolves around the conflict of the good frontiersman and the good aristocrat. This was only a few years after Frederick Jackson Turner had promulgated his frontier hypothesis and one sees something of a climate of opinion here in Churchill's more or less unconscious assumptions along the same line. At the same time the novelist continued to operate on his basic assumption that nobility of character depends upon a genteel background.

This ambivalent attitude is present both in Churchill's comments in the novel and in the characters themselves. After a short stay at his aunt's plantation Davy reminisces, "A longing came upon me for the old backwoods life, with its freedom and self-reliance, and a hatred for this steaming country of heat and violent storms, and artificiality and pomp. And I had a desire, even at that age, to make my own way in the world." Here is apparent the naturalness of the frontier compared with the artificiality of the seaboard area; later he pictures this same West as the Garden of Eden which men can attain only with great sacrifice.

Henry Nash Smith has termed one of the dominant themes in American thought "The Myth of the Garden." He suggests that Americans, including Frederick J. Turner, have felt that the European or Easterner entered into the frontier atmosphere and there, in contact with nature, he sloughed off the artificial veneer of corrupt institutions and traditions and emerged as the good natural man.[8] Something of this is seen in *The Crossing*, although there is little explicit discussion of it; at that point in his life Churchill was not so systematic in his thinking. Most of his pioneers, however, are presented as natural men of the woods, led not by the formalized rules of society, but by the same moral law which guided the actions of Cooper's Leatherstocking.

Davy certainly worshiped the buckskin men of the West, but those he most admired have qualities which distinguish them from the typical frontiersman, qualities which are a product of civilization. And these are virtues which Churchill associated with a gentleman. Writing of Nollichucky Jack Sevier, Churchill says:

> I saw him coming from the porch of the house, a tall, slim figure in a hunting shirt — that fitted to perfection — and cavalry boots. His face, his carriage, his quick movements and stride filled my notion of a hero, and my instinct told me he was a gentleman born.[9]

Even Clark, who in many ways personified the man of the West in this novel, is described as a man "whose power was reenforced by that strange thing called an education. It was this, no doubt, gave him command of words when he chose to use them."[10] The logical conclusion is that the West simply brought out the nobility of character already present in those of aristocratic background; it provided an ideal environment for the development of inherited characteristics.

Churchill also followed the pattern of his previous novels in endowing his pioneer heroes with the same quality of personal magnetism that characterized his earlier heroes. Throughout the book Davy is always adulating someone — Sevier, Boone, Clark, etc. These men are born leaders whom others follow instinctively, and upon their actions depend the future of the West. Speaking of Clark as he went to a meeting with the Indians, Churchill observed, "Here was the spectacle of one strong man's brain pitted against the combined craft of the wilderness."[11] For Churchill the settlement of the West was the conquest of a ruthless wilderness by the daring of great leaders whose nobility of character was brought out by the challenge of the West.

This was the side of the westward movement that Turner eulogized and Smith pictured in the "Myth of the Garden." The other side was the inevitable conquest of the wilderness by the advance of the American, and the subsequent creation of a new civilization; and in Churchill's version, this idea of manifest destiny involved the current myth of Anglo-Saxon superiority. Contrasting the French citizens of Kaskaskia with Clark's army, Churchill made this apparent.

> On the one side, not the warriors of a nation that has made its mark in war, but peaceful peasants who had sought this place for its remoteness from persecution, to live and die in harmony with all mankind. On the other, the sinewy advance guard of a race that knows not peace, whose goddess of liberty carries in her hand a sword. The plough might have been graven on our arms, but always the rifle.[12]

These men of the Anglo-Saxon race would conquer the wilderness by force. With reference to the leaders of the Wautagua settlement, Davy says, "These captains dwelt on the border-land of mystery, conquered the wilderness, and drove before them its savage tribes by their might."[13]

This is presented by the author as inevitable, as almost a divine mission; America was fulfilling God's purpose. Men of such a race were not likely to be balked by such small things as the Mississippi River or the legal possession of territory by another nation. A French merchant told Davy that any student of the Anglo-Saxon race must come to the conclusion that the United States would one day take Louisiana. "You have seen for yourself how they have overrun and conquered Kentucky and the Cumberland districts, despite a hideous warfare waged by all the tribes. Your people will not be denied, and when they get to Louisiana, they will take it, as they take everything else."[14] Davy himself later speculated on this and used the same reasoning partially to justify Clark's actions in that connection.

> The support given to Wilkinson's plots, to Clark's expedition, was merely the outward and visible sign of the onward sweep of a resistless race. In spite of untold privations and hardships, of cruel warfare and massacre, these people had toiled over the mountains into this land, and impatient of check or hindrance would, even as Clark had predicted, when their numbers were sufficient leap the Mississippi. Night or day, drunk or sober, they spoke of this thing with an ever increasing vehemence, and no man of reflection who had read their history could say, that they would be thwarted. One day Louisiana would be

> theirs and their childrens' for the generations to come.
> One day Louisiana would be American.[15]

Given his belief in the justness of the Anglo-Saxon march to the sea, Churchill's attitude toward those who stood in the way is understandable. His picture of the Indian, like his characterization of the Negro, was tinged with contemporary racism. His Indians follow the pioneer stereotype — crafty, cruel, easily cowed when brought face to face with a man like Clark. Consequently, when the captains of the Kentucky settlements "drove before them its savage tribes by their might," little thought is given to the fact that these savages were defending their homes. When Davy scalps an Indian that he has killed, he thinks to himself: "Nor did I have any other feeling than fierce hatred of the race which had killed my father."[16] The Anglo-Saxon — warlike, marching forward with irresistible power — had no time to worry about the destiny of inferior races.

Churchill, then, combined in his own thinking the same dual image of what the West had been that Henry Nash Smith found typical of the general American attitude toward the frontier. On one hand, it was the Garden in which men sloughed off the artificiality of older societies and lived as the natural man under the vague guidance of the moral law. This is a rather strained image in Churchill's case, however, since he pictured the Garden as a hostile environment which must be conquered by men who were slightly larger than life. On the other hand was the idea of manifest destiny, combined in Churchill's mind with the march of the Anglo-Saxon, whereby the Garden must inevitably yield to the conquering hand of the American and a new civilization would emerge out of the wilderness. These two myths are logically self-defeating; the results of manifest destiny would mean the end of the Garden; there would be nowhere to escape from the constrictions of society, no frontier to bring out the best in men. As has been noted many times, this is a contradiction that bothered Frederick Jackson Turner in the 1890's as he sought, unsuccessfully, to replace the geographic frontier with an economic one, somehow to make the Andrew Carnegies the logical successors of the George Rogers Clarks. Churchill understood the contradiction less clearly. Rather than worry about what would happen to the natural man in an industrial society, he chose to worry about the nature of the union now that it had been transformed from a group of states clustered around the Atlantic ocean to a vast continental expanse that stretched from sea to sea. At this point he was concerned with the elasticity of a political system, not, as Turner was, with the ability of the good man to survive in a world where he was surrounded by the institutions and traditions of society. Thus, in this novel, Churchill turned his attention for the first time to the nature of government.

This new interest, especially with regard to the validity of the Constitution in 1900, is not an integral part of the story and may well have been a concern which arose in his mind fairly late in the composition of the novel. It occurs in more or less isolated speeches and more particularly in the Afterword. In all probability it is an indication of his increasing interest in the politics of his own day, and here again he is torn between his democratic faith and his aristocratic assumptions. His attitude toward the French Revolution is a good example. As a good American he could not totally oppose an event or movement which replaced a monarchy with a republic, yet he had great sympathy for the French aristocracy and had his hero marry an émigrée. Whatever he may have thought about the principles involved, he describes the French Revolution as a bloodbath and denounces those Americans who favored it. He makes Davy a stout Federalist and speaks rather harshly of Jefferson, to whom Davy refers as the "saint of American Jacobinism."

The facet of his own republic that most disturbed Churchill was its lack of gratitude toward those who had served it. This is a recurrent theme throughout the novel. Clark first broached it when he says to Davy, "Some day you will learn that foresight sometimes comes to men, but never to assemblies. But it is often given to one man to work out the salvation of a people, and be destroyed for it." Later he advises the boy to "serve the people, as all true men should in a republic. But do not rely on their gratitude." Davy himself comes to this conclusion when the men who served with Clark are given only small land grants for their service, and he ponders "this injustice to the men who won an empire and were flung a bone long afterwards."[17]

Could a form of government which treated its heroes in so cavalier a fashion survive the growing pains of continental expansion? Churchill stated the question in Davy's thoughts on the future of Louisiana.

> What had God in store for the vast land out of which the waters flowed? Had He, indeed, saved it for a People, a People to be drawn from all nations, from all classes? Was the principle of the Republic to prevail and spread and change the complexion of the world? Or were the lusts of greed and power to increase until in the end they had swallowed the heaven? Who could say?[18]

Although Churchill could not answer these questions, he could state what seemed to him in 1904 to be the essence of the problem. In the Afterword he leaves his readers, not with a summation of what the great westward expansion meant, but with a question.

> The political faith of our forefathers, of which the Constitution is the creed, was made to fit a more or less homogeneous body of people who proved that they knew the meaning of the word "Liberty." By Liberty, our forefathers meant the Duty as well as the Right of man, to govern himself. The Constitution amply attests the greatness of its authors, but it was a compromise. It was an attempt to satisfy thirteen colonies, each of which clung tenaciously to its identity. It suited the eighteenth-century conditions of a little English-speaking confederacy along the seaboard, far removed from the world's strife and jealousy. It scarcely contemplated that the harassed millions of Europe would flock to its fold, and it did not foresee that, in less than a hundred years, its own citizens would sweep across the three thousand miles of forest and plain and mountain to the Western Ocean, absorb French and Spanish Louisiana, Spanish Texas, Mexico, and California, fill this land with broad farmsteads and populous cities, cover it with a network of railroads.
>
> Would the Constitution, made to meet the needs of a little confederacy of the seaboard, stretch over a continent and an Empire?
>
> We are fighting out that question today. But *The Crossing* was in Daniel Boone's time, in George Rogers Clark's. Would the Constitution stand the strain now that the once remote haven of the oppressed has become a world-power?[19]

While he was writing an historical romance dealing with American expansion across the hills of Kentucky and into the trans-Mississippi West, Churchill's interest began to shift from the early nineteenth century to the early twentieth century — from the romance of the past to the problems of the present. *The Crossing* marks the beginning of his transformation from an historical romancer to an analyst of his own society.

The Winston Churchill who wrote historical romances considered himself to be a practitioner of his craft or profession, and he expended about as much thought on theories of art as a practicing lawyer gives to theories of jurisprudence. One of the few times that he wrote about the nature of his craft was at the beginning of his career in response to a copy of Paul Leicester Ford's article on the historical novel that Brett sent to him in 1897.

> Before reading Mr. Ford on the subject I had written a few notions to guide me, and I do not now find them changed, but strengthened. Historical characters, as he says, if properly brought in surely impress reality upon the story. I would say further, that they should by no means be principal characters; otherwise an untrue and distorted biography would result. But they should breathe the life and spirit of the time, and be of a part with the fictitious characters. If painted true they cannot be out of harmony.
>
> A writer, especially a young writer, must be sure which kind of an historical novel he wishes to make. My conception has been that the story must move easily along, not so fast that the reader will be out of breath: that he cannot for speed see the trees and fields and houses by the roadside, or stop to talk with the people at the street corners. And he must not be taken back to a period in order merely to be given a fleeting and unsatisfied glimpse. You must satisfy his craving. Let him have a good look. Let him wear gold buckles and lace awhile, and comprehend how it feels. On the other hand, he must not be gorged, or he will rebel. What is historical romance if it is not taking a man to a strange country, which he longs to see and never can? And when he arrives their [sic] he must be given the best time possible; a full-time; and a typical and likely

time. A time to think of with a lingering delight
when he has put down the book.

He should be a good story-teller, but not a good
liar. For he must stamp his pages with a truth which
is of infinitely more value than historical accuracy . . . .

Your old moralists were pleased with Sir Charles
Grandison, and cannot conceive of the first President
of the United States with a glass to his lips and a
wager in his note-book. Dignity is not merely a
quality of statuary, nor are heroes reproofs to levity.
And Mr. Washington, of Virginia, was by no means
a Puritan.

It can do no harm, but much good, to accentuate
the fine in a great man. But we must be sure first
of what the 'fine' consists . . . . It is not necessary
to have a pulpit printed on the fly leaf, nor need
virtue be served out as medicine.[20]

This is a good statement of what Churchill tried to do in his
historical novels and of his approach to the medium. He introduced his readers to true historical figures but never allowed these
figures to take the lead roles; he took the reader for a leisurely
(sometimes too leisurely) stroll through past epochs. And from
the letters and reviews it would seem that many readers were left
with a "lingering delight" after they finished the story. Without
sacrificing historical accuracy, he tried to be an artist in the sense
that the artist transcends the merely factual to a new realm of
truth. Here, for the modern reader, Churchill fell short of his goal,
but his contemporaries thought they found such truth in his
novels. In the above letter one can see Churchill's suspicion of
literary creeds, of art for art's sake, which tended to forget the
reading public. He had little patience with novelists who wrote
only for each other and the critics.

It is not difficult to determine what Churchill was trying
to do in his historical romances; assessing his actual accomplishments is another matter. Undoubtedly he brought to the writing
of historical fiction a new dimension, namely an awareness and
close study of the facts of history. In his own day he had a
reputation as an accurate historian; this is the reason for all the
letters and articles pointing out errors in detail. Professor A. B.
Hart contended that Churchill had given the best literary portrait
of Lincoln, and when asked who was the best writer of historical

fiction at that time (1902) replied: "Winston Churchill, who visualizes his periods and characters in a style reminiscent of Thackeray. He handles history with an accuracy betokening un-flagging application to its study."[21] This feeling was supported at the time by another famous historian, James Ford Rhodes, and in the present day by Henry Steele Commager. Although he has little respect for Churchill's later work, Commager is enthusiastic in his praise for *The Crossing*. "The story of the folk movement into the West," he says, "is one of the thrilling episodes of the book, thrilling not only for its picture of the pioneers, of the skillful pathfinders, and of Indian fights, but for its picture of nature." The historian describes Davy's first fight with the Indians as "one of the best in our literature," and goes on to suggest that "if you want your history straight you can read this story in Theodore Roosevelt's wonderful *The Winning of the West*; if you prefer it in novelized form you cannot do better than *The Crossing* . . . . "[22] It is possible that if Churchill had turned his later energies to straight history instead of problem novels, he could stand in the august company of such amateur historio-graphical greats as Parkman, Prescott, Motley, and their only successor in the late nineteenth century — Henry Adams. But the day of the professional, "scientific" historian, trained as a special-ist in his craft, had arrived by this time, and the continuation of history as literature may well have been impossible. As it was, Churchill was known as an historian to vast numbers of high-school students in England and Australia, as well as the United States, who read inexpensive editions of the novels as textbooks in American history.

Why did American readers at the turn of the century devour novels that today impress most people as being long-winded, stereotyped, and downright dull? A. E. Hancock, writing at the time, suggests that, whereas the mere historian recorded only the facts, Churchill was "perceiving the heart throb of the life, of which the fact is the spiritless record. Americans love big things; they are proud of accomplishments; they are interested in the deeds of their progenitors. These are the real reasons why Mr. Churchill is read by the million." Carl Van Doren, writing later, suggests that in Churchill America found "a romancer full of consolation to any who might fear or suspect that the country's history did not quite match its destiny."[23] Both of these comments bear on the question of why Americans at the turn of the century preferred historical novels to other forms of fiction. The nation was just emerging onto the world scene and perhaps they wanted to be reassured that their historical past had prepared them for their new role. Also, the glorification of the American past that was found in historical novels was in sharp contrast to the more strictly literary authors of American fiction who had harped upon the idea that American society was not a fit subject for the novel because it had no structure — no court, no upper-class aristocracy, no romantic peasants, no beautiful old churches.[24] Perhaps also Americans were simply looking for escape from the difficulties of an industrializing society, an escape into a past that for all its problems was a much simpler world than the one in which they lived. Maybe they just wanted to read a good story.

In any case, the relatively simple question of why Americans at the turn of the century preferred historical romance to the realism of Howells, James, Crane and Norris, does not explain why they were especially addicted to Churchill's books. Nor can this be explained simply by saying that he rode the crest of a wave by consciously catering to his audience. There were a great many hack writers of historical novels who did try to do these things, as there are hack writers in every period and in every art form. And Churchill's historical novels had appeal for too many intelligent men and women to base his popularity on the grounds of human stupidity. The only logical answer would seem to be that Churchill was a master of his craft. He wrote well the kind of things that people at the time wished to read, and his historical novels have stood the test of time in the sense that they are still excellent examples of the genre. They have all the faults that are inherent in the historical romance; they also have the virtues.

But by 1904 and the publication of *The Crossing*, Churchill's own interests were beginning to change — one of the two major shifts that were to occur during his lifetime. As early as April of 1903, Churchill indicated in an interview that he intended to abandon the historical novel. In the same interview he said that he would enter the field of general literature and, if he had any specialty, it would be political.[25] He had by then served his first term in the state legislature and the problems that now interested him were not those which centered upon the evolution of a great nation, but in just what had gone wrong in the process of this evolution. Before turning to these novels it is essential that the groundwork be laid for his political education, an education that was to change the course of his life and occupy much of his attention for almost two decades — a period that would witness his emergence as a politician of national reputation and an analyst of contemporary society.

CHAPTER VII

The Beginning of an Avocation

On a crisp autumn morning in 1912, Winston Churchill announced that he was the candidate of the Progressive Party for the governorship of New Hampshire. Alongside his idol, Theodore Roosevelt, he would stand at Armageddon and battle for the Lord. With this step the popular man of letters entered one of the most interesting national political campaigns in American history, a battle which astute political observers predicted would lead to the election of the first Democratic President in twenty years and the first Democratic governor in New Hampshire in sixty years. In retrospect his stand appears a futile and amateurish gesture, but at the time it seemed the logical culmination of a decade-long battle. For both Roosevelt and Churchill it was an act of optimistic conviction, not one of desperation; it was to be the ultimate victory, not the final defeat.

Churchill's earliest observations on politics are in his Annapolis notebooks where he advised himself to eschew political activity or debate because the two parties in America were corrupt factions rather than real parties. At Annapolis he listed himself as a Republican, but it is doubtful that this had much meaning for him. In the political atmosphere of the 1890's, his background and training inclined him toward the sterile Republicanism of William McKinley and away from the agrarian radicalism of William Jennings Bryan. As a natural conservative and as a proponent of the war with Spain, he undoubtedly voted for McKinley in 1896 and 1900.

Symbolically, his first participation in politics was connected with the career of Theodore Roosevelt. As early as 1901, he was associated with attorney Guy Murchie in a plan to boost Roosevelt as the next Republican presidential candidate. If the death of McKinley had not made Roosevelt President, Churchill would probably have become politically active before he did. Certainly his own ideas were moving along the lines which would be developed by Roosevelt. These early views were expressed in a letter which he sent to several of his friends in the fall of 1902. He had been toying with some notions about the nature of the American political system and wanted to get the reaction of his friends. The letter is a good expression of his early belief in the positive role of a strong central government.

> I believe that almost anybody will agree with me when I say that many of the present evils of government arise from a lack of Federal strength. The state governments, originating as they did accidentally in the thirteen colonies, have served their purpose up to the present, although they have been responsible for a great deal of trouble. The state government, at least in a majority of the states, seems a waste of time and men and money. It is also, next to the city government, (and perhaps in a long run will prove more so than city government) a source of corruption, and an opportunity for politicians.
>
> Of course such a drastic measure as the abolition of the state government would never get through in a thousand years. But it seems to me, with the amalgamation of this country going on at the present rapid rate, that some of the state powers could be with great benefit conferred upon the general government . . . . The trusts are by no means undesirable things in themselves, but most undesirable if organized under a lenient and perhaps venal law in a small

state. Whether the present powers of Congress are sufficient to give the proper regulation in trusts and strikes, does not greatly matter, except in regard to the relative difficulty of the task. Perhaps the constitution may have to be changed. If labor unions, whose members comprise citizens of many states, were compelled to organize under Federal law, the Federal courts, and in extreme cases, the Federal troops would be the remedies.

My idea is to work for the establishment in all of our cities of clubs to be known as Federal clubs. The nucleus and backbone of these clubs is to be composed of young university men. I do not mean that there should be only one club in a city, but many. And I shall aim at establishing them in the various universities from California to Maine. Such an organization would not be called a party or any portion of a party.[1]

A number of ideas are displayed in this letter which should be noted, if for no other reason than that they contradict the myth, accepted by both Churchill's friends and critics — perhaps even by the novelist himself — that he entered the political world knowing nothing of the interaction of politics and business. None of these ideas are new, but they do indicate that Churchill had done some serious thinking about the proper ordering of a state and that he was aware of some of the evils in the existing governments. His "radical" solutions shocked his friends, who were appalled both at the idea of increasing federal power and at his implication that the Grand Old Party be abandoned in favor of some new organization.[2]

These political notions were probably stimulated by Churchill's entrance into the world of practical politics. The previous summer (1902) he had announced his intention to stand for the state legislature and that September had won Republican endorsement. Why a person enters politics, unless he is an obvious self-seeker, is usually a complex matter. This is especially true of men who later become controversial political figures. Certainly it is true of Winston Churchill.

From the time of his first campaign until the present day, the assertion has been made that Churchill entered politics in order to obtain material for a novel. This charge gained some credence when he published *Coniston*, a study of New Hampshire politics, at the end of his second term in the legislature. But it is doubtful that this was his original intention. It seems more likely that during some stage of his work on *The Crossing* he became aware of the importance of politics in the development of the nation. At the same time his attempts to achieve forestry reforms and good roads convinced him that nothing could be done for these causes without political support. Both *The Crossing* and his own outside interests pointed to the importance of political action. In all likelihood the idea of writing a political novel occurred to him after he had gone to the legislature, where he began to hear interesting stories about politics and politicians and learned at first hand about the corruption that existed. Also this was a period during which a number of literary men were running for political office.

Nor can one entirely neglect the rather simple idea of the public-spirited citizen quietly doing his duty. To be a member of the New Hampshire legislature was no great honor; it was the largest assembly in the entire country and almost anyone who really wanted to be a member could become one. There is also some evidence that Churchill had been offered local political positions, including that of Selectman, before he ran for the legislature, and there is every reason to believe that he was solicited for the position of representative as well. He had an independent income, he had just begun work on his next novel after having published a runaway best seller, and as a candidate for the legislature he could perform a public service while at the same time having an entertaining diversion from the difficult task of writing novels. Why not try it?

Newspapers across the country and in England made note of the fact that another man of letters was entering the political arena, several of them suggesting that this was just an opening wedge for Churchill's real aspiration, which was for a seat in Congress. Churchill received immediate encouragement from a number of the state's political leaders. Ex-governor F. W. Rollins, head of the Society for the Preservation of New Hampshire Forests, was delighted to have an active member of his organization running for the legislature; the Secretary of the State, Edward Pearsons, expressed his hope "that the proposed service may be so agreeable to you and so acceptable to the public that a seat in the House may be but the first step to much higher political honors."[3] Indeed, some state Republican leaders, apparently convinced that they could make political hay out of this famous political neophyte, relished the prospect of his winning the seat from Cornish. Churchill must have been a bit amazed at the amount of political intrigue necessary to win a mere nomination in his small community. Certainly some of the actions engaged in by his supporters, while they were obviously common practice, went beyond the bounds of mugwump campaigning. One of them wrote him about a young man in Boston, a legal resident of Cornish, who would gladly assist Churchill with his vote, but who did not feel he could afford to come to New Hampshire at his own expense. If his expenses were to be paid, that was another matter.[4]

This campaign, which Churchill almost certainly entered with the notion that it would involve little effort, served mainly to educate him in the intricacies of local elections. It was good training in practical politics. And almost immediately he was drawn into state and national politics. Henry M. Cheney, editor of the Lebanon *Granite State Free Press*, informed Churchill that he was running for the speakership of the House and promised the novelist every opportunity in the legislature. United States Senator J. H. Gallinger congratulated the author on his election and solicited Churchill's support in the upcoming Senate contest. Churchill had now entered a new world in which favor was balanced against favor, an atmosphere far different from the protected realm of mugwump detachment in which he had been reared.

Even before he arrived in Concord, Churchill found himself the recipient of honors and encouragement. In December the Governor-elect, N. J. Bachelder, wrote:

> Allow me to invite you to accept a position upon my
> military staff with title of Colonel. I will consider it
> a great favor if you will honor me with acceptance,
> regarding the matter confidential for the present.[5]

Although Bachelder had encouraged Churchill from the beginning, he was also being pressured to make this appointment. One of the men applying the pressure was George H. Moses, Secretary of the

Forestry Commission and an important newspaper editor, who said that he had taken the liberty of suggesting to Bachelder, "who is under some obligation to me," that Churchill be appointed to the staff.[6] Many of the men who supported the appointment later opposed Churchill's modest reform proposals, and one is led to suspect that their interest in placing him on the Governor's staff was to insure that a popular, well-known, and potentially influential legislator would be in their camp on any important issues that might arise. Churchill was an aristocratic young conservative, not a political maverick. The political leaders were not trying to buy him; this was not yet necessary. They were simply insuring his regularity as a party man by giving him the recognition his fame seemed to warrant.

When Churchill interrupted his work on *The Crossing* to return from St. Louis for the opening session of the legislature in Concord, his arrival and every subsequent activity were widely publicized. The fact that the Churchills rented a house in Concord undoubtedly gave credence to the charge that they lived in an offensively ostentatious manner. Most legislators were not wealthy enough to do this, and if they were, they had no desire to appear so affluent. The great majority of them simply rented rooms. Certainly the Churchills were at the center of much of Concord's social life, entertaining regularly and attending many receptions and dinners in their honor. But Churchill was not only the social lion of the season; he was also a popular legislator whose geniality and hard work won him the respect of his peers. The way in which the novelist took hold as a working legislator came as a surprise to some observers, including some of the local newspapers. One editorial exclaimed:

> Quite a surprise to the present legislature, however, is the celebrity from Cornish, Col. Winston Churchill of Gov. Bachelder's staff . . . . He is head over heels in three departments of legislative activity here at the Capitol, for good roads, for forest preservation and in all educational matters. More and more he is being sought out by gentlemen interested in these subjects, and more and more are his opinions being consulted.[7]

The biggest problem with which the 1903 legislature had to deal was prohibition, a question about which Churchill had no strong feelings one way or another. The second most important problem, however, was the summer resort business and this was a subject that definitely interested him. If the tourist trade in New Hampshire was to be stimulated, two steps had to be taken: preservation of the area's natural beauty through a program of forest conservation, and improvement of the roads in the state. In both matters Churchill was given a chance to see what he could do — as chairman of the Forestry Commission and as a member of the Committee on Public Improvements. His maiden speech dealt with the question of forests, and he was instrumental in the passage of two joint resolutions which embodied at least part of the program of the New Hampshire Society for the Preservation of Forests. The first of these appropriated five thousand dollars for a forest survey of the White Mountain region; the other authorized tax exemptions for lands planted in timber or lands upon which lumbering was conducted on scientific forestry principles. His bills for highway improvements, however, did not fare so well.[8]

Churchill possessed his full share of the current spread-eagle patriotism and he was concerned about educating the people in the nature of the union and the structure of their governments. In this connection he introduced a bill requiring the reading of the state and national constitutions in all New Hampshire schools, and endorsed another requiring all cities and towns to purchase flags for the public schools. One of his other bills, dealing with bridges across the Connecticut River connecting neighboring Vermont and New Hampshire towns, was more controversial. Churchill originally favored construction of a bridge connecting Plainfield with Hartland, Vermont, because this would increase the summer resort business in the Cornish area; for the same reason, most of the summer residents opposed the idea. They did not want the area opened up further and opposed spending money to build a bridge which would make it easier for tourists to pester them. Churchill's constituents as well as the summer residents were more interested in abolishing tolls on existing bridges across the river than in replacing the Plainfield ferry with a bridge, and he introduced a bill to abolish them.[9]

When he had introduced his bills and defended them, Churchill left Concord to resume work on *The Crossing*. While the bills were being debated and voted on he was making his research trip to St. Louis, New Orleans, and Nashville. When he returned to attend the closing sessions of the legislature he discovered that his most important bills had not become law. His political education was just beginning. As an inexperienced politician, he assumed that since his bills were in the best interests of the state (in his opinion), they would be passed automatically and signed by the governor. But things did not work out quite that way.

Part of the difference of opinion between Churchill and those who opposed these bills stemmed from the fact that he viewed New Hampshire as an area which had to solicit tourist trade if it was to survive economically. Most of the politicians, as longtime residents and as prosperous citizens, did not see the future in the same light. To Churchill it seemed the common sense of the matter to invest money in things like a New Hampshire building at the St. Louis Exposition which would advertise the beauty of the state and increase the number of tourists; to many others such activities were unnecessary expenses which would increase taxes — money which would come out of their pockets. Certainly this was the tenor of the criticism leveled against the novelist by his chief critic, Henry Putney, editor of the Manchester *Mirror* and the political power behind Governor Bachelder, his brother-in-law. Putney viewed Churchill as a wealthy outsider, ignorant of what the people of New Hampshire needed or could afford, and he was pleased that Churchill's expensive bills were defeated. Actually, Putney himself was in bad odor with a number of the newspapers who suspected him of less than honest dealings, as was Governor Bachelder, who was criticized for holding a number of other offices at the same time he was governor.[10]

Some of the obstacles which Churchill's bills encountered resulted from personal differences. According to one newspaper account, Churchill was in favor with the party leaders until he gave a dinner for the notables in Concord and failed to invite Putney. From that point, his legislative measures encountered opposition and Putney began to criticize him in his newspaper. This notion was substantiated by Churchill's friend Henry F. Hollis, a lawyer in Concord who was in close touch with the political scene.[11]

One result of this situation was Colonel Churchill's resignation from his position on Bachelder's staff. Many of the newspaper accounts stated that he resigned out of pique over the vetoing and defeat of his bills; others suggested that he had parted company with the rascals associated with Bachelder and Putney. Whatever his motivation may have been, his course of action called forth a steady stream of letters (from both politicians and plain citizens) approving his resignation, praising the bills he had introduced, and encouraging him to continue in politics. Hollis, delighted with Churchill's action, said he thought Bachelder was the most unpopular governor in a long time and that the people were ready for a revolt against the Republican machine.[12] It is doubtful that Churchill shared Hollis' sentiments about the machine at the time, and he does not appear to have associated the failure of his bills with any basic flaws in the state party. Although he was associating with such outspoken critics as Hollis and the Remick brothers, he still maintained a working relationship with Speaker Cheney and James E. French, who were leaders in the Republican party. There were those who understood that New Hampshire's political problems were far more involved than the personal honesty of a few men, but Churchill was not yet among them. It would take additional knocks and more exposure to actual conditions to convince him that good government could not be achieved simply by eliminating the villans.

Churchill's education in practical politics was continued at the Republican National Convention of 1904. As the renomination of Roosevelt was a foregone conclusion, the convention itself was a dull affair and public interest turned to the celebrities who were present — including Churchill. All of the Chicago papers carried stories about the famous author who had come to help nominate Roosevelt and he was constantly harrassed by reporters. He wrote Brett that the only reporter who succeeded in getting to him was a Hearst man who wanted him to cover the convention for their chain. This offer, like a previous offer from *Collier's*, he turned down. "I talked with him for a few minutes on Convention subjects, and when I returned to the East I discovered that they had printed an account of the Convention by me in all their papers."[13] The two articles appeared in the Chicago *Examiner*, among other newspapers, and Churchill was indeed named as author.

More important consequences arose from the election of the National Committeeman from New Hampshire. The interpretations of this event are conflicting in the extreme, but the facts are fairly clear. When the elected National Committeeman died, Mark Hanna, as chairman of the National Committee, had to appoint someone to take his place. Of the various aspirants for the position, two men — Senator Jacob H. Gallinger and Frank S. Streeter — were the front runners. Gallinger was a professional politician, capable and seasoned; Streeter was head counsellor for the Boston and Maine Railroad and a man with more political ambition than experience. The railroad counsellor was extremely bitter when Hanna decided on the professional. Then, before the 1904 convention, Gallinger made a public statement that he did not wish to continue as National Committeeman. This opened the way for Streeter, but Hanna and Roosevelt both urged the Senator to continue and it was commonly assumed that he would be elected by the New Hampshire delegation as a matter of course. He was not. By a vote of seven to one, with the Senator himself casting the only dissenting vote, the delegation elected Streeter.

After the convention the action of the delegation was severely attacked by Gallinger and by many New Hampshire newspapers. The gist of this attack was that Streeter's election was the result of a crooked deal designed to strengthen the lawyer's chances for a seat in the United States Senate. It was suggested that the support of the other delegates had been purchased by promises of the railroad's support for other political plums and that Churchill had been promised Frank Currier's seat in the House of Representatives. Five of the delegates, including Churchill, published a reply to these charges in which they contended that they did not know Gallinger had changed his mind about standing for reelection.[14]

One authority on New Hampshire political history has suggested that Churchill was an innocent whom the party leaders used as they saw fit; "particularly when . . . he was induced to vote for Streeter as National Committeeman without the slightest idea of the issues involved."[15] Doubtless Churchill was an innocent and was used in this instance by Streeter and others. It is difficult to see, however, what issues were involved. The apparent issue, of course, was the control of New Hampshire politics by the Boston and Maine Railroad. Since Streeter was chief counselor for the railroad, it appeared that the railroad was making an open move for control of the dominant party in the state. Two facts contradict this interpretation. In the first place, the railroad already had control of the Republican party and did not need to make such a clumsy and overt grab for power. In the second place, Streeter's superior, Boston and Maine president Lucian Tuttle, opposed Streeter's election and was on record, privately and publicly, in support of Gallinger. If this was a grab for power, it was a matter of personal power for Streeter. Churchill, in his usual fashion, made his decision on the basis of personal feelings. Streeter was a friend and he had decided to vote for his friend.[16] There is no evidence to indicate that Churchill acted on any other grounds than these personal feelings, but the uproar which ensued provided later political enemies with ammunition and may have convinced some of the regular party leaders that he could not be relied upon. It also taught the novelist that in politics personal friendships are shaky foundations upon which to base a decision.

Another result of the accusations which came out of the Gallinger-Streeter battle was Churchill's decision, in the summer of 1904, to retire from politics. In the face of rumors that he would run against Frank Currier for the Republican nomination to Congress (and there is some evidence that he had contemplated such an action), he supported the incumbent's renomination. He also let it be known that he did not intend to run for reelection to the legislature.[17]

The basic reasons for this decision are outlined in a letter to his old political ally, William Sisson, in which he states that he had been "very unjustly accused by Senator Gallinger of making a political trade" and "I wish to convince the people of the state that I do not care to force myself into any office." Sisson, surprised to discover that he was about to lose his most prized political asset, replied that he had discussed the matter with other local leaders and they were all agreed that "it is folly for you to withdraw your name now if at any time in the future you wish anything that the town might give."[18] Churchill received many similar letters and, whether it was because of this pressure from the local politicos or for some other reason, he did change his mind. It seems quite obvious that he wanted to remain in the legislature, but he did not want to be put in the position (especially after Gallinger's charge) of seeking the office. Throughout his political career he was extremely sensitive about this kind of thing; he always took any comment that he was seeking to further his own ambitions through political office as a personal insult to his honor as a gentleman.

He was nominated and reelected to his seat in the legislature. Again he worked closely with the man behind the scenes in Cornish, Vene Bryant. Bryant had worked to elect him as a delegate to the national convention earlier in the year and continued to guide his political fortunes during the fall campaign. After the election, however, they had a disagreement and Churchill wrote him a letter that demonstrates his feelings about several matters.

> I have received your letter with the somewhat stupendous town election expenses. You must know, as I have frequently told you, that I cannot stand for this sort of thing, and will not. I would much rather get out of politics altogether. I am serving [in] the legislature this term to the neglect of my professional duties, and I hope for the betterment of the state. I have done a good deal of thinking in the last year, and I have come to the conclusion that the only way for a man in my position to obtain political preferment is not to seek it. To seek it, and to pay a price for it, would give it no value for me. I have come to regret the fact that I went so far as to pay the sum of five hundred dollars as a retainer in case I went to Congress .... [19]

Their correspondence leaves little room for doubt that Bryant was a paid political worker, or that he was influential in getting Churchill elected as a delegate and as a legislator. Churchill was not denying his effectiveness, only the size of his bill.

In the fall of 1905 Churchill again had to consider his future as a politician. By November he had made up his mind to run for the state senate and wrote to Bryant, Sisson and others to see what they thought of the idea. After being assured of their support, Churchill suggested that Sisson leak the news to the press.[20] Events, however, were to alter the novelist's aspirations considerably before the state elections of 1906. One of the most important changes was his growing interest in reform. His relations with the Remick brothers had grown closer in the years since his first session in the legislature and he had already established contact with Robert Bass, the man who would ultimately lead the reform cause in New Hampshire. Churchill's disenchantment with the Republican party in New Hampshire came as a process of education through exposure to the system, and one of the men who helped to educate him was William E. Chandler. Chandler was an arch-foe of the railroad interests that controlled New Hampshire politics and a former United States Senator who had been defeated for reelection, at least in part, by the influence and money of his railroad enemies. As early as October of 1904, Chandler asked the young legislator to return his free pass to the railroad if he were elected and to pass a bill preventing the railroads from providing free transportation for legislators. Churchill did not return the pass (though it is doubtful that he ever used it), but Chandler kept up the pressure.[21] In the following months he wrote Churchill several letters in which he explained how the railroads dominated the state and even suggested that Churchill might be the man to break this control. "I am too old to make the fight any longer. I can only entreat and advise. In my dreams sometimes I see arise in N H [sic] a conscientious brave strong man like Roosevelt or LaFollette to destroy the system. Sometimes he takes your shape — and then I awake."[22]

Churchill himself was not then being opposed by the railroads in his bid for a seat in the state senate. In a letter to Sisson, he reveals: "The Boston and Maine attorneys, whom I know very well, have assured me voluntarily, in even stronger terms than I can write, that the railroad will not oppose my election, and on the other hand will not require me to give any pledges, which of course they know I would not give."[23] So in January of 1906 Churchill intended to stand for the senate; he had the backing of some prominent men, and the assurance that the railroad would not oppose him. But before the fall elections, publication of his fourth novel, *Coniston*, changed the whole course of his public career by making him an anethema both to the state Republican party and to the railroad which dominated that party.

CHAPTER VIII

The Novel That Set The Stage

Why would a man who had achieved fame and fortune as an historical romancer suddenly abandon that genre for the uncertain field of the political novel? Most of the scholars who have looked into this question have concluded that Churchill, with an almost uncanny perception of public tastes, decided that the historical romance was passé. *The Crossing* had not done as well in the marketplace as *The Crisis*; the public was buying fewer historical novels in general. Public taste had switched from a romantic glorification of the past to an interest in contemporary problems. John Chamberlain suggests that "Churchill found himself taking stock of his position of popular novelist thrown suddenly into a decade whose popular clamor was for muck."[1]

These interpretations are based upon a number of false assumptions, the most notable of which is that the era of the historical romance was dead. Although the great age of historical novels in America had passed, people continued to buy large numbers of such novels for years to come; indeed, they have never stopped buying them. In the second place, this interpretation assumes that Churchill surveyed the market and then went home to write a novel which would fit the mood of the public. It is true that in the beginning he viewed writing as a business, and he entered this particular business as a means of making a living. But his attitude toward the novel and toward his own work underwent a slow and subtle change over the years. This is not to say that he ever forgot that his income was derived from his novels or that he was ever uninterested in the sales that they achieved. It is simply to suggest that after 1905 he told the public not what he thought they <u>wanted</u> to hear but what he thought they <u>should</u> hear. A story teller he always remained; beyond this he wrote to point up current problems and to stir his contemporaries to such a degree that they would take actions to solve those problems.

Still, the change from historical romance in *The Crossing* to political reform in *Coniston* is not a sudden break. Part of *Coniston* takes place in a time setting earlier than that of *The Crisis*, and many of the contemporary critics viewed the book as a continuation of his series on the American past rather than as a radical new departure. The book is, in fact, neither an historical novel nor a reform novel, but a transition between the two. Before this time Churchill had written only of the American past; from this point he would write only of the society of his own day. This change in focus coincided with that of a large part of the American reading public and Churchill's novels continued to sell as well as before.

The novelist's own summary and description of *Coniston* are contained in a letter Churchill wrote to an editor.[2] "Coniston," he says, "deals primarily and psychologically with the life of Jethro Bass, the son of a rough tanner among the hills of a certain state in New England . . . . " Jethro falls in love with Cynthia Ware, "the daughter of a minister, who was far above him in social station. She loved him for the strength she saw in him." Jethro also discovers a way to achieve political control in Coniston. He works behind the scenes, but Cynthia surmises that he is behind the movement and begs him to stop. When he tells her it is too late for that, she leaves him in anger and goes to Boston, where she marries a "kindly but weak man, named Wetherell." They have a daughter who is also named Cynthia, but the mother dies shortly thereafter. Ill and broken, Wetherell brings his daughter back to Coniston, where they are befriended by Jethro, who transfers his love for the mother to the daughter. When Wetherall dies, Jethro — now the political boss of his state — adopts Cynthia.

Jethro's lifelong enemy is Isaac Worthington, who makes a fortune in a neighboring mill town and uses this money to gain control of the railroads in the area. Worthington's son, Robert, falls in love with Cynthia just at the time when Worthington is attempting to consolidate the railroads. While Jethro and Worthington battle for domination of the state Cynthia reads a newspaper story about Jethro's illicit political methods. When she confronts Jethro with these charges, he confesses; "and a scene which is a curious repetition of a scene he had in his youth with her mother takes place. He makes a supreme sacrifice in the shape of a compromise with his enemy Worthington, in order that his son may marry Cynthia, and the railroads' control is thus effected."

Many of the components of Churchill's earlier stories are present in this one. The usual amount of attention is given to the historical setting, although the scene is much more narrow than in the earlier novels with the action set among the New Hampshire hills which the author knew so well. Churchill admitted that the towns portrayed in the story were actual New Hampshire towns: Coniston is really Croyden; Brampton and Harwick in the story are Newport and Claremont in real life; and Cornish Flat he renamed Clovelly.[3] The action in the novel takes place between the 1830's and the 1880's, but New Hampshire had not undergone drastic changes since then and by describing what he saw around him in 1905 Churchill could present a fairly accurate picture of his state a generation or two before. His flair for narrative descriptions of scenery and local color is put to its best use in *Coniston*, and the reviewers had high praise for his portrait of rural New Hampshire. The local characters, too, ring true to life, particularly the small-time politician Bijah Bixby and the delightful Lucretia Penniman.

Although he was willing to admit that the towns in *Coniston* were patterned on actual villages, Churchill was careful to deny that any of the characters (except Jethro) were fictional portraits of individual people. This does not, of course, preclude the possibility that the characters were composites of local people whom the author had encountered in New Hampshire. Certainly the critics found the characters true to the spirit of rural New England. One of the most favorable critics contended that "no American novelist since the days of *The Scarlet Letter* has so finely and inspiringly set forth the soul of New England on paper."[4]

Churchill's handling of the background material is not different from his earlier works except for the relatively greater skill in presentation, and even this is probably the result of his more intimate acquaintance with the scene of the story. And his two heroines are, if anything, less real and certainly less interesting than such predecessors as Dorothy Manners and Virginia Carvel. The villainous Isaac Dudley Worthington, as blackhearted a scoundrel as Churchill ever created, also follows a preestablished pattern.

The real difference between *Coniston* and the earlier romances is the lack of a hero. In the earlier novels the reaction of his characters to a given situation was automatic and predictable. If he was a "good guy," he responded in one way; if he was a "bad guy," he reacted in another. But beginning in an elementary way in *The Crossing*, Churchill became increasingly interested in more serious problems, and a necessary aspect of this was a new look at the questions of human motivation and of the ability of man to control his own destiny.

The growing complexity of the Churchillian world by 1906 is most clearly revealed through the life and career of the political boss, Jethro Bass. Jethro was accepted by both contemporary critics and later commentators as Churchill's supreme achievement.[5] It was as both man and symbol that Jethro achieved fame, and therein lies the real problem. *Coniston* is both the story of a man and a tract for the times; this double level writing was new to Churchill and it cannot be said that he solved the problem of uniting the major and minor themes.

In point of fact, Jethro emerges more clearly as a human being than as a symbol. He is introduced as a tall, ungainly tanner from the bottom of Coniston's social scale, unlettered but literate, he speaks with a decided stutter. Although he was low-born and, therefore, in the Churchillian world, lacking in native nobility of character, Jethro does have certain sensibilities. When the younger Cynthia asks the man whom she has come to look upon as a father if the charges against him are true, Churchill exonerated Jethro of any real villainy.

> It was thus that Jethro Bass met the supreme crisis of his life. And who shall say he did not meet it squarely and honestly? Few men of finer fiber and more delicate morals would have acquitted themselves as well. That was a Judgement Day for Jethro; and though he knew it not, he spoke through Cynthia to his Maker, confessing his faults freely and humbly, and dwelling on the justness of his punishment; putting not forward any good he may have done, nor thinking of it, nor seeking excuse because of the light that was in him. Had he been at death's door in the face of nameless tortures, no man could have dragged such a confession from him. But a great love had been given him, and to that love he must speak the truth, even at the cost of losing it.[6]

And the novel has a happy ending for Jethro. He has enjoyed politics but is no longer content with such activities because of Cynthia's feelings. After Jethro's voluntary retirement from power, Churchill says:

> Never, I believe, did man, shorn of power, accept his lot more quietly. His struggle was over, his battle was fought. A greater peace than he had ever thought to hope for was won. For the opinion and regard of the world he had never cared. A greater reward awaited him, greater than any knew — the opinion and regard and the praise of one whom he loved beyond all the world.[7]

Jethro is a man with faults and virtues, a man who triumphs and fails, who makes mistakes, who loves and hates and is in turn loved and hated — he is a human being.

But when one moves from Jethro the man to Jethro as an example of the political boss, problems arise. In the first place, Churchill does not explain why a man should strive to become the political boss of an entire state. Nor does he make it clear whether or not he holds Jethro responsible for the political corruption that existed. Certainly corruption follows in the wake of the unlettered tanner. Politics had been quite "clean" in Coniston; affairs had been run by the best people until the victory of Jethro and his Democrats. Of this victory, Churchill says, "There is no moral to the story, alas — it was one of those things which inscrutable

Heaven permitted to be done." Jethro sets the upheaval in motion but apparently is powerless to stop it. Writing of the meeting between the first Cynthia and Jethro when she comes to plead with him not to seize power in the town, Churchill says, "But what she asked was impossible. That wind which he himself had loosed, which was to topple over institutions, was rising, and he could no more have stopped it then than he could have hushed the storm." Nor is this confusion mitigated by later events. At one point Churchill writes that "Jethro Bass himself was almost wholly responsible in that state for the condition of politics and politicians." But later he speculates about the boss: "Who will judge him? He had been what he had been; and as the Era was, so was he. Verily, one generation passeth away, and another generation cometh."[8]

Some light is thrown on this problem by the Afterword to the novel. Here Churchill contends that the political conditions revealed in his book are typical of the whole United States at that time. Men have strayed from the principles of government laid down by the Founding Fathers.

> Self-examination is necessary for the moral health of nations as well as men, and it is the most hopeful of signs that in the United States we are today going through a period of self-examination . . . . Thus the duty rests to-day, more heavily than ever, upon each American citizen to make good to the world those principles upon which his government was built . . . . In America today we are trying — whatever the cost — to regain the true axis established for us by the founders of our Republic.[9]

What all of this seems to mean is that Jethro was responsible for the corrupt political conditions in his own state, but that the boss was himself the product of a corrupt age in American politics — a state of affairs that Churchill (like the rest of the mugwump-liberals) tended to blame on the Jacksonian movement and the introduction of the spoils system. In his own day, Churchill believed, people were becoming aware of the evil situation and were on the verge of doing something about it.

But between the end of boss rule and the beginning of the Progressive revolt a new group of political manipulators had their day. Although Churchill does not make a particular point of it, the union of Cynthia with her lover is achieved at the price of turning the state over to the railroads. On a personal level this is a moral act, a sacrifice on Jethro's part to the happiness of his ward; on a political level, however, it means turning over the affairs of state to an influence which all seem to recognize as far more pernicious than Jethro's. This, again, is part of the difficulty of the novel's bilevel construction. The conversion and sacrifice are necessary for Jethro's rise as a moral man, but they hamper his use as a model of the political boss. It is not impossible that a political boss would willingly surrender control of his state to the railroads; it is unlikely.

Jethro is almost unique among Churchill's characters in yet another way. One later commentator states:

> Churchill seemed absorbed with the fact that Jethro had a personality which could attract people. People, in the Churchillian world, are not usually attracted by personalities of evil cast . . . . In Jethro Bass, then, Churchill wanted to show the potentially good man whose mischievous actions resulted from one false step. Seen in this light, Jethro's conversion provides a fitting climax for a story of individual struggle in which the hero experiences a change of heart.[10]

It seems doubtful that Churchill intended Jethro to be a hero or to imply that all his actions resulted from one false step, but he did accord to the political boss the power of personal attraction which he normally reserved for the hero and the historically great.

The association of good character with family background, however, remained a part of Churchill's outlook. In one place he remarks, "After all, people with consciences are born, not made."[11] Later, in telling of young Cynthia's first realization of her passionate love for Bob Worthington, Churchill says that for a brief moment love burned out all reason — but this was only for the moment. On another occasion Churchill indicates that Cynthia's self-restraint might rest more on inbred instinct than upon reason, but in any case the training of generations seems to be the thing which instills this good character and self-restraint, whether it operates through reason or some other faculty.

The actions of the genteel few may be guided by reason and restraint but those of the common herd are not. Throughout the book there is the implication that the old families who controlled

Coniston before Jethro seizes power are motivated only by justice.
The motives of the men who come to vote for Jethro in his first
battle at Coniston are quite the reverse.

> Some . . . came through fear; others through
> ambition; others were actuated by both; and still
> others were stung by the pain of the sleet to a still
> greater jealousy and envy, and the remembrance of
> those who had been in power. I must not omit the
> conscientious Jacksonians who were misguided enough
> to believe in such a ticket.[12]

Here certainly is the aristocratic, mugwump distinction. The best
people are guided by justice; the common herd — and particularly
the politician — by fear, ambition, jealousy, and envy. Although
Churchill admits the possibility that some may have been conscientious in their beliefs, even these are misguided.

He does recognize, however, that even the moral man may be
caught up in the swirl of corrupt politics. Mr. Merrill, the president
of a small railroad, is such a man. Churchill says he is "a good
man, as men go," but he is slowly drawn into Jethro's circle.
Merrill realizes that what Jethro has done is wrong; on the other
hand, he has a duty to the stockholders in his not-too-prosperous
railroad. If he does not cooperate with Jethro these innocent
people will be hurt. Beyond this, he recognizes that his choice
lies not between boss rule and clean government, but between
Jethro and domination by Worthington's railroad syndicate.

So Churchill saw something of the complexity of the problem, but his tendency (for purposes of the story) to reduce
principles and forces to the personal level tends to obscure this
complexity. While he was aware of the fact that the rule of the
railroads would be more tyrannical than Jethro's he ignores this
fact when he praises the boss's sacrifice of his power for his love
of Cynthia. Yet, the direct result of this action is not simply the
personal happiness of the two young lovers; it is also the political
and economic debasement of an entire state. In the last analysis,
however, it must be recognized that Churchill was still a historical
novelist. The boss system, historically, did develop a symbiotic
relationship with the corporations (although it is again an over-
simplification to say that boss rule was replaced by corporate
control). If he was to present the facts, if he was to continue to
be the historian of American life, the railroads had to win. The

only real alternative to making Jethro voluntarily relinquish power was to have the railroads defeat him — an action which would have destroyed his portrait of Jethro as a master politician.

The public response to *Coniston* was prompt and enthusiastic. It was soon translated into several foreign languages and, in spite of the parochial setting, was also successful in other countries. The country store in Croyden appropriated the name Coniston; A. Schuman and Company of Boston brought out a line of Coniston suits for ladies.[13] Innumerable letters again came to Harlakenden House from far and wide, from men of distinction and unknowns, from politicians and ministers. Senator Albert Beveridge gave the novel generous praise,[14] and President Roosevelt suggested that his author friend had put his finger on one of the great abuses of modern times.

> Mrs. Roosevelt and I have just finished "Coniston," and we like it so much that I must write you a line to tell you so. She, of course, was appealed to by it most from the standpoint of the story. My interest in it was even greater because I think you were dealing with one of the real and great abuses of this generation. I do not know whether I abhor most the wealthy corruptionist, or the sinister demagogue who tries to rise by exciting, and appealing to, the evil passions of envy and jealousy and hatred. In the last analysis the two supplement one another.[15]

A letter from James Ford Rhodes, the famous American historian, indicates the high esteem in which Churchill was held by many learned men.

> Mrs. Rhodes and I have just read your Coniston with great interest and pleasure. It seems to be a gratifying advance from Richard Carvel and The Crisis . . . . It is nice to know Jethro Bass and Cynthia and you have enriched for us our list of characters of fiction, on whom we shall love to dwell. There is fun in the book and there is true pathos in the development of the two great characters. Some of the scenes seem to me to be drawn with a very artistic touch.
>
> The picture of political life was especially interesting to me. It is lifelike and has the mark of freshness, which only work drawn from the original sources can possess . . . . [16]

The vast majority of the critics agreed with Rhodes that the book was a definite success, and many called it the best book Churchill had ever written. Several critics held that it was the best American novel to come out in years. A surprising number, viewing the novel as a love story rather than a tract for the times, did not emphasize the political side of the story so much as one might expect. This approach may explain why they did not object to *Coniston*, as they did to his later works, on the grounds that it was too didactic. This may also explain why the New Hampshire newspapers, most of which were under the influence of the Boston and Maine Railroad, joined the rest of the world in praising the book. Most of the critics, however, did interpret the book as an exposé of the boss system in politics, and it was this use of Jethro as the symbol of a corrupt system that made trouble for Churchill locally. He had presented fictionalized portraits of actual people before, but this was the first time he had presented such a person as a corruptor of the state. James Yeatman and his friends did not object to his fictionalization as the saintly Mr. Brinsmade, but Ruel Durkee's friends did object to Churchill's openly using the deceased New Hampshire political boss as the model for Jethro Bass. Ironically it was William E. Chandler who was the chief (and in many ways most important) objector. Chandler, who had known Durkee intimately and had liked him, was so upset that he published a forty-page pamphlet, entitled *Jethro Bass Unreal*, in which he tried to prove that Durkee was a model citizen who never corrupted anyone or anything.[17] He also wrote letter upon letter to the local newspapers to combat the image of his friend which Churchill had set forth. Chandler received support from Vene Bryant, who had directed Churchill's first campaign and had been a minor lieutenant under Durkee. Bryant described *Coniston* as "a nawful mean book."[18]

Churchill's sources of information about Durkee (consisting largely of stories related to him by older politicians who had known the man) were undoubtedly a mixture of fact and fantasy. But Fred Louis Pattee, who knew Durkee well, supported the novelist's version of him. "The actual Ruel Durkee did say that he carried the State of New Hampshire in his vest pocket," Pattee states, "and there was truth in what he said."[19]

The national press picked up the Chandler-Churchill debate,

but gave much more publicity to the statements of B. B. Odell, ex-Governor of New York and at that time political boss of the same state. Odell claimed that it would have been impossible for such an unschooled and uneducated man as Churchill's Jethro to have attained political leadership, and that the system which Jethro was supposed to have used to build up his power would not have worked. Churchill's picture of Jethro, Odell suggested, simply demonstrated that the author knew nothing about politics. Churchill did not reply to Odell's criticism, but many letters to editors of newspapers around the country show that numerous people did not agree with the New York boss.[20]

There can be little doubt that Churchill over-estimated Durkee's power, but there is even less doubt that the tanner was part of the power structure in the state. In his excellent biography of Senator Chandler, Leon B. Richardson says that in the years immediately following the Civil War Chandler's "relations with that eccentric and powerful rural politician, Ruel Durkee, were especially close." Richardson traces Durkee's career in much the same way that Churchill had presented it and then makes this assessment of his role in New Hampshire politics:

> He was a man of little education, who, through innate force and the power of personality, had come to assume a wide influence in the State. He never held public office or aspired to it (except that of select-man of his native town), but at each political convention and at each session of the legislature he was sure to be at hand, conspicuous in the dress of the backwoodsman, showing all the mannerisms and speaking with the nasal twang of the traditional Yankee, but displaying a keenness of mind equalled by few of his compeers, a reticence broken only by some pithy utterance when something really important was to be said, a capacity for gaining the liking and even the affection of those with whom he came in contact, complete reliability in keeping his word when it was once given and a genius for political management which made him a power always to be reckoned with in the councils of the party. He was not the supreme boss that he is sometimes pictured as having been (particularly in the novel, Coniston, by Winston Churchill) — there were too many ambitious men in the State aspiring for leadership to

permit that — but he was never to be ignored in the deliberations of his associates.[21]

This scholarly assessment of Durkee's character, personality, and ability is not very different from the novelist's description of Jethro Bass.

CHAPTER IX

A Mugwump Revolution

Churchill, like Rousseau, believed men were born free and yet everywhere he found them in chains. He did not go back to a state of nature to explain this paradox, but he did return to a time when New Hampshire was ruled by a natural aristocracy. This rightful rule of the natural aristocracy had been usurped by the political boss and his followers; their power in turn had been taken over by the "interests," in this case the railroads. Now the time had arrived for the people to rise and restore the state to its rightful rulers.

By the middle of June, 1906, Churchill was ready to make a fight of it. This was a decided change from his position just two months before. At that time an editor of the New York *American* wrote to ask whether Churchill thought a newspaper investigation of the corruption of the legislature by the Boston and Maine Railroad would be newsworthy. Churchill did not think the time was "propitious" especially since "there is a decided reaction of sentiment just now against the so-called 'muck rakers'."[1]

Churchill still was planning to run for the state senate at that time, and the Boston and Maine had not yet decided to oppose his election. Nor had *Coniston* yet appeared. He was going back into politics as a reformer but, at this point, as a reformer with no clear program. In line with the sentiments expressed in his

108

novel, he was intent upon running this campaign without the help
of the local political boss, Vene Bryant. He informed Bryant that
he did "not intend to solicit support. If my books and my good
intentions and loyalty to the state are not sufficient to convince
people that it is worth while sending me I shall be very well
content to remain in private life."[2]

It can be doubted, however, just how content he would have
been. While it was true that he clung to the aristocratic notion
that the honorable man does not seek public office but allows it
to seek him, and it is also possible that his childhood doubts about
his own virtue may still have plagued him, there can be no doubt
that he was increasingly drawn into politics. It seems likely that
by the time he finished writing *The Crisis*, Churchill had sensed
a national identity crisis in his own day. His novel at this point
turned to the development of a hero who could deal with this
crisis as the great heroes of his romantic historical novels had
dealt with the emergencies of their period. He had welcomed
Theodore Roosevelt as the hero of the present crisis, but the
novelist felt the President needed active help to unite the people
and return the republic to its natural virtue.

At this point, however, Churchill moved slowly and tentatively into the role of activist. For the governorship he had tentatively
committed himself some time before to the candidacy of Rosen-
crans Pillsbury, manager of the Union Publishing Company, which
published the Manchester *Union*, one of the most powerful newspapers in the state. At forty-three Pillsbury was a prosperous
young man, a dilettante in several fields and a specialist in apple
culture, who had engaged in manufacturing with his father. He
had served two terms in the legislature and was now pursuing what
from all indications was the great ambition of his life — the
governorship of New Hampshire. The previous summer, Pillsbury
had written to Churchill soliciting his support for this position.
Churchill replied: "It is quite easy for me to say that I will
support you heartily against any candidate now in the field I
believe in you and in your principles, as you know, and I have no
other affiliations whatsoever."[3]

By June of 1906, Churchill and a number of others, disenchanted with the Manchester publisher's weak platform, decided that a new organization and a new candidate were needed. The timing of this revolt was probably influenced by the publication of *Coniston*; certainly the novel was largely responsible for Churchill's nomination for governor by the Lincoln Republican Club. His own account of his selection is fairly accurate:

> After finishing the book I went to Concord and asked Judge Remick if he would be a candidate for the Governorship on a platform to free the state and its government from railroad domination. He said he could not, but we got together Mr. Cook, Mr. Niles and Mr. Sargent, and talked over the situation, and we urged President Tucker of Dartmouth to be a candidate. While expressing every sympathy with the movement, he, too, was unable. Judge Remick sent out invitations to his friends, and as a result thirteen men, the original Lincoln Club, met on the night of July 2nd, 1906, and decided that, while there were many drawbacks, I was the only man who was in a position to make the fight.[4]

It is probable that the movement would have been launched even without Churchill's support; some of the other men involved had been interested in fighting the machine for some time. Churchill's book and his availability as a candidate simply precipitated events. Most of the other men involved had private interests or professional commitments that militated against their actually leading the movement. Churchill's position was unique; he had just published a book and could afford to take time off to make the fight. Perhaps even more important, his livelihood would not be endangered if he should lose.

The original thirteen members of the Lincoln Club were all respectable and respected professional men, established and prosperous members of the community. The most conspicuous absentee from the original list was Chandler. He was the most famous politician in the state and his anti-railroad views made him a logical leader, but his biographer points out that Chandler did not know anything about the movement until after the organizational meeting. Since the idea was to have the campaign run by respected men in various communities who had not been associated with earlier attacks on the railroad, Richardson suggests, it was thought best not to have the old advocate of railroad reform associated with the organization of the club.[5] This is logical, but is not the whole of the matter. Churchill and Chandler were, after all, engaging in a battle over the author's characterization of Chandler's friend Durkee. And beyond this, some members of the Lincoln Republican Club did not trust the ex-Senator. Churchill, himself, suspected Chandler's motives and was convinced that the old rebel was actually working for Pillsbury, whom the author described as "a milk-and-water candidate . . . . "[6] And despite his biographer's contention that Chandler embraced the new movement "with alacrity and enthusiasm," there was solid ground for the suspicions of the Lincoln Republicans; Chandler did end up supporting Pillsbury.

Churchill's own political ideals at this time are expressed in a letter he wrote to accompany an advance copy of *Coniston* that was sent to President Roosevelt.

> I cannot refrain from adding my congratulations to the thousands which you must have had for your recent magnificent achievements. I have always been a Federalist; an American, rather than a citizen of any state, and a believer that in general the size of the statesman is in proportion to the size of his constituency. This, I am aware, would make the average senator a small man. The state, and especially the small state, is a fertile breeding ground for the small politician. You, as Mr. Croly, a neighbor of mine has very aptly put it, have nationalized reform.[7]

From the beginning of Churchill's career in politics he had been an ardent nationalist, a firm believer in the extended powers of the federal government. His affection was for the union, and he saw the New Hampshire reform movement as only one cog in the wheel of national reform which was being set in motion by Roosevelt. He was already impressed with the ideas of Herbert Croly, ideas later expressed in *The Promise of American Life*, the philosophical rationale for Roosevelt's New Nationalism in 1912. Possibly Churchill introduced Roosevelt to Croly's writings, for he certainly took an active interest in furthering the career of his taciturn but brilliant young neighbor. And when Churchill used the word Federalist in 1906, Roosevelt understood what he meant. In replying to Churchill's letter, the President wrote, "I shall read 'Coniston' at once, and, I am sure, with the interest and pleasure I always feel in your books. I thank you for your letter, too, oh my fellow-Federalist! I wish I could see you and talk matters over with you."[8]

But in 1906 the fight was to be made on the state level. Robert M. LaFollette had already pointed the way in Wisconsin, where by the end of 1905 the insurgents had initiated reforms that would soon be incorporated into the statutes of many other states. The objectives of the New Hampshire insurgents closely resembled those being fought for by similar groups in other states at the time: to rescue the government from the malefactors of great wealth, and return it to the people. The pattern of operation differed, however, from that of the states farther west. From Wisconsin westward the Progressive movement was tinged with the remains of a far more radical reform movement — Populism. Western Progressivism was a combination of radical Populism and the general prosperity of the first decade of the new century. In the East, where Populism had never had a strong appeal, the reforms were milder and less sweeping in nature, a combination of moral indignation and what Richard Hofstadter has called the Status Revolution.[9] It seems beyond question that some of the Progressives in New Hampshire were victims of this Status Revolution which had replaced the local gentry with the new giants of industry and finance as the primary political force and guardians of the state. But it is wrong to stop at this point. These men were also genuinely concerned about the state of the nation, and their moral indignation was a necessary ingredient in the rise of the revolt in New Hampshire, as in the other states of New England. This indignation is evident, as is the essentially conservative nature of the movement, in Churchill's statement accepting the nomination of the Lincoln Club.

Here he stated his belief that the majority of the citizens had awakened to the evils of the political machine in New Hampshire.[10] The solution, as for most Progressives, was a simple one. " . . . I have at last come to the conclusion which is in your minds, that good government in New Hampshire, as in other

states, can only be restored in one way, by a direct appeal to the
people. They can always be depended upon, and if they will go
into the caucuses and nominate their own candidates to the convention it will be an easy matter for them to resume the reins of
government." He then set forth the political philosophy of the
group.

> I take the liberty of suggesting that the broad issue
> and general platform of the Lincoln Republican Club
> of New Hampshire should be the non-interference of
> the Boston and Maine Railroad or of any other cor-
> poration in the politics and government of the state.
> We should make it clear to this and other corporations
> that we do not come as enemies of theirs, that our
> intentions and platform in no way concern the cur-
> tailing of their legitimate rights: but, on the other
> hand, we should make it plain to them that their
> interests, as heretofore, should not come first —
> should not prevail to the detriment of the interests of
> the people of the state at large.

To members of the Lincoln Club the existing political situation in New Hampshire was monolithic. The railroad maintained
an army of lobbyists in Concord whose job it was to pick candidates for all important offices who would pledge to protect the
interests of the railroad. This same lobby, working through both
parties in the legislature, blocked legislation detrimental to the
railroad. To put the legislators in a receptive frame of mind, the
railroad issued each member a pass which allowed him to travel on
the railroad free of charge. It also issued these passes to most of
the lawyers in the state. The passes given to the lawyers stated
that the pass was to be accepted as a retainer, which meant that
anyone who wanted to sue the railroad would have considerable
difficulty hiring a lawyer. The Lincoln Club further contended
that right-minded men had repeatedly urged the railroad (and the
other corporations involved) to relinquish voluntarily their grasp
on the government of the state — only to have the officials deny
that they exercised such power. The only alternative solution was
a direct appeal to the people of New Hampshire. Churchill then
specifically states the aims and objectives of the Lincoln Club:

If we win we pledge ourselves to the enactment of

> such progressive laws as will give the people a better
> control of their government, among which I would
> suggest the following: a direct primary law, a law to
> abolish the lobby, and a law on the lines of that
> enacted by the Federal government to do away with
> the evils which attend the giving of passes within the
> state.

These men were neither anti-business nor anti-railroad; they were concerned only with removing the Boston and Maine's political domination. The way to accomplish this seemed fairly simple. They would appeal to an aroused electorate which would put them in office, where they could pass a few equally simple laws that would destroy evil and insure that in the future control of the government would remain where it belonged. Here is no plea for social justice, no offer of laws to redress the grievances of the underprivileged groups in a growing industrial society. This was a movement to restore the old order by taking political control out of the hands of the self-seeking nouveau riche and return it to the people, who would then elect their rightful leaders from the local gentry — as was proper in any well-ordered society.

The handicaps which the Lincoln Club faced were formidable. Churchill was still looked upon by many people as an outlander, and these same people regarded his statements that they were slaves of the Boston and Maine with something less than enthusiasm. The railroad-controlled machine dominated the committees that directed the town caucuses where the convention delegates were elected. With the possible exception of Chandler, no state Republican leader of any influence supported the Club, and the Lincoln leaders themselves were mostly political neophytes. Nearly all of the local newspapers opposed them, and a good percentage of the liberals in the state had already endorsed Pillsbury. Churchill's group had six weeks to change this situation before the town caucuses met. The one favorable condition was a factional split in the regular Republican organization. One group supported the nomination of Charles H. Greenleaf, a wealthy hotel proprietor from Franconia; the other group backed Charles M. Floyd, a Manchester merchant. Floyd had the support of the indomitable Henry Putney, state railroad commissioner and editor of the

powerful Manchester *Mirror*, who had given Churchill such a hard
time when he was in the legislature. Greenleaf had the backing of
Senator Gallinger, undoubtedly the most powerful man in New
Hampshire politics at the time. To add confusion to the situation,
Chandler's newspaper, the Concord *Monitor*, was also supporting
Greenleaf. Chandler and his editor, George Moses, were having a
fine row during the summer about who controlled the editorial
policy. Moses had hitched his star to Greenleaf in order to please
Gallinger and to gain a larger role for himself and for the paper in
state politics. The fiery ex-Senator (who theoretically supported
Churchill) had agreed that Moses could support Greenleaf but insisted that he was to go easy.[11] This left Churchill as the only one
of the four candidates who did not have a major state newspaper
working for his nomination.

In light of these difficulties, the Lincoln Club wisely decided
to concentrate on state affairs and ignore, for the moment, the
question of the Congressional delegation. Churchill was not interested in waging a campaign against individuals at this point.
Indeed, some of his opponents, men like Frank Streeter, were
personal friends of the author and he considered them not so much
evil as misguided.

> I have never openly revolted, but I never "trained
> with the gang." Many of them are pleasant men to
> meet — good men, if you can differentiate between
> the morals of a man in private life and the morals of
> the same man in politics. I have nothing against any
> one of them personally. Collectively I have every-
> thing against them.[12]

These were men with whom he had hunted and fished, played
poker and dined; he still considered them good men who had
fallen prey to the system. Such loyalties tended to dissolve,
however, in the bitterness of the campaign that followed.

Since Churchill had so few state newspapers on his side, he
was forced to conduct a rather old-fashioned campaign. Both he
and the other members of the Lincoln Club, usually operating in
teams of two, took to the stump and conducted a whirlwind cam-

paign of the state. At the outset Churchill was by all accounts a
poor speaker. One friendly observer noted: "His speech is not
clear, and lacks the beauty and fluency of his writing. There is a
nervousness in his bearing and gesture, more characteristic of a
schoolboy than of a political orator."[13] Newspaper accounts indicate that he improved considerably by the end of the campaign.
Perhaps more important, the people who came to listen went away
convinced that whatever his deficiencies as an orator, he was a man
of sincerity and deep personal conviction.

One of the major difficulties in the campaign was the diffu-
sion of leadership in the Lincoln Club. Edmund S. Cook, as Secretary of the Club, was to coordinate the activities from Concord
but he had even more problems than exist in the usual campaign.
Most of the men involved were mature leaders in the community,
many of them had risked their future financial careers in the fight,
and each was sensitive to criticism from the others. As an experienced politician and an original anti-Boston and Maine man,
Chandler naturally thought of himself as the political strategist of
the movement, and he did not hesitate to bombard Churchill and
others with directives. Dan Remich was another inveterate letter
writer who was certain that victory could be grasped only if all
the others did as he said. Churchill, an extremely proud man himself, was not partial to criticism, especially if it reflected in any
way upon his personal honor. But in this campaign he seems to
have taken most of the suggestions in his stride and he may have
been the moderating influence which held together a potentially
factious movement.[14]

The campaign could not be waged, of course, by the original
thirteen members of the Lincoln Club alone, but dozens upon
dozens of letters poured in from citizens across the state and each
received a reply urging him to form a local Lincoln Club and work
for the election of Churchill delegates. The Club also had a few
paid workers whose primary job was to tour the state, to assess
the enemy strength in various areas, and to encourage the people
to vote for Churchill men in the caucuses. Late in the campaign,
Churchill also acquired a publicity man and speech writer. Evidently, he had written his own speeches until that time. Most of

the money for the hired workers, in addition to that for most of the other campaign expenses, came from Churchill's pocket. The official expenses of the Club came to $4915.59; the novelist contributed $4358.[15]

The campaign speeches followed the basic ideas expressed in Churchill's letter of acceptance — that the state was in the grip of the Boston and Maine to such an extent that no laws were passed, no chairmen of legislative committees named, no major state officials elected without the approval of President Tuttle. He did not charge that Tuttle was a despotic or evil ruler, but simply that it was degrading for the citizens to have any ruler at all. A war had been fought in 1776 which removed the king and made New Hampshire a republic, Churchill maintained; now a new war must be fought to remove the king in Boston and reestablish the republic. To break the system the lobby had to be destroyed and the pass system abolished.

The Lincoln Club campaigners did not contend that the railroad passed laws which directly oppressed the people, for the railroad lobby was far more concerned with seeing that certain laws were not passed. The railroad paid a lower tax rate than the average citizen and was anxious to see that this continued. But it did pay a high percentage of the state tax and was therefore determined to keep state expenditures as low as possible. Consequently, the railroad lobbyists opposed such improvements as the building of roads and conservation measures. Finally, the railroad lobby prevented the passage of any laws which would force the railroad to abolish dangerous grade crossings and build safe bridges designed to handle modern traffic.[16]

These were the issues upon which the Lincoln Club wanted to do battle, but they were not the only issues that arose. One persistent issue that Churchill considered extraneous was the question of prohibition. He had held a liquor license when he was operating an inn on his land as a public accommodation (it had since been converted to a private residence), and rumors were circulated that he was a heavy drinker. This was an important issue with many of the voters, with none more so than Churchill's puritanical friend Dan Remich. Consequently, he was forced to restate his position that the existing local option laws with high license fees were the proper approach; he came out further for such additional laws as would absolutely prohibit licenses in towns which had voted against them.[17]

Another issue that Churchill had to contend with was his connection with race track gambling. The New England Breeders' Club, of which Churchill was a member of the Board of Governors, was rumored to be supporting an attempt to pass a betting law at the next legislative session. Dan Remich insisted that Churchill's connection with the club was seriously injuring his political future, and the novelist finally resigned from the board.[18]

Churchill undoubtedly hoped that now he had put to rest the fears of the puritans and the campaign could proceed on the basis of the real issues. But, in fact, he was tilting with an invisible adversary that did not directly enter the field against him. Public opinion against the Boston and Maine was strong enough that few wanted to come out openly in its defense. Most of the support of the railroad appeared in the local newspapers in New Hampshire and centered upon two contradictory assertions. The newspapers denied, on the one hand, that the Boston and Maine engaged in political activity, and, on the other hand, asserted that the railroad — as the largest taxpaper in the state — had the most at stake in any political decisions and therefore was forced to defend itself by encouraging the election of candidates favorable to its interests. But the principal device used against Churchill was innuendo. One rumor averred that Churchill had gone to see President Tuttle to solicit the railroad's backing for Frank Currier's seat in the House of Representatives, and that he had been told that the railroad would not interfere in the choice of congressman. In spite of Churchill's vehement denial, the rumor continued.[19] It was also charged that the real reason Churchill was in the race was to stimulate the sale of *Coniston*. These remarks were natural, especially since the Lincoln Club had made the novel an issue in their open letter inviting Churchill to be a candidate. In this statement they declared that *Coniston* was as timely as *Uncle Tom's Cabin* had been; the local press simply picked up the challenge. Indeed, this issue and the length of his residence in the state — his frequent trips and lengthy stays outside the state — were the main arguments they used against him. Although Churchill was a legally qualified seven-year resident, this did not still the fears that he was an outsider. The local newspapers were further incensed by Churchill's constant charge during the campaign that they were subsidized tools of the railroad.

Outside New Hampshire, the announcement of Churchill's candidacy for the gubernatorial nomination was carried in newspapers across the country. Most of the early stories treated his candidacy in a light vein, stressing the human-interest angle of the novelist in politics, and they, too, pointed out the free publicity that would be given his books by the campaign. As the campaign rolled on, out-of-state newspapers maintained a careful coverage of the events, and they became more and more impressed with the Lincoln movement. Their main emphasis ceased to be human interest and became that of connecting the New Hampshire campaign with reform movements all over the country. The longer the campaign continued the more they viewed it as a legitimate insurgent movement, and the tone of the articles and stories changed accordingly. By the time of the convention the national press was already congratulating Churchill on having made the grand fight, and quite a few reporters were convinced that he really had a chance of being nominated. During the campaign Churchill developed into an effective campaign orator, and one reason for the change in the tone of the newspaper coverage was that he was now looked upon as a professional who was conducting a real political fight.[20]

Churchill also received support and publicity from many individuals outside the state. Letters came from Finley Peter Dunne, Mark Sullivan, Fred Lewis Pattee, Albert Shaw, George Brett, Richard Harding Davis, and O. S. Marden, among dozens of others. Sullivan and Dunne wrote articles favoring his campaign; Davis and Pattee offered their personal services in any way that would help. In addition he received letters from ordinary citizens all across the country offering their support and encouragement.[21]

Although this outside support was doubtless encouraging to the battle-weary young author, it changed few votes. Fortunately for his own peace of mind Churchill realized all along that the odds were against him, but as the race neared a close it seemed to some that the Lincoln Club might have a chance at victory. Because Putney and Gallinger disagreed as to which of them should control the organization, the machine would enter the convention with its vote split between two candidates.

A canvass of the state in late July showed Churchill to be running a weak fourth, behind Greenleaf, Pillsbury, and Floyd. Then the local caucuses began to meet, and in these meetings there seemed to be extraordinary excitement and considerable corruption. As the results started to come in, it was evident that Churchill had more delegates pledged to him than was expected. The climax of the Lincoln Club effort came when they defeated a Greenleaf slate in Concord that was headed by Gallinger himself. Frank Streeter was also defeated in this same ward, which meant that neither man could officially attend the convention. This was a great victory for the reformers, and more of the newspapers began to speculate that Churchill might have a chance.[22]

As the day for the convention arrived, the Greenleaf and Floyd supporters were at each other's throats and the machine was running scared. Interest around the country was almost as high as it was in New Hampshire, and the event more than lived up to expectations. The floor of the convention hall was a scene of turmoil, and it was nearly impossible to tell whether those present and voting were legal delegates or not. As a result three of the nine ballots were pronounced invalid because more votes were cast than there were legal delegates.[23]

Because of limited accommodations, the public was excluded from the hall for the first time and huge crowds assembled outside to remain at their posts during the proceedings, which lasted without intermission from eleven in the morning until ten at night. Churchill was nominated by James Remick with a flourish of rhetoric. "We began in ridicule and abuse for apparently a hopeless cause," he said. "But the early caucuses made our hearts glad, and after the Waterloo in Concord we found our candidate was a Wellington."[24]

On the first ballot Churchill was, as expected, in fourth

position. Greenleaf had 232 votes, Pillsbury 204, Floyd 200, and Churchill 157. The next three ballots, (two of which were declared invalid) brought little change, but on the fifth Floyd pulled ahead of Pillsbury. Pillsbury then withdrew from the race and advised his followers to support Floyd. Many of Pillsbury's followers refused to follow his defection to the enemy camp, and the author-politician found the tide surging in his favor. On the eighth ballot (which was also invalid) Churchill took over the lead with 299 votes to 268 for Floyd and 243 for Greenleaf. It looked as if the reformers were to carry the day, but they led solely by virtue of the personal split between Floyd and Greenleaf and their respective supporters. At any point in the proceedings the machine could have won the nomination by uniting its support behind one or the other, and at this point the party regulars put on enough pressure to force the issue. On the next and decisive ballot Floyd won the nomination with a vote of 408 to Churchill's 335. The short and lively campaign had concluded with the expected and perhaps inevitable result.[25]

The one positive development to come out of the convention was that the principles set forth by the Lincoln Club won a place on the party platform. Newspapers and journals claimed that the machine was frightened by the insurgents and accepted the reform planks to placate an aroused public. Certainly this was something of a victory, more in theory than in fact as it turned out, and many people were impressed by the success of Churchill's political neophytes. The Boston *Transcript* wrote, "The moral victory in this contest beyond all question rests with the Lincoln Republican Club and Winston Churchill." A similar sentiment was expressed in *Outlook*, which ran an article entitled "Mr. Churchill's Virtual Victory," and coined a phrase that was used by newspapers around the country.[26] The old idea that he was in the race for publicity or material for a new book disappeared almost entirely as the national press now assumed that he would continue the fight and that he would win.

Many people urged Churchill to enter the race as an independent candidate. Such an action on his part would have blocked Floyd's victory in the election itself, but that is all it would have accomplished. There was almost no chance that Churchill could win a clear majority as an independent and, if the election were thrown into the Legislature, the heavy majority of Republican regulars would elect Floyd anyway. As it was, the novelist had stirred up dissension within the party that took years to erase.

Actually, Churchill had developed too much political sagacity by this time to listen to the siren song of those who urged him to run independently. Before the convention he wrote a letter to James Remick which he told the judge to keep to himself until after the convention, and then release it. Here he said:

> About a month ago I told a reporter in confidence that in the event of my not being nominated I did not intend to run independently . . . . If losing the regular nomination, I were to run independently and get the governorship I should undoubtedly run the risk of losing the splendid organization which we have begun to build up and which in a few years we hope to make invulnerable. One man in the governor's chair without a council, a senate and a house behind him could not do much.[27]

Indeed this was the lesson Churchill learned in the fight of 1906. The great problem, he felt, was to make reform practical and lasting; to do this it was essential that a strong organization be built, an organization, as he phrased it on one occasion, which would replace "the bad pieces of the old machine with good new metal."[28]

In the months that followed, the new political leader found plenty of activity as he spent most of his time that fall in political work. For one thing, his relationship with Roosevelt, who had not taken any part in the campaign, became even closer in the months that followed. In part, this stemmed from the personal affection between the two men, but Churchill's new position in New Hampshire politics was also an important factor. This can be seen in a letter from the President written right after the convention.

> Next winter Mrs. Roosevelt and I want Mrs. Churchill and you to come down either for one of the dinners, or if you would prefer it, for one of the

> receptions and the supper afterwards; and then I
> want you to come alone to lunch with me or else
> give me a couple of hours when I can go over at
> length the whole political situation with you. Ask
> Mrs. Churchill which dinner or reception she would
> prefer.[29]

This was not the first time that the Churchills were invited to the White House, nor the last, but it is the first written evidence that the President was consulting with the novelist on politics.

From the beginning of the Lincoln movement Churchill had performed a variety of time-consuming tasks and the number of these increased in the latter months of 1906 and the early part of 1907. The Club itself was an informal organization without a constitution or by-laws, operating largely through the office of its secretary, Harry Sargent. The president of the Club, and in many ways its most respected member, was James Remick, a former Justice of the State Supreme Court and a lawyer in Concord. For reasons of health, Remick was forced to resign his office in December of 1906, and his duties were assumed by Churchill.[30]

His major duties as acting president were to remain in Concord during the legislative session of 1907 and do what he could to see that the Republican platform was enacted into law. The first issue which arose, however, was the question of whether or not to oppose the reelection of the incumbent Senator Henry E. Burnham. Burnham was a member of the old guard and some of the insurgents, notably Dan Remich and Chandler, felt that the reformers must put up an opposition candidate. They argued that if the movement was to mean anything it must fight at every turn. Chandler contended that he and Churchill, since they had both incurred the wrath of the Republican machine, should stand aside in favor of someone like Judge Remick. But the Judge, Churchill, and the majority of the Lincoln Club members felt it would be useless to put forward their own candidate and that such an action would appear as a self-seeking move to the people of the state. This disagreement brought about a definite break between the Churchill-Remick group and Chandler.[31]

Even though Floyd and Burnham achieved victory, Churchill felt the Lincoln Club had gotten through the situation as well as could be expected.[32] The reformers, he suggested, had been hampered by lack of time in the summer campaign and had therefore elected only forty-five men to the legislature, and it was impossible for this small group to elect one of their own to the Senate. They had, therefore, simply cast a protest vote for Congressman Currier because he was popular with all elements of the party and might possibly have picked up enough outside votes to block the election of the more conservative incumbent. The reformers stood no chance of defeating Burnham and there was no sense dissipating their strength fighting windmills. There were more important things to be done.

Aside from the Senatorial hassle, Churchill's political activities in the spring of 1907 were of three sorts — his lobbying efforts for enactment of the Republican platform, his attempts to get federal patronage for the reform group, and a continued attempt to educate the citizens of the state through speeches on the issues involved. As the official representative of the Club in Concord, Churchill received advice from every quarter. Herbert Croly, James F. Colby, James Remick, and Dan Remich all bombarded him with suggestions for laws that would improve the state. As usual, Dan Remich was the most dogmatic and presumptuous of the group. He sent Churchill actual drafts of bills which he wanted the author to submit to the legislature. Despite the fact that neither he nor Churchill was a member of that body, Remich appears to have been under the impression that he was going to draw up the legislation for that session and Churchill was going to see that it passed.[33]

Actually, despite the efforts of Churchill and a number of others, the reform group was hampered by factional differences on matters of strategy. The most notable example was Chandler. The uneasy entente with the volatile ex-Senator broke down in the fall of 1906 when Churchill refused to back anyone for the Senatorial election. Burnham was the man who had defeated Chandler in 1901, and the old man felt it was essential for Burnham to be removed — an action which might conceivably result in the reinstatement of Chandler himself. Beyond that, he resented Churchill's use of his old friend Durkee. He held off his criticisms until after the primary, then unleashed the attack which was discussed earlier. In both cases he tended to lose sight of the issues involved and concentrate on attacking those who disagreed with him. He openly accused both Churchill and Judge Remick of having selfish personal motives in the course they took on the Senatorial election, and a breach was opened in the reform ranks that was never to be healed completely.

Although Churchill did work diligently to hold the small block of reformers together, his efforts accomplished little. The reformers were vastly outnumbered in the house and practically non-existent in the senate. The only bill of any consequence which they got through was an anti-pass law forbidding the railroads to give passes to public officials or members of the legislature. If there was a change in attitude it is measured more by two events that occurred than by any legislation that was passed. Early in the session a representative from Concord rose in the house to charge that Churchill had done more harm to New Hampshire than 10,000 Jethro Basses could ever do. No man, he said, had ever defamed the state so falsely as Churchill or with such blatant motives of personal aggrandizement. By the end of the session the mood of that body had changed to such an extent that Jim French, ruler of the legislature for twelve years, was booed and had things thrown at him when he attempted to filibuster a reform bill. Change was slow but it was coming.[34]

Later historians have tended to agree with Chandler that the major trouble with the reform movement at this point was that Churchill and some of the other leaders were more inclined to take noble stances than to engage in practical politics. This charge is not true. Churchill was fully aware of the necessity for organization. The Lincoln Republican Club had been accused of trying to build up a machine, and in one of his speeches Churchill confessed:

> There is no use in being hypocritical about it, we are
> trying to do just that. One of the greatest problems

> in American government today is to make reform
> practical, and still keep the "reform" in spirit as well
> as the letter. We are trying to build up an organiza-
> tion within the Republican party — a machine if you
> like, but a machine every cog and crank and wheel of
> which will be made of the best metal to be found in
> the State.[35]

Churchill also understood the necessity of having loaves and fishes
for the faithful. Since the machine still controlled the state patronage, such rewards had to come from the federal government, and
here Churchill's connection with the President was important. The
two men conferred twice in January of 1907, and it can be assumed that one of the main topics for discussion was the political
situation in New Hampshire. [36] But Churchill and Roosevelt looked at the problem from different points of view. Churchill's position is obvious. The political philosophy of his group and that of
the President were almost identical; the federal patronage should,
therefore, be used to strengthen the reform element. Following
this line of thought, Churchill wanted the federal office holders
who supported the machine removed and replaced with deserving
reformers. Roosevelt, however had to contend with the fact that
the party in New Hampshire was still in the hands of the Republican machine and with the problem of Senatorial courtesy. He
pointed out to Churchill that he could go only so far. While he
would not appoint men he knew to be incapable, neither could
he appoint men whom the New Hampshire Senators opposed.[37]

   Although his mind was almost completely absorbed by
politics during these months, Churchill was a professional writer,
not a professional politician. He may have preferred to devote
even more time to practical reform, but he had to earn a living.
At this time he handled his dual commitment by writing another
political novel.
   Mr. Crewe's Career, published in May of 1908, took up the
story of politics in New Hampshire at the point where Churchill
had left it in *Coniston*. This novel had its setting in Ripton, New
Hampshire, and centered upon the activities of five main characters; Hilary Vane, chief counsel of the Imperial Railroads; his son

Austen; Augustus P. Flint, who had appeared in *Coniston* as the stable influence behind the vitriolic Worthington and who had now become president of the consolidated railroads of the state, the Imperial Railroad; Flint's beautiful daughter, Victoria; and, finally, the millionaire Humphrey Crewe.

The hero and center of interest in this novel is Austen Vane, not Humphrey Crewe. In this drama Austen plays both the hero and the Greek chorus, participating in and explaining the events that take place. His theme, reiterated again and again, is that the corrupt political conditions were the result of evolution. The novelist was confident, however, that the evil and corruption of the existing institutions could and would be corrected. In the past men had become careless. Engrossed in the pursuit of wealth, they had allowed the corruption to creep in. But, since man is both good and creative, he is free to reform or remake his institutions in the light of his reason. The new generation was becoming aware of the evil conditions which had evolved while its predecessor's back was turned. The course of evolution would now be altered as the new generation exerted its creative powers. Such was the optimism which Churchill shared with a large number of his contemporaries.

The novel was as well received as Brett and Churchill could have hoped. The usual shower of letters of praise arrived, including congratulations from Roosevelt and Upton Sinclair. The reviews were not quite so good as those for *Coniston*, but it was frequently noted that some of the more serious critics, who had been inclined to pass off Churchill's efforts in the past, were enthusiastic about *Mr. Crewe's Career*. The consensus was that of the many political novels being published at the time, this was the best; the characters were well realized, the story well told. Both contemporary critics and later commentators have accepted the novel as an accurate presentation of political conditions in New Hampshire at the time.

The amount of political detail in the story led to the most widespread criticism of *Mr. Crewe's Career* — that the book was a tract rather than a novel.[38] This same criticism is one of the two criteria on which later critics have rejected it. Literary critics have said that it is too didactic, while political analysts have contended that it provided no real answers to the problems of the day.[39] What most of the latter group are really denouncing is the fact that Churchill was a progressive and not a radical. John Chamberlain, for example, criticizes Churchill for believing that reform can come without organization along class lines, and for the fact that his reformers always come from the upper classes as "paragons of self-sacrificing purity, good-breeding and disinterested intelligence." [40] This latter charge is true. It is also true (as Chamberlain partially realizes) that these same things could be said about the attitudes of most Progressives.

One of Churchill's own rare comments with regard to the artistic side of his novels was made in connection with *Mr. Crewe's Career*. Brett had written to him suggesting that the love scenes near the end of the book be lengthened and that the postscript should indicate the future of the major characters more explicitly. He referred his author to Dickens' postscripts as a model. Churchill replied that he appreciated the spirit in which the letter was written but did not agree with the advice.

> That postscript chapter was intended for a final piece of irony, and was really an afterthought. I had even believed it a kind of inspiration, and my critics here agreed with me. The idea of it is that Mr. Crewe, after whom the book is named and who is mockingly taken as the hero throughout is forgotten in the stress of real events: and the making of this chapter of two lines was supposed to be highly sarcastic . . . . Remember that my postscript will have to be a forecast, because Mr. Flint's last remarks were made only yesterday.[41]

Brett agreed that from an artistic point of view Churchill's postscript was the correct one, but he was thinking of the general reading public which likes "to have its ideas spelled out, leaving nothing to the imagination." [42] And the publisher had his way. Churchill added a longer postscript in which he pointed out what happened (in a general way) to the main characters, but he saved his original postscript and added that as the final two sentences in the book.

As one might expect with a novel of contemporary politics, *Mr. Crewe's Career* led to considerable speculation about the identification of characters. Most of the minor politicians were patterned on those the author had encountered in his own political career, and people made great sport of identifying them. The center of speculation, however, was the millionaire, Humphrey Crewe. Churchill stated again and again that neither Crewe nor any of the other characters was drawn from real people. They were, he contended, all "types." [43] The newspapers ignored these protestations and went ahead to identify such worthies as Vene Bryant, Senators Burnham and Gallinger and others. They achieved their greatest unanimity, however, on the identity of Humphrey Crewe; this pompous political aspirant had to be the comic relief in the New Hampshire reform movement, George Leighton.

The problem was that most of his contemporaries took the novel too seriously. Certainly Churchill had a message to convey which was serious enough in itself, but, to a greater extent than in any of his writings since *The Celebrity*, he lightened the novel with humor and irony. He said all along that this book had been fun to write. Surely much of this enjoyment was a result of his tongue-in-cheek approach to the title character. Crewe was a composite all right — a composite of Churchill's experiences and Leighton's characteristics. The reviewers recognized the characteristics but not the experiences. Churchill never admitted that he had had Leighton in mind, but in 1908 he did identify the experiences as his own.

> In order not to make my book banal, it was necessary that the so-called reform element in it should not be too angelic, and open to more or less criticism. This is life. Some of the incidents in the career of Mr. Crewe happened to me, when I was a little more green than I am at present. [44]

Some thirty-three years later he again alleged that *"Mr. Crewe's Career* in particular was more or less autobiographical. I like to think that I was making fun, perhaps more or less unconsciously, of myself." [45] And this is almost certainly the case. He saw in Leighton a magnification of his own characteristics at the time he was in the legislature, and, with a greater ability for self criticism than he is usually credited with, Churchill presented his reading public with Mr. Humphrey Crewe.

CHAPTER X

The Development of a Seasoned Politician

During the months that *Mr. Crewe* occupied his attention, and the period following its publication, Churchill had participated in the political scramble on every level from the local caucus to the national convention. At the local level he parted ways with Vene Bryant, and in April of 1908 Bryant defeated the Churchill group to maintain his forty year reign as boss of Cornish. According to the author, he accomplished this by using the liquor interests and the Democrats against Churchill's faction. But in September, Churchill came out on top. "We beat Mr. Bryant in one of the most dramatic caucuses ever held in this state," Churchill wrote, "and we beat him by clean, honourable, American methods."[1] It is doubtful that the methods of the two groups varied that much, but it is typical of the Progressive mind to see nefarious bosses as the only possible reason for their defeats.

Most of Churchill's time, however, was devoted to a reorganization of the Lincoln Republican Club for its second convention fight. "To commit the dominant party in a state to certain definite principles and to fight until those principles are enacted into law, is the most practical way to obtain good government," he contended.[2] And the most practical way to commit the dominant party was through organization. He told a group of Dartmouth

130

alumni, "There seems to be no question that, under our system, an organization or 'machine' is an absolute necessity."[3] With this idea in mind, Churchill tried to pull together the splintered remnants of the earlier movement. In addition to writing many letters to former members of the Lincoln Club, he worked to obtain the support of other groups that might unite with the insurgents. Frank Streeter, now out of the railroad's employ and a self-professed insurgent, had an extensive correspondence with Churchill, as did the Democratic lawyer Henry Hollis, James Lyford, a Republican moderate, and Pillsbury.

A preliminary meeting of what came to be called the "Committee of Fifty-Two" was held in November, 1907, to form the nucleus of a new organization to replace the Lincoln Club. By the following July, the group was ready to act. After a meeting in Concord the Platform Republicans became a working organization designed to put the government back into the hands of the people by the enactment of the 1906 Republican platform. Under the leadership of Professor James Tufts of Exeter, they formed committees in each county to campaign for legislators committed to that platform. Although they did commend Pillsbury and denounce Henry B. Quimby as the railroad and machine candidate, they were not prepared to give a definite endorsement for governor at that time.[4]

One of the chief problems was still the opposition of the local newspapers. Churchill told Brett to send copies of *Mr. Crewe's Career* to only seven designated papers in the state because the others were so bitterly against him that it would not be wise to send copies to them.[5]

Another major local problem which the Platform Republicans faced was the position of the old warhorse, William Chandler. Chandler at seventy-two still had an opinion on everything and an available forum in his newspaper and publishing house. Even Leon Richardson, his highly sympathetic biographer, has to admit that his course of action during this time is confusing. It was "according to the phrase which grew to have a definite meaning in New Hampshire, 'Chandleresque'."[6] In the fall of 1907, Churchill and Chandler tried to reach an understanding, but the attempt was unsuccessful and by the late summer of 1908 Chandler was again attacking the author in the columns of his newspaper. Still,

Chandler was known as a reformer in the state and could not be ignored. The insurgents had to try to work around him without unnecessarily stirring up his vitriolic pen.

The Platform Republicans had little trouble agreeing on principles, but when it came to nominating a gubernatorial candidate, the old personal feelings emerged. Part of the difficulty arose when Churchill endorsed Pillsbury without bothering to consult with his associates. Soon after the 1906 convention Pillsbury had announced that he would run again in 1908. Churchill evidently had no such intention. If he did, his enthusiasm was dampened by several letters urging him to step aside in the interests of party harmony. He had been the one to lead the fight and had attracted the hatred of the machine and the railroad; they would, therefore, fight harder against him than they would against a new man. Even his old friend and staunch supporter, James Remick, thought that Churchill should step aside.

The problem of a gubernatorial candidate was compounded by Churchill's desire to send to the national convention a New Hampshire delegation that was solidly committed to Taft. His determination to hold the party together for Taft meant that he had to avoid an open battle for the governorship. In pursuit of this unity, he and Pillsbury issued a joint statement in May of 1907 that they would work together on the election of delegates to the National Convention. The statement added, "It is distinctly understood that neither of us has agreed to support the other for any office."[7] But Churchill was also making plans for the future of the local reform movement beyond 1908, and during the summer of 1907 he came out in open support of Pillsbury. The reasons for this switch demonstrate his increasingly realistic outlook. In the first place, he suggests that the Lincoln Club may not have been fair to Pillsbury in the previous convention, since by the time of the convention, Pillsbury was advocating what was practically the Lincoln Club platform. When the Churchill group steadfastly refused to pull out and give him its support, Pillsbury threw his delegates to Floyd out of personal pique. Since that time, in spite of the tremendous resentment against his actions at the convention, he had continually demanded in his Manchester *Union* that the platform of 1906 be enacted. At the present time Pillsbury was a candidate and would have the large city of Man-

chester on his side. In addition Pillsbury would contribute the influential Manchester *Union* to the cause. Then, if no candidate on
the reform side should appear against him, the editor surely would
feel that he had been fairly dealt with. Whether he obtained the
nomination in 1908 or not (and apparently Churchill never believed he would), he would feel committed to the insurgents and
his newspaper would remain on their side in the future.[8]

Churchill's reasons for publicly supporting his enemy of two
years before seem sound, but they stirred up a hornets' nest
among his old friends. This, together with his association with the
still-suspect General Streeter, brought an avalanche of protests
from many other insurgents. Pillsbury's actions at the previous
convention were unforgiveable in the opinion of many; others
simply opposed a public commitment at that time. Even James
Remick, who felt they would end up supporting Pillsbury, said
Churchill's action was politically inexpedient.

Churchill still was more concerned about stopping the two
conservative candidates, Bertram Ellis and Henry B. Quimbly,
than he was about nominating Pillsbury, but he worked for
Pillsbury in earnest. Frank Streeter jumped on the Pillsbury wagon, but many of the others were a problem and at the time of the
convention the reform vote still was not consolidated. Some of
the insurgent votes went to Ellis, a larger number to Quimby —
both of whom had been associated with the machine in the
past — and a few voted for Edmund Cook, former secretary of
the Lincoln Club. With the reform vote scattered to the winds,
Quimby was easily nominated. The problem then was whether
the Churchill-Remick-Pillsbury group would support Quimby in
the upcoming election. Churchill, more interested in the election
of Taft than in the slight possibility a Democrat might be elected
Governor, was eager to maintain party unity by rendering tacit
support to Quimby. James Remick bolted completely and threw
his support for the first time in his life to a Democrat, Clarence E.
Carr, who was conducting his campaign on the issue of emancipation from the railroad-dominated Republican Party. Most of the
other insurgents decided that they would neither oppose nor
support Quimby; they would sit out this campaign.[9]

The absence of Churchill and the other insurgents from the
campaign trail was a boon to the Democrats, and they capitalized

on it. The author found himself in the curious position of being praised by Democratic speakers who used his own material on the domination of the Boston and Maine over the Republican party against his candidate. The combination of this maneuver with the active support of James Remick and a few others was effective. While Taft swept the state, Quimby won by with the narrowest of margins. [10]

It was the Taft contest that really interested the novelist-politician. There are two primary reasons for this. In the first place he knew that Roosevelt wanted the portly Secretary to succeed him, and he was convinced that Taft would carry on the President's policies. In the second place, Churchill was concerned about state patronage. If his group was successful in sending a solid Taft delegation to the national convention, they could expect to get the federal patronage that was necessary to build up a solid state organization. Throughout 1907 and 1908 Churchill pressured Roosevelt to throw all possible patronage bones to his group, and he always added that he was willing to do whatever was necessary to ensure Taft's nomination. [11] A Taft Association was formed early in January, 1908, and Churchill again found himself closely associated with the former counsel for the Boston and Maine, General Streeter. Opposition came from two sources. Chandler in his usual unpredictable way was supporting LaFollette and was, consequently, in the same camp with the conservatives, led by Gallinger, who wanted to send an uninstructed delegation to the convention. [12]

The relationship between Churchill and Taft was warm. In Taft's mind at least, Churchill's support was essential for his success in the state. Taft and Churchill were both guests at a banquet of the Fitchville, Massachusetts, Board of Trade in March of 1908, and Churchill said that he "sat next to Taft and talked to him all through a very long dinner." Churchill was particularly delighted with Taft's account of having met Leighton, whom he had instantly disliked and had put down hard. The candidate's treatment of Churchill was the exact opposite. "Taft," he wrote, "treats me like a prince." When they were standing at the railroad station, some photographers came to take pictures of the Secretary and Churchill started to step aside; Taft called him back, saying, "Come along, Churchill, you can't expect to escape the consequences of the Taft boom." [13] The author was naturally pleased by Taft's attention and this added a personal tie to the political commitment he felt toward the candidate. Consequently, Churchill placed both his time and his purse at the disposal of the Taft Association. He persuaded Dan Remich to stump the state with him, picking up the bills for renting the halls himself. They tried to convince the voters that Taft was the only man who could be relied upon to carry on Roosevelt's work.

As events turned out, the Taft Association's efforts were unsuccessful. New Hampshire Republicans had never sent an instructed delegation to the National Convention except to support an incumbent President, and even then only rarely. This precedent they followed again in 1908. Their delegates ultimately cast five votes for the victorious Taft and three, including Gallinger's, for Charles W. Fairbanks.

Churchill, deeply disappointed by the decision of the state convention, was convinced that once again the machine had subverted the will of the people. [14] In spite of the lack of success in New Hampshire, Taft wrote to thank Churchill for his efforts. Thus encouraged, the novelist continued to make speeches for Taft throughout the summer. Even with this activity, he did not feel that his enthusiasm was being fully utilized by the Taft Association. He wrote in July, "The Taft Association is afraid to send me out because the old line Republicans hate me so, and are showing a tendency to come onto the band wagon." With no apparent bitterness, and with a keen eye for political realities, he accepted this as a fact of life — one of the results of having tried to derail the machine. [15]

By the end of the 1908 campaign Churchill was well on his way to becoming a seasoned politician. He had acquainted himself with a wide range of political issues and problems, and had learned to think in terms of political tactics and achievable goals. Even his abilities as a speaker had improved markedly with the experience he had obtained since 1902. And he used his talents outside New Hampshire as well. In 1908 he spoke for Taft in New Haven, Connecticut, spoke for Everett Colby in New Jersey, and addressed the Intercollegiate Civic League at Harvard. That same year he was elected as the third vice-president of the National League of Republican Clubs at their convention in Cincinnati.

Churchill, himself, was not to receive a rumored appointment to Taft's cabinet, but two of his friends were elevated to such positions. Charles Nagel, a St. Louis lawyer, became Secretary of Commerce and Labor; and Franklin MacVeagh, a supporter of the Platform Republicans in New Hampshire, became Secretary of the Treasury. [16] Churchill was consequently able to bring inside pressure to bear on the Taft administration with regard to the important patronage positions, and he did so. Nor did he stop with the cabinet. His relationship with Taft allowed him to go straight to the top with his requests. The first federal appointment in the state, however, went to George Moses, the editor of the Concord *Monitor*, and a man whom Churchill had once described to Roosevelt as "without doubt the cleverest political scalawag in the State." [17] Moses had been campaigning for appointment as Ambassador to Greece since 1905, and when his appointment was made public, the insurgents sent angry letters of protest to the President. Taft replied to Churchill's letter by saying that he was aware that Moses had abused both the novelist and himself, but that his appointment would appease Gallinger and give him (Taft) leverage which he could use with regard to future appointments. A few days before, when he first informed Churchill of the appointment, Taft quipped, "You see I have sent Moses as far away as possible!" [18] Churchill accepted Taft's explanation and went on to other battles. The big one came over the appointment of Frank Musgrove, one of the most outspoken insurgents, as Supervisor of the Census. As editor of the Hanover *Gazette*, Musgrove had taken an active part in the preceding progressive campaigns and had earned the undying enmity of the two New Hampshire Senators. Churchill and the other insurgents bombarded the President with letters supporting Musgrove, and he was ultimately appointed. [19]

In spite of the continuing friendship between Taft and Churchill, the novelist's enthusiasm for the President cooled quickly. A year after Taft's election, Churchill confessed that he was "profoundly disappointed, from all outward appearances, with Mr. Taft's administration." [20] Churchill, along with most other insurgents, was upset by the passage of the Payne-Aldrich Tariff — a clear violation of the Republican promise in 1908 to revise the tariff schedules downward. And this was only the beginning of a series of events which were to disillusion most Progressives with the President.

On the state level, the legislative session of 1909 demonstrated the inroads which the insurgents had made on the Boston and Maine machine's ability to control legislation. After that session the railroads could issue passes only to its own employees and to people on charity. The use of passes to tie up the legal talent in the state, one of Churchill's most serious complaints against them, was a thing of the past. Equally important was the establishment of the direct primary for the nomination of state officials. Although the law did not provide for the direct nomination of candidates for Congressional seats, it did furnish a tool for the nomination of an insurgent governor.

Churchill's satisfaction with the progress that was being made can be seen in a letter he wrote to his friend, Norman Hapgood.

> You will be glad to hear that the so-called reform forces have won what was at this time an unforeseen and almost complete victory over the railroad lobby. We have carried the whole platform, for which we have been fighting for three years, into law, with the exception of a taxation measure which was to arrive at some businesslike method of assessing the public service corporations . . . . The credit is due, of course, to public sentiment, and secondly to the parliamentary ability developed by certain young men of our side.[21]

One of the most important of the young insurgent leaders Churchill mentioned was Robert Perkins Bass of Peterboro. A man of considerable wealth and ability, a graduate of Harvard and Harvard Law School, he had made his first political appearance in 1906 when he was appointed to the State Forestry Committee. He performed yeoman service in that position and then was twice elected to the House. In 1909 he served in the state senate, where he framed, introduced, and directed the passage of the direct primary bill and was instrumental in obtaining passage of other progressive legislation. Churchill, who had known Bass for some time, maintained a close correspondence with him during the 1909 session. [22] By the fall of that year Bass had emerged as one of the leading insurgents in the state.

When the time came for a decision about a gubernatorial

candidate for the following year, Bass and Churchill were at first in opposite camps. It was Bass's feeling that the reformers should concentrate on electing their own kind to the legislature and not challenge the machine directly by putting up their own candidate for governor. Churchill opposed this approach. "I put my nation before my party," he wrote Bass, "and far sooner would I retire from politics than enter into a 'love feast' with those men [Gallinger, Sulloway, and Burnham] merely for the sake of keeping together a body of voters in the state who should be known as Republicans." "On the tariff issue and every other issue of importance, national and state, they are wrong. I would rather be a Democrat." [23] He insisted further that people across the country, partially as a result of Roosevelt's leadership, had begun to focus their attention on the executive branch of government. If the insurgents had no candidate for chief executive of the state, they would be unable to arouse popular interest. Here again, Churchill was viewing the situation in a practical way. He had become thoroughly disillusioned with the Pillsbury-Streeter group, but he was convinced that faction would have to back the candidate selected by the insurgents because of the support the reformers had given Pillsbury in the previous campaign. If they could find a gubernatorial candidate who would stir the people, then the campaign could center on what he felt to be the real issues, and the insurgents would stand a strong chance of sweeping both the executive and legislative branches of the state government.

And Churchill thought he had the man they needed in Sherman Burroughs, who had joined the Churchill-Remick(h) group after the 1906 convention where he had been Pillsbury's floor leader. Burroughs was a relatively young man, a graduate of Dartmouth and of Columbia Law School, and a lawyer in Manchester. He had served one term in the legislature and was widely regarded as a genuine reformer, as well as a highly reasonable and respected gentleman. He had been neither a candidate for office nor a prominent member of the activist legislature of 1909 and, consequently, had not stirred the wrath of the conservatives as had Churchill and Bass. Indeed, except for a disinclination to run for public office, he had almost no political liabilities.[24]

During the crucial month of December, Churchill was trying

desperately to finish his new novel and still keep abreast of the political winds. Consequently, he was absent from the meeting on the twenty-second at which Burroughs agreed to enter the fight, but he was delighted with the news. They were still not out of the woods, however, for early in 1910 Burroughs again changed his mind and definitely decided not to make the race. The mantle of the insurgents then fell upon Bass, and a roar of outrage erupted from their old nemesis, William E. Chandler. According to Chandler's biographer, even though the old warrior did not know Bass, he was convinced that the party would not accept the man. From conservatives in the party he learned that feelings against Bass ran high in that quarter. They considered him an outsider who had bought his way into politics, a young upstart with wild ideas who was in too much of a hurry.[25]

During the months preceding the primaries, the insurgents again received help and encouragement from outside the state. William Allen White continually gave Churchill both reassurance and advice (especially the latter), and Senator Albert Cummins of Iowa wrote to say, "I sincerely hope that you will succeed in awakening the spirit of the people of New Hampshire and that under your leadership the East will join the ranks of the 'insurgents'." More important in publicizing the cause of New Hampshire insurgents was an article by Ray Stannard Baker that appeared in the March issue of *American Magazine*. The well-known muckraker contended that of all the eastern states New Hampshire was the one closest to insurgency. This, he said, was because it was exploited by the Boston and Maine "with a degree of absolutism not equaled by the rule of the Russian Czar."[26] Certainly Baker overestimated the power of the railroad in 1910 and, consequently, underestimated the work which the reformers had already accomplished, but he did give nationwide publicity to their cause.

The Bass campaign started slowly. During the early weeks, there was no opposition in the field and the insurgents devoted their time to building up local organizations. Churchill was well satisfied with the way things were moving, but he was overly optimistic. In the middle of July he noted, with considerable irritation, that Speaker of the House Bertram Ellis had entered the fight for the gubernatorial nomination. Ellis was known as a friend of the railroad machine, and as Speaker had appointed the old boss, Jim French, as chairman of the powerful Appropriations Committee. In this campaign he did make some liberal pronouncements, but he was supported by the attorneys for the railroad and by the conservative Congressional group.[27]

Equally as important as the nomination of a reform governor was the election of a progressive legislature. It was crucial to have an insurgent file for the primary in each district and to make certain that progressive men did not file against each other. Since the job of coordinating insurgent candidates had to be handled by someone who was not running for office himself, Bass asked Churchill to undertake this rather thankless chore. The novelist had long understood the necessity for getting dependable men into the legislature and he devoted full time to the job. During the late spring and the summer he wrote innumerable letters, seeking information about men who would be willing to serve and attempting to coordinate filings for the primary.[28]

At the same time he maintained almost constant contact with Bass to discuss details of the campaign. And, although there is some indication that Bass was trying to keep the controversial author from becoming an issue in the campaign, Churchill did make a number of speeches. The opposition had spread the idea that the Bass-Churchill group were really Democrats in disguise and urged all true Republicans to support Ellis. This was a powerful argument in a solidly Republican state, and Churchill did his best to counter it. He openly admitted that there was a split in the party at both the state and national levels, but he insisted that his group was the one that was adhering to true Republican principles. It was the members of the railroad machine who were not party regulars; they would use either or both parties to maintain their hold on the state. He further contended that Republican difficulties on the national level were the work of the trusts and their hirelings. The obvious course was for the party to admit it had made mistakes and to stand by its principles. The embodiment of those principles was, of course, Robert Perkins Bass.[29]

One of the problems that the reformers faced was stirring up public interest. Churchill felt that the solution might be to bring in national problems by running a candidate for Congress and perhaps in the future to form a third party. In the course of a lengthy letter to Sherman Burroughs urging him to run for the House of Representatives against the conservative incumbent Sulloway, Churchill states, "We have all probably, long foreseen the time when we should have to hitch on to the National Progressive campaign. . . . In my opinion the next administration [National] will be either Democratic or Progressive Republican." He went on to suggest that the people were beginning to think seriously about such national issues as the tariff and conservation. A real fight for a national office would, therefore, add to the interest of the Bass campaign, which the machine, he contended, was trying to kill through apathy. "None of the things which are agitating the man in the street are coming into it; his enthusiasm has no outlet."[30]

In the light of these statements about a third party, it is interesting to note that both Churchill and Bass were in close communication with Roosevelt, lately returned from hunting lions to discover that his successor was not running things to his liking. They urged Roosevelt to speak for Bass after the reformer was nominated; he replied, "I have written to Bass asking him if you and he cannot come out and lunch with me, if you are to be in the neighborhood of New York. Of course if I can, I am going to do what you desire."[31] Apparently this meeting was to be kept secret. Churchill said they would be glad to come and would keep the meeting quiet. What plans, if any, were made with regard to the next presidential election is not known, but Roosevelt did come to speak for Bass and two years later both New Hampshire men joined Roosevelt in his fight against Taft.

They received no help from Roosevelt's successor. If they had any hope of assistance from Taft, it faded when George Rublee, a friend of Churchill's and a prominent Republican, "volunteered the information that we could not expect in our fight here any help or good will from the Taft administration."[32]

Contrary to Churchill's concern about public apathy, New Hampshire's first direct primary brought about seventy percent of the state's Republicans to the polls, where they accorded Bass a landslide victory of almost two to one. Although quite a number of the reform candidates for other offices were defeated, Churchill was satisfied with the outcome.

The ensuing campaign against Democratic nominee Clarence

E. Carr lacked the fire of the previous battles. About the only real excitement was Roosevelt's appearance in Manchester in October, when he fulfilled his commitment to the insurgents. Disgruntled conservatives like Gallinger had no place to turn in opposing Bass, since the Democratic platform was nearly identical to the Republican and Carr was just as liberal as Bass. This fact also explains the substantial majority which Bass received in the November election, an election in which the Democrats carried all other gubernatorial races east of the Mississippi River. Given a choice between two reform candidates, the people of New Hampshire simply expressed their normal Republican allegiance. The triumph for the insurgents came in the primary; the election itself was anti-climactic.

The victory went to another, but Churchill received his fair share of the credit. Typical of the comments in the national press was an article in the New York *Evening Post* which contended that had it not been for Churchill's persistent work over the previous years, the Democrats would have won in New Hampshire as they did elsewhere in 1910. [33] The feelings of many of the state insurgents was expressed by Edmund Cook, the original secretary of the Lincoln Club and in 1910 the chairman of the New Hampshire Republican Committee.

> I want to say to you that I think the work you have done during the campaign and before the campaign has contributed largely to the result of Nov. 8th. It must be a great satisfaction to you to have the principles for which you have so long and so earnestly contended ratified by the voters. Personally I think that you, as much as any one man and perhaps more than any one man, are entitled to the credit for what has happened. [34]

It would be difficult to dispute Cook's contention that Churchill, as much as any other individual, including Bass, was responsible for the insurgent victory. He was the publicist of the movement; he had borne the standard when no one else was willing to take the risk; and in 1910 his presence in the campaign served to attract much of the machine's outraged squeal away from Bass.

During this campaign, Churchill became closely connected with insurgent movements around the country. He corresponded with Judge Ben Lindsey of Colorado, whom the author congratulated on his fight against the "interests" in that state. He was also involved in Albert Beveridge's campaign for the Senate. The two men had become acquainted some time before through the Indiana Senator's admiration for Churchill's novels, and each had subsequently followed the other's political career. As early as July, Beveridge realized he was in trouble at home and asked Churchill to campaign for him. Churchill was reluctant to leave the New Hampshire fight, but by September it was obvious that the Senator was fighting for his political life and he practically begged Churchill to go to Indiana. If Churchill could not, even a letter of support that Beveridge could publish would help. Yielding to these entreaties, Churchill made three speeches for the Senator in October, but to no avail. [35]

He made one other excursion into the Midwest in 1910. In September of the previous year, under the leadership of Richard S. Childs, a Short Ballot Association was established. The following month Woodrow Wilson was elected as the first president of the Association, with Churchill and William U'Ren of Oregon serving as his vice presidents. [36] The short ballot was a subject which had increasingly interested the novelist, and he accepted an invitation from Harold Ickes, a future Bull Mooser and later Franklin Roosevelt's Secretary of the Interior, to address a gathering of insurgents at Peoria, Illinois, on this topic. In the speech he emphasized that the long ballot allowed boss control of politics. Contrasting the English system of responsible government with the American system of voting on men for all positions, he said, "Our voters on election day are called upon to vote for so many people that they either have to vote at random, or else rely blindly on party machines." [37] The adoption of the short ballot would make it possible to hold the governor responsible. He would be an elected boss, as opposed to the old-style corporate-controlled boss, and could use his appointive powers to carry out the people's will. In politics, as in his novels, Churchill was drawn to the image of the dynamic hero-executive who would lead the people back to the path of natural virtue.

By the end of 1910, Churchill was convinced that the fight in New Hampshire had been won and that he could retire from politics. After Bass's nomination, he wrote, "I did not realize four years ago that such a brief time could see the accomplishment of so much, and I am now glad of the opportunity it offers me to retire from politics to a work which I have in mind to do."[38] Churchill was so pleased with the way things were progressing that he even made peace with Chandler.

One of the things which may have led Churchill and some of the others to view the situation somewhat over-optimistically was the apparent withdrawal of the Boston and Maine from the political scene. The New Haven Railroad had acquired a controlling interest in the Boston and Maine, and shortly after Bass's nomination President Tuttle resigned. He was replaced by Charles S. Mellen, who became head of both roads, and he let it be known that henceforth the Boston and Maine would have nothing to do with politics. [39] In line with this policy, Edgar J. Rich, General Solicitor of the railroad, informed Churchill that he had been entrusted with working out problems in New Hampshire. He said that his ideas about the methods to be employed were in line with those which Churchill had advocated but that "the working out of this policy of non-interference in political matters is not so easy as it might seem." Rich felt that the insurgents should support him in his efforts and suggested that Churchill arrange a meeting for him with some of the reform leaders. There also were some things that Rich wished to submit to Governor-elect Bass, since "we have cut ourselves off from the customary means of reaching the legislature . . . ." This letter is an open admission that the railroad had been interfering in politics up to that time, and it is also a recognition of Churchill's position in the insurgent group that the approach should be made through him. There were several further exchanges of letters which indicate a cooperative feeling on both sides.[40]

None of this, however, was to allow Churchill to return to full-time literary pursuits. He was too involved in the insurgent movement to sit by quietly just because they had won the executive office in the state. Almost immediately after the election he set about writing letters to the newly elected legislators in a successful attempt to get Musgrove elected as Speaker of the House. Bass stayed in close touch with him, asking for suggestions for appointments to committees, and advice in regard to his message to the legislature. When his legislative program ran into trouble, the Governor asked Churchill to come to Concord and help get the platform measures through an obstructionist state senate.[41]

The major battle centered upon the creation of a Public Service Commission and the corollary issue of an increase in railroad rates. Before the legislative session the railroad officials went to the state Railroad Commission (still staffed with members of the old machine) and secured an authorization for a new issue of stock. This still did not provide the railroad with the desired increase in income, and Mellen went before the 1911 legislature with a request for higher rates. Theoretically this was impossible because the provisions of the Railroad Act of 1883 and the Consolidation Act of 1889 had stipulated that there were to be no rate increases. The railroad, however had already violated these provisions by several advances in rates. Chandler was violently opposed to any such concession and ranted at the insurgents, including Bass, for even considering it. But, these men were placed in a dilemma by the fact that the old machine was able to control enough votes in the senate to hold up all of the progressive legislation that had been passed by the insurgent-controlled house. The situation obviously called for a compromise, and the insurgents agreed to validate the higher rates that the railroad had been charging for two years, during which time a body of experts would attempt to work out the situation. The logjam in the senate immediately broke, and that body allowed the establishment of a Public Service Commission with broad powers over all public-service corporations in the state. This was the first such board in New England and one of the first anywhere in the country. It was a large victory won by small concessions.[42]

This same legislature put into law a large part of the rest of the platform. By the end of the session New Hampshire had a State Tax Commission, a law forcing publicity of campaign expenses and receipts of lobbyists, one prohibiting campaign contributions by corporations, a workman's compensation law, a child labor law, and a factory inspection law. The insurgents failed to win ratification of the federal income tax amendment, and the attempt to broaden the application of the direct primary was unsuccessful. On the whole it was a record of which the insurgents could be proud, and since they had won control of most of the party machinery they could look forward to many more victories in the future. Subsequent events, however, were to kill this possibility, and Churchill, who had done so much to make the victories possible, was equally responsible for the fall from power.

CHAPTER XI

The Failure of Insurgency

1912 was the year of decision for Republican insurgents. Should they continue to fight for control of the regular party organization or part company with the Aldriches and the Gallingers and strike out on their own? Churchill had toyed with the possibility of a third-party movement since 1902, and by 1911 many political leaders were thinking in these terms. Followers of the great Wisconsin Republican insurgent, Robert M. LaFollette, Sr., launched a National Republican Party in January, 1911, and Churchill (writing to Oswald Villard, then editor of *The Nation*) embraced the idea of a third party.[1]

Within the state of New Hampshire the insurgents were moving along smoothly as Churchill, Chandler, and Bass worked together with no apparent friction. The Remick(h) brothers retained some doubts about Bass; they suspected that the Governor's ethical sense was exceeded by his political ambitions. When Bass indicated a desire to withdraw from the next gubernatorial race in favor of Churchill, they advised the novelist to move with caution. New Hampshire would be electing a United States Senator as well as a governor in 1912, and they felt that Bass might be trying to eliminate Churchill as a rival for the more prestigious position.[2] Churchill, deeply engrossed in a new novel, was not interested in involving himself in politics more than necessary, and he seems never to have questioned the motives or actions of the Governor. The two men remained close and both stayed in touch with Roosevelt, who was sounding more and more like a candidate.

By the winter of 1911-12, it was obvious that insurgents in many states would not accept Taft, and on February 24, Roosevelt overcame whatever reluctance he may have had and announced his candidacy for the Presidential nomination. The New Hampshire Progressives reacted quickly, and Churchill was named to the Executive Committee of the Roosevelt Republican League of New Hampshire. Although he was at a crucial point in the composition of his novel, he took time to write letters and make speeches urging Roosevelt's nomination.[3]

The campaign moved slowly until Taft defeated Roosevelt for the Republican nomination at the Chicago convention in June. Roosevelt had tried to persuade Churchill — who was not a delegate — to attend the convention, writing that "it will be a very real pleasure and advantage to me if you can get to Chicago." But Churchill was not too disappointed about Taft's victory. He was looking for a real fight and was convinced that it had to come through a third party. On the day of Taft's nomination he telegraphed Roosevelt, "In my opinion people all over this country desire intensely new, clean party and you to lead it. The time has come."[4] A few days later he pledged his support to Roosevelt and promised to finish his novel within a month so that he could hit the campaign trail.

An organizational meeting of the New Hampshire Progressive Party was held on July 20, placing a great many state insurgents in an embarrassing situation. After a six-year fight they had captured control of the state Republican party. If the new party failed, they would lose all they had gained in the past years, and would in addition, leave the Republican party in the hands of the conservatives. Yet if they hoped to carry the state for Roosevelt they had little choice but to launch a third party in the state and submit a full slate of candidates. Many of the letters written to Churchill show an awareness that the third-party movement was likely to be disastrous on the state level, and no one saw this more clearly than Chandler. He poured out his sorrow in a letter to Bass and Churchill, predicting that the third-party movement would destroy insurgency in New Hampshire.[5] The two leaders were attacked in the press on the same grounds. Their reply was that the new party would draw together progressives from both old parties and unite them into a more dependable working organization. Beyond this, they could not support Taft and it would be impossible to run as Republicans in New Hampshire and Progressives nationally. It was all or nothing, and they chose to gamble their political futures and their past accomplishments in one great battle.

They did not nominate candidates for every office in the state. Bass and Churchill agreed that the best strategy was to wait until after the state conventions and then support progressive Democrats or Republicans in districts where they had been nominated; third-party candidates would be put forward only where both old parties had nominated unacceptable men.[6] Since they were already committed to the Roosevelt movement, neither Bass nor Churchill campaigned for nomination by the Republican convention. As Chairman of the Provisional Committee on Organization, Churchill did create a functioning Progressive group which was to stay under cover until after the convention.[7]

Until the middle of August it appeared that Bass would be the Progressive candidate for governor. Then Bass decided that his health was not good enough to make the fight, and Churchill consented to run. Since the Progressives had agreed to make no public moves until after the state Republican convention in September, this decision was kept in strictest confidence. Churchill did not even mention it in his report to Roosevelt.

In any case, Churchill did not attach much importance to his own candidacy. During the campaign he wrote advice to himself in his datebook, and the constant theme was to play down the importance of his election. And he followed his own advice; nearly all of his activity was devoted to the election of Roosevelt and of insurgent legislators. Whether or not he believed he had a chance is difficult to estimate.

As predicted, the third-party movement split the insurgent ranks in the state. Such veterans as Rosecrans Pillsbury, Sherman Burroughs, and James Colby openly fought against Roosevelt, and Pillsbury and Chandler were both active and honored participants in the State Republican Convention that nominated Frank Worcester for governor.

Churchill's political philosophy had matured considerably by 1912. One important source for his new approach to politics and economics was his relationship with Herbert Croly. Churchill and Croly had been acquainted for years, and their friendship developed into one of some affection on both sides. Indeed it was Churchill who called Brett's attention to Croly's famous *Promise of American Life*, the book that formed the philosophical foundation of Roosevelt's Square Deal in 1912. The novelist read the manuscript and recommended it as "one of the ablest books on political subjects which I have read in a long time."[8]

Prior to the 1912 campaign, however, Churchill still had reservations about some of the reforms that were being put forward. He was contributing funds to the New Hampshire Direct Legislation League for example, but he was concerned about certain aspects of its program. "I am particularly shaky, up to the present time, on the question of the Initiative," he wrote. He had similar reservations about the recall of elected and appointed officials. "I regret to have to admit to you that I have not yet made up my mind about the Recall. It is an issue which has not yet come up in this state, probably on account of the short term of our Governor. Our judges are appointed, as I believe judges should be."[9] By the time of the 1912 campaign he espoused all three of these reforms.

Two other issues that divided Progressives harassed the novelist. The question of woman suffrage was one which had at one time divided the Churchill family and, consequently, provided good copy for the press. In 1903 there had been a campaign for an amendment to the New Hampshire Constitution that would have allowed women to vote. Churchill opposed the amendment, but Mrs. Churchill signed a petition in its favor, initiating speculation in the press about domestic quarrels on this issue.[10] This was not the case, but Churchill continued to drag his heels on the matter. In reply to a request that he accept appointment to an advisory committee that was seeking adoption of the suffrage amendment in 1911, he replied, "Although I am in solid sympathy with the suffrage cause I should rather not . . . take a public part in it at present." Two months later he declined an invitation to speak before the Boston Equal Suffrage Association because he was finishing a novel, but he added, "I should have liked to go on account of my wife and my friends who are much interested in

Woman Suffrage, in which I believe on the grounds of universal and individual responsibility of women as well as men for government."[11]

The liquor debate attracted him even less than woman suffrage but cropped up with persistent tenacity. In 1912 Rev. J. H. Robbins, Secretary of the Anti-Saloon League in New Hampshire, insisted that the Progressive platform must deal with the question. Churchill's reply shows that he was neither well informed on the issue nor concerned about it.[12]

Churchill's views on the important questions in 1912 were presented in an open letter which was published as his acceptance of the gubernatorial nomination. [13] After paying tribute to Bass, he moves immediately to the principle of social justice which he contends is the keynote of the Progressive Party's platform. His new conviction regarding the intimate connection between social justice and Christianity permeates the statement.

> With the Twentieth Century there springs up with new vigour that transforming force, the Public Conscience. No longer in a government deriving its authority from a Christian people may the persuance of a selfish and ruthless individualism be tolerated and condoned. No longer do the citizens of our republic regard with complacency a system in which men and women and even little children are exploited in mills and mines and factories like cattle; in which our young women, for lack of food and clothing in the midst of plenty are sold into the vilest and most hopeless of slaveries with the cynical connivance of our politicians. No longer is it thought right for the injured workmen to be thrown on the human dump heap and his family left to starve.

Here, as in all of his writings in 1912, can be seen a recognition that simple political, procedural reforms are not sufficient. He continued to advocate political reforms, but they were now a means to a much more positive end. And for Churchill, as for Charles Beard, the main obstacle to reform was the Constitution. "The farmers of our government set up, instead of an hereditary line of kings, an <u>automatic monarch</u> in our Constitution, an Eighteenth Century sovereign who will put his veto relentlessly on certain modern measures necessary for the advancement of humanity." For this reason, one of the most important measures (at

The successful novelist with his dogs
Courtesy Mrs. Mabel Butler

Churchill as a child in St. Louis
Courtesy Mrs. Mabel Butler

Churchill with his daughter Mabel in 1906.
Courtesy Mrs. Mabel Butler

Churchill at about the time of WWI.
Courtesy Mrs. Mabel Butler

The novelist-politician working on his Cornish, N. H. grounds
Courtesy Mrs. Mabel Butler

both the state and the national level) was to devise an easier method of amending constitutions.

To accomplish this change it was necessary for a new, vital party to take the floor.

> It has rapidly been growing apparent that no political party can continue to exist half corporation and half free: that the time was bound to arrive when all the people who think alike . . . would unite in one party. That party has come. It is the Progressive Party, the party of social democracy, the party of the people. And over its door these words are written,
>> "No admittance to Bosses."

The new party offered a program that was "no mere jumble of phrases, the result of no compromise of conflicting interests, but the most comprehensive and practical programme of social democracy ever put forward." It was a platform designed by the finest minds in the universities, not by log-rolling politicians; professors and experts in various areas, like Jane Addams and Gifford Pinchot, drew up the planks in their areas of specialty. These people recognized that "an unequal distribution of wealth (particularly in a land of plenty) is an artificial condition which is in the power of modern government to cure." The masses must be raised "out of the depths of darkness in which they toil, educate them, give them the leisure and relief needed so they may grow into right minded and healthy citizens." The money to do these things would be provided by the Social Surplus. "The Social Surplus of a nation is that wealth left over every year after that which has been consumed has been deducted. We are beginning to see that the Social Surplus produced by our farms and workshops, by the community, should be spent on the community." This surplus could be collected by the government through an income tax and a reform of other tax laws so that they would fall heavily on the hidden wealth of the favored few. In another speech, Churchill made a point of "the most serious condition that now confronts the nation, and that threatens to bring on a violent revolution if it is not corrected — the concentration of wealth in a few hands."

The Progressive platform and Churchill both made a strong play for the labor vote in this election. Churchill contacted labor

leaders in New Hampshire, seeking the names of men in the factories who might be willing to help the cause.[14] And in his speeches
he went to some lengths to show that the reforms they were
advocating were both practical and useful.

Two major issues absorbed most of Churchill's attention —
the tariff and the trust. He favored the Canadian Reciprocity
Treaty passed under Taft, but was appalled at the passage of the
Payne-Aldrich Bill. During the years preceding 1912 Churchill had
become friendly with Oswald Villard and in their correspondence
had expressed strong views on the tariff question.[15] In his open
letter of acceptance he also took a firm stand. On this issue his
position was close to that of Roosevelt's chief opponent, Woodrow Wilson. He disagreed with Wilson, however, on the extent to
which lowering the tariff would benefit the average citizen. The
difference between Churchill and Wilson on this matter resulted
from the differing roles which each would assign to the federal
government, and especially on the proper way of handling trusts.

In theory, the national campaign of 1912 gave the country
a clear choice between the two methods of dealing with trusts.
Roosevelt espoused the control system proposed by Herbert
Croly; Wilson preached a return to true competition by breaking
up the trusts. Churchill's position was squarely in line with that of
Roosevelt and Croly. The all-purpose speech which he used
during the campaign opened with a blast at Wilson's failure to
alter the incorporation laws in New Jersey and went on to denounce the Democratic Party's devotion to states rights.

> Mr. Wilson and the Democrats claim that if you
> take this privilege away from New Jersey [the right
> to charter trusts], you will be interfering with the
> doctrine of States Rights. They cling to their interpre-
> tation of the Constitution, and cling to states rights
> even when they become national wrongs . . . .

Churchill believed that

> any attempt to dissolve the trusts (which the Dem-
> ocrats advocate) must result in the farcical procedure
> of President Taft's administration in regard to the
> Tobacco and Standard Oil Corporations . . . . The
> Progressive Party, taking its stand with the best
> authorities on economics in every university of prom-
> inence in the land, acknowledges that trusts are an

> evolution of the times, and that in most cases they
> can no more be dissolved than the earth can be dis-
> solved back into the gases that originally formed it.
> The Progressive doctrine is modern and practical,
> and proposes to use the cheapened methods of trust
> production for the benefit of the consumer. Wood-
> row Wilson and the Democrats would apply to the
> Twentieth Century the Eighteenth Century doctrine
> of Thomas Jefferson, who never heard of a trust.[16]

The virtue of the Progressive position was that it saw the possibility of using the fruits of the large corporations without
having the political and economic system totally dominated by
them.

Churchill was willing to accept the results of such control
in a more sweeping way than most of his contemporaries. In 1912
he wrote in a private letter:

> Since the counteracting effect of competition has
> been removed, we must replace it by another ele-
> ment — that of government control. I am in favor of
> federal incorporation, and the control of prices by a
> federal commission. That such a course will eventu-
> ally, in the more or less distant future, end in Govern-
> ment Ownership I have not the least doubt, but I
> don't see how it can be helped.[17]

The national Progressive campaign stirred public interest in
the political issues of the day and helped to educate the public,
especially on the matter of the trust. It demonstrated that there
was a via media between those die-hards who contended that
giant corporations must be allowed to go their own way, and
those on the other side who insisted that this menace must be
destroyed. Perhaps it even helped to educate Woodrow Wilson.
It did not, of course, achieve victory. Just as the three-way race in
the nation placed a representative of a national minority party in
the White House, so the entrance of a third party in New Hampshire placed the nominee of the minority Democratic party in
office. Samuel D. Felker won a strong plurality of the votes, and
a coalition of Democrats and Progressives in the state legislature
made him the first member of his party to occupy the Governor's
mansion in thirty-eight years. And this was but the beginning.
Wilson carried the state, and the Democrats won both Congressional seats. The state council was Democratic, and the Progres-

sives held only a balance of power in the legislature, where they formed a working coalition with the Democrats.

The real blow to conservatives in New Hampshire came in the battle for the Senate seat of retiring Senator Burham. The obvious Progressive candidates were Bass and Churchill, and the party (with Churchill's complete support) settled on the ex-Governor. The Democrats united behind Henry F. Hollis. It became evident that the two Republican factions hated each other more than they feared the Democrats, and Hollis finally was elected.[18] It is doubtful that Churchill, who was in California during the long fight, was unduly upset when Hollis ultimately won. The new Senator had been associated in law practice for years with progressive leaders Harry Sargent, Ed Niles, and James Remick. He shared most of their ideas and ideals, but was an incorrigible Democrat. Over the years he and the Churchills had become trusted friends, and this relationship continued long after this battle was concluded.

Why this complete Republican rout in 1912? Speaking specifically about Churchill's defeat, the novelist Ernest Poole (another close friend of Churchill's) felt that the key issue was taxes. He contended that after Bass had gotten a more realistic assessment of railroad property, the railroad paid the increased taxes, then sent men through the state to check appraisals of farms; "and when most such appraisals were found also to be too low, so many farmers turned against 'that reform crittur Bass' for his 'land-appraisal monkeyshines' that when in the next election Churchill ran for Governor, they flocked to the polls to vote him down."[19] This may have been involved in the gubernatorial contest, but it does not explain the election of Democrats to so many other offices. The real reasons are probably even simpler than Poole suggests. The Republican vote was split and the Democrats moved into the breach. In all probability, neither the personality of the candidates nor the record of the Bass administration had much to do with the outcome.

While Roosevelt realized soon after the 1912 fiasco that the Bull Moose movement was dead, Churchill and many other leaders were determined to create a viable organization which would continue the fight. Addressing a mass meeting of Progressives in Tremont Temple on November 11, 1912, Churchill sounded the call to arms. They were meeting to celebrate a victory, he said, not to mourn a defeat. The enthusiasm of the rank and file had raised their hopes too high in this battle, but this was only the first of many campaigns. "We recognize now that it was too much to expect that an entirely new theory of government and political science could be immediately absorbed and accepted by a majority of the electorate of our states." [20] They had managed to scuttle the old Republican party, and Churchill felt that refuge of ultra-conservatism would last for no more than one further national election before it disappeared as an organization. The Democratic Party had now elected Wilson, whom Churchill called "an able and sincere gentlemen," and that party, too, would splinter into its component elements under the strain of accession to power. This would lead to a realignment in politics.

> After the Democratic party shall be purged, the country will divide on two conceptions of democracy, the conservative conception and the liberal, the old and the new. Mr. Wilson stands for the old conception, the Eighteenth Century conception that [it] is the best government which governs least . . . .

> The old democracy is directed against the old bugaboo of tyranny by government. Hence the doctrine of States Rights, the unwillingness to concentrate and increase the federal power. The new democracy, that of the Progressive Party, is directed against a modern and more sinister tyrant, the "invisible" tyrant of the financial interest, whose dark shadow we now perceive looming up behind the legislatures of the people. [21]

To carry out their ideas and educate the people, Churchill advocated the formation of local Progressive clubs affiliated with and coordinated by a permanent state organization, operated by a permanent salaried staff. Above this would be a national organization. The money to finance the campaigns of education and election would be gathered from the people themselves and not from interest groups, so that no one would be beholden for office to any individual or group. And, finally, he made a strong plea that women should be admitted to the organization on equal terms with men.

He was hoping to move out of active personal participation in politics, however, and soon after the Tremont Temple meeting he left for California. The local party had no intention of allowing him to retire in peace. A meeting in Manchester in December voted to continue the organization and passed a resolution, introduced by Bass, expressing their gratitude to Churchill for the fight he had made. At another meeting the following spring in Portsmouth, letters from Churchill and Roosevelt were read, and the meeting was closed with three cheers for the next President and Vice-President — Roosevelt and Churchill.[22]

As the months passed, however, the New Hampshire Progressives were forced to admit that Wilson was doing a good job, and many of them were at loss about how to proceed under these circumstances. In May of 1913 Bass wrote that he had seen Roosevelt, who wanted to speak with the two of them about the national outlook, but the ex-Governor too felt that Wilson was doing all right and should not be criticized at that moment.[23] The problem arose first at the local level, where Governor Felker was making an effort to attract the Progressives into the state Democratic organization. Felker wrote Churchill that he intended "to appoint some Progressives to office during the coming two years. In fact, I am in hopes this struggle for political and social equality and justice will in the near future bring it about so that we can act together as a party."[24] Actually the Democratic administration accomplished little in the state, and while the local Progressives were impressed with the Wilson administration, they were unimpressed by Felker's efforts.

The election of 1914 again faced the New Hampshire Progressives with a choice between two evils. The Republican nominated Rolland Spaulding, a man of progressive tendencies. If the Progressives supported Spaulding they would endanger their party organization for the big fight in 1916. If they opposed him and retained their organization, they were certain to split the Republican vote and again the Democrats would win the executive chair. They chose the latter course and nominated Henry D. Allison. Churchill supported their course of action and denounced Spaulding as a back-sliding reformer. But for the first time since 1906, he said his professional work would prevent his participation in the campaign. Both he and Bass tried to keep in the background since the novelist in particular felt the New Hampshire voters had seen enough of him for awhile.

> It is long since I arrived at the conclusion that New
> Hampshire has had an awful dose of me. I have been
> rammed — or rather rammed myself — like a purga-
> tive down her unwilling throat. And I believe that
> part of wisdom, both for the party in the state as well
> as for myself, is to make what speeches I can, after I
> shall have finished my book, for the national party.[25]

In the 1914 election the Progressives did not even draw
enough votes to defeat the Republican regulars. Spaulding was
elected; and, in spite of his campaign oratory about uniting all
Republicans, the Progressives found themselves on the outside
after this election. The result of the local revolt in New Hampshire was almost exactly the same as the results on the national
level. The Old Guard was left in control of the Republican Party,
and the Progressives had to choose between returning to an increasingly conservative Republican Party or taking the long walk —
so distasteful to many of them — over to the Democratic Party.
Churchill chose to withdraw from local politics and was never
again to participate in a state campaign.

This did not isolate him from a plague of requests to address
various Progressive organizations around the country. Owing to
his travels and the pressure of his own work, most of these requests were turned down. He did, however, speak at a dinner
which the Progressives of Los Angeles county gave for Hiram
Johnson while Churchill was in California. Nearly a thousand
people gathered at Scottish Rites Hall to honor California's new
Senator and the visiting celebrity from the East. Johnson introduced Churchill as "a true exponent of the new party." According to
one newspaper account, "Churchill proved to be an entertaining,
epigrammatic speaker, and he kept his hearers cheering and
laughing continually by his sallies."[26]

Churchill's own political posture was complicated by the fact
that the President was his tenant in Harlakenden House for three
summers, but he does appear to have approved, in general, of
Wilson's policies. He wrote Wilson to this effect in 1915, and his
statements indicate that he was convinced the Progressive Party
was moribund.

> The Progressive Party in most states has all but dis-
> appeared; and most of those who, like myself, have

> been Progressives on principle have been willing to aid
> by any means in their power the legislation you have
> endorsed and carried into effect.[27]

The legislation which Wilson had "endorsed and carried into effect," included the lowering of the tariff schedules, the establishment of the Federal Trade Commission, and the strengthening of the trust legislation with the Clayton Anti-Trust Act. All of these were measures that had been urged by the Progressive platform, so there was little Churchill could do but approve.

By the summer of 1916 Wilson had moved far enough away from his laissez-faire pronouncements to attract many former Progressives. The social legislation he had scorned in 1912, he had reluctantly accepted in 1916. The Democratic Party was a minority party in the nation; he had been elected in 1912 only because of a split in the Republican ranks. In all likelihood this split would not appear in 1916, and the only hope Wilson had of keeping his Party in power was to unite all the progressive elements behind his own brand of reform.

Churchill clung to the Progressive Party so long as it had any possibility of success. He and Bass continued to correspond on political matters throughout 1915, but by 1916 both men knew that the revolt had failed. Bass wrote that he did not even want to attend the Progressive convention in Chicago because he did not like the idea of meeting simultaneously and in the same city with the Republicans. He was, however, under strong pressure to be a delegate and said he would go if Churchill would go along — adding "I hope you will take part in the last act of the drama."[28] Both men did attend the funeral of their movement that summer, and afterwards Churchill even wrote a defense of Roosevelt's incredible actions in recommending Henry Cabot Lodge for President. The article, entitled "Roosevelt and His Friends," appeared in *Collier's*, and Churchill laid the blame for the whole debacle on the other Progressive leaders. His basic defense of Roosevelt centered upon the notion that the Republican platform was an acceptable one for Progressives and that the party must unite to rescue the country from the hands of the Democrats.[29]

It should have been clear from this article that Churchill was going to follow his mentor and his own strong Republican feelings in supporting Hughes in the election. Yet attempts were made to enlist him in an independent group that was backing Wilson. Ellery Sedgwick and Norman Hapgood made the overtures, but Churchill had made his choice.

> As I wrote you earlier in the season, I am supporting Mr. Hughes. This does not in the least mean that I am one of those who have been railing against Mr. Wilson. I have a great respect and liking for him, although he made no attempt until this election to ally himself or consult with Progressives most kindly disposed toward him.[30]

Churchill was invited to attend the official notification ceremony informing Hughes of his nomination, and he was actively sought as a speaker. The National Republican Committee complained that they were having a difficult time getting the usual coverage in the press because of the war, that only the biggest names were getting publicity, and they were anxious to know how many speeches he would be able to make for Hughes. Despite their assumption that he would enter the fight, he did not do so. He did allow his name to be used by the National Hughes Alliance, an organization that was working outside regular party channels to attract Progressive and Democratic voters to the Republican nominee.[31]

The most positive move Churchill made for Hughes was to join Hamlin Garland in drafting a statement that the authors of the nation were for the Republican candidate. Garland and Churchill had been mutual admirers since the noted author of the middle border requested an autographed copy of *The Crisis*. The two men corresponded frequently after that and in the early months of 1916 worked with George Perkins, the "angel" of the Progressive Party, to push Roosevelt into actively campaigning for his own nomination. They also cooperated in forming an organization of authors to support Roosevelt's candidacy; when this fell through, Garland wrote to suggest they turn their support to Hughes.[32] Churchill's reply indicates that he was not particularly impressed by the Republican nominee.

> I have contributed to Mr. Hughes's campaign and I am not for Mr. Wilson. Yet I am not so keen about Mr. Hughes so far that I am likely to lose my head with excitement and enthusiasm.
>
> When you get your statement written let me see it

and perhaps I may sign it.[33]

When he received the statement, he wrote Garland a most candid assessment of his feelings about Hughes.

> I don't think I can honestly say that I can declare my intention of advocating the election of Charles Evans Hughes. I shall not have the time, and, to use a George Ade expression, he hasn't enthused me with the "pep". I am for him. I believe in him very much as I believe in the future of the world. He may come true . . . .
>
> I think the legend "We the undersigned authors" etc is weak — like the rest of Mr. Hughes's campaign.[34]

Moderate reform, prosperity, plus "He kept us out of war" kept Wilson in the White House. Churchill made no public statements about Hughes's defeat, but it is unlikely that he cared much one way or the other. His feelings about Hughes had not been strong, and Wilson was moving in the direction of preparedness during these months, a move that Churchill approved wholeheartedly. In any case, his interest in practical politics had declined to the point of disappearance. The future held far different interests.

Churchill had served the cause of reform in his state in much the same manner that Roosevelt had served it in the nation as a whole. His fame had dramatized and publicized the evils that existed; his courageous fight had inspired others. And just as Roosevelt's efforts culminated in the passage of progressive legislation under Wilson and then the disappearance of reform under the party the old Rough Rider had made more conservative by his revolt, so Churchill saw at least part of his program enacted under Bass and then the same return to power of the conservatives in the party he had first tried to reform and then had abandoned to those he had helped to defeat.

CHAPTER XII

An Artistic Achievement and a Long-Awaited Journey

Churchill's political career did not seriously hamper his other activities. Except for a few months during the height of each campaign, he enjoyed the life of a successful novelist — traveling, studying, writing, and visiting with his friends. When he was in Cornish (and much of the time when he was traveling) he devoted himself to broadening his knowledge of history and literature or pursuing his interest in contemporary social and political problems.

Although he said he enjoyed the work of such diverse talents as Howells, Barrie, Kipling, Wharton, Twain, Herrick, and Garland, Churchill did not actually read much current fiction. He cherished "the still, small voice of Mr. William Dean Howells crying out the true way," but his favorite author was Rudyard Kipling.[1] This affinity for the poet of English expansion probably had something to do with the fact that Churchill shared the paternalistic attitude toward "backward" peoples that permeated Kipling's stories and verse. The rolling cadence, grandeur, and sentimentality of Kipling's writings undoubtedly appealed to the suppressed romantic

161

strain in Churchill, and he enjoyed the Englishman's sense of humor. Churchill was a serious man (perhaps too serious for his own good), but he did have a sense of humor. In addition to ponderous treatises on the tariff, his datebooks contain such quips as "Blessed are the ugly, for they shall not be tempted."[2]

The types of public speeches that he was being asked to give during these years indicate that Churchill had won the respect of the academic community. Invitations to give commencement addresses at the University of Kansas and Smith College, a talk on corporation problems and business interference in politics at the annual meeting of the American Academy of Political and Social Science, and a lecture on the modern novel for a University of Chicago lecture series, were among the requests (most of which he declined).[3] He was still ill at ease on the podium and he preferred to speak only on those topics that he had studied in detail. The addresses that he did give before 1910 were of a political nature, and most of them were delivered in New England.

Other demands on his time and energy continued at a high level. He accepted membership in the Navy League and the National Institute of Arts and Letters, and agreed to serve on the Advisory Council of the American Society for the Judicial Settlement of International Disputes. He was asked to write articles running the gambit from the *Christian Endeavor World* request for one telling young Christians how to gain influence in politics, to a sketch of Brett for *American Magazine*.[4] People he did not even know sent him books to read, suggested themes for novels (usually reforms of some sort), requested permission to name children after him, and made pathetic pleas.

> Won't you please fix this story "up" for me? I want to sell it to a magazine. I will pay you for the trouble when it sells. I have a mother to care for — 94 years old. We have nothing only what I earn reporting for a [smeared word] newspaper. I get $4 or $5 per month — that is all. We have had fierce times this winter and now mother is ill with grip. This story is not deep enough — is it? And not up to magazine requirements. Won't you help me?[5]

Such requests were common, and Churchill handled them by relating his own early experience of having to rewrite his stories many times before they were published. Usually he gave some mild encouragement but naturally refused to rewrite anything.

As he approached the age of forty, Churchill remained a very reticent human being. His early advice to himself to maintain a respectable constraint was carried out even in the privacy of his own datebooks. Only on occasion, and then in anger, did he allow his emotions to break through the calm exterior. And the same characteristics are seen in his relations with his family. Mrs. Churchill was an active and vigorous woman with a warm personality and an open frankness. She also had a touch of wanderlust in her, and when Churchill could not accompany her, he wrote to her almost daily. These letters are written in restrained but affectionate terms, bragging just a bit on occasion, and complimenting her own entertaining letters with their vivid descriptions of people and places.[6]

As a father, Churchill displayed the same quiet affection that is evident in his role as husband. When his daughter Mabel was born in 1897, he was the normal proud father, and as she grew up they developed a warm and friendly relationship.[7] John, his first son, was born in December, 1903, and by the time he was six, he sometimes remained with his father during the frequent absences of the female members of the family.

Churchill continued to prefer the company of old friends or people in other lines of endeavor, to that of other writers. Although he maintained contact with many contemporary literary figures, his disinclination to enter actively into the society of the literary world is indicated by his reaction to Hamlin Garland's numerous efforts to interest him in the Chicago literary group, the Cliff Dwellers. The two authors were friends for years and worked together on several projects of mutual interest, but Churchill's admiration for Garland (and for the Cliff Dwellers as a group) was never intense enough to draw him into their activities. He did participate, however, in the social activities of such men as John D. Rockefeller, Jr., the renowned Judge Learned Hand, J. P. Morgan, Bishop Lawrence, and British Ambassador Thomas Spring Rice — in addition to Lord Dartmouth and Lord Bryce, both of whom were guests at Harlakenden.[8] It was with men such as this, as well as politicians from all over the country, that Churchill liked to spend his leisure time. Why he preferred the social whirl to the more esthetic company of his fellow writers is

frequent

difficult to say. Perhaps he felt ill at ease with those authors who considered writing an art rather than a craft; perhaps, too, he was dazzled by the fact that he had become so successful that the nation's elite sought his company. Also he may have needed periodic reassurances that his youthful fears that he was not quite good enough to be intimately associated with the "best" people were unfounded. He could get this reassurance more easily by associations with the socially respectable than with the sometimes less reputable creative artists.

After the 1908 campaign, Churchill did considerable traveling in such company before he settled down to the composition of his next novel. In February the serious illness of his uncle, James Breading Gazzam, called him to St. Louis, where he remained until two weeks after his uncle's death in late March. Mrs. Gazzam returned to Cornish with him and remained with the Churchill family until her death in 1917, becoming an integral member of the household and a source of joy to the children.[9]

Depressed by his uncle's death and not in good health himself, Churchill had difficulty settling down to concentrated work, but an autumn publication date and a planned trip to Egypt forced him to write under pressure. Completed late in December 1909, *A Modern Chronicle* marked another plateau in Churchill's evolution from historical romancer to social philosopher. At the same time he was breaking bread with the industrial moguls and the social elite, Churchill was developing ideas that would have given his dinner partners severe indigestion. His two previous novels had argued that the corrupt political conditions of the late nineteenth and early twentieth centuries had evolved because men had been engrossed in money-making and had not been sufficiently aware of the state of the nation. He had further stated his belief that men in his own day were becoming aware and would remedy the situation by their own positive actions. Churchill now examined the influence of modern civilization on the sensitive individual. He states the ostensible theme of *A Modern Chronicle* in these terms.

> It was the poet Cowper who sang of domestic happiness as the only bliss that has survived the Fall. One of the burning and unsolved questions of to-day is, — will it survive the twentieth century? Will it survive rapid transit and bridge and Woman's Rights,

the modern novel and modern drama, automobiles,
flying machines, and intelligence offices; hotel, apartment, and suburban life, or four homes, or none at
all?[10]

The central concern of the novel, however, is neither to analyze
the institution of marriage nor to study the social consequences of
divorce; the theme is the individual's search for self-integration
and moral roots in an industrial civilization devoted to business
and competition.

The search is made by Honora Leffingwell, who was born
about 1870 in Nice, where her father was the American consul.
When her parents are killed in an accident, the infant goes to live
in St. Louis with her father's brother, Tom Leffingwell, and Tom's
wife Mary. Honora's early life has already been discussed in connection with Churchill's childhood; her escape from a constricting
environment comes with her marriage to Howard Spence, a young
businessman. Although the gauche financier becomes a financial
success (more through his wife's charm than by virtue of his own
limited abilities), Honora can find no meaning in the life they
lead. She turns to philanthropy and social work and meets Hugh
Chiltern, a modern "Viking." After much agony, he convinces her
to get a divorce and marry him, but life with Hugh brings Honora
no more real happiness than her first marriage. When Hugh is
killed in an accident, Honora takes a small apartment in Paris to
live out her life alone.

Some years later (after her first husband died), Peter Erwin,
who has loved Honora since she was a child, comes to see her. It is
Peter who now represents in her mind all the good things that she
has missed in life. He has not compromised with evil, nor sold his
soul on the auction block of commercialism; yet he is a famous
and respected lawyer. Spence was the modern commercial man
without ideals, Hugh the aristocrat who could find no place in
modern society, and Peter Erwin the man who maintained personal integrity in the modern world by adhering to the standards
of an earlier era. Like most of Churchill's moral men, Peter has
good blood in his veins but has to prove his worth by rising on his
own. Peter, the moral man who denounced Honora's divorce, can

marry her now that both of her previous husbands are dead. And Honora can finally have what she has sought — to be wanted, to be needed, to be useful.

The novel attracted considerable attention when it was published, both because of the extensive advertising campaign which Macmillan launched and because Churchill by this time had a loyal following which eagerly awaited the publication of each new novel. Since he published only every two or three years, the public appetite for his work was never satisfied. Even Brett was pleased by the early sales. The sales, however, did not hold as Brett had expected and by fall he was worried about the future.[11]

In contrast to the comparatively unenthusiastic public response, the critical reception given A Modern Chronicle was encouraging. Favorable views predominated, and the critical comments were generally on the author's position concerning divorce. The more emancipated reviewers were bothered because he did not openly advocate divorce, while the Christian Work denounced the novel as "unmoral." Many of the reviewers were puzzled by the moral problem posed in the novel. It seemed a condemnation of pleasure seeking and divorce; yet, Churchill did not destroy Honora for her sins.[12]

Nearly all the reviewers conceded that this was Churchill's most artistic novel. Some were impressed by the picture he presented of various social circles in American society, but the majority were more fascinated with Honora. A number of reviewers compared Honora favorably with Thackeray's Becky Sharp. It was the heroine who fascinated the English; and as one of his old friends put it, Churchill had "done what some people thought you couldn't do — draw a woman." Later critics have agreed with their predecessors that A Modern Chronicle is, in many ways, the best novel Churchill was ever to write — largely because of the heroine.[13]

One commentator has suggested that "only in the creation of the faithful Dobbin, Peter Erwin, and in the happy ending did he surrender unconditionally to literary convention and to his own idealism." [14] It is true that the characterization of Peter (and of Spence) is weak. Peter is as boring as Stephen Brice; Spence is a caricature. Indeed, the only male character of any real interest in the novel is Hugh Chiltern. But the portrait of Peter and the happy ending were much more the product of Churchill's own beliefs than of a surrender to literary convention. He still felt that it was possible for the individual to rise above the chaos of the modern world and become a unified person. Honora was saved not because of the necessity of a happy ending but because she had persisted in a search for a goal that was achievable. A tragic ending would have been out of line with the essence of the novel and with the idealism of the novelist.

While Churchill was applying the final touches to *A Modern Chronicle* in December of 1909, Brett handled the arrangements for his prize author's well deserved vacation trip to Egypt, where the Churchills had been invited to go up the Nile in a dabbiah with a group of Bostonians. Little Mabel and John were installed in a rented house in Dedham, Massachusetts, under the capable rule of Mrs. Gazzam, a governess, and a trained nurse.

The Churchills boarded The Lusitania in New York Harbor December 29, 1909, and arrived in London a week later. Churchill went to hear David Lloyd George speak in Kensington Tabernacle, and the future Prime Minister made a considerable impression on him.[15] After only two days in England, they crossed the channel and traveled by train to Marsailles, where they boarded the ship for Egypt. They began the journey up the Nile on January 15, pausing the following day for an excursion through ancient Memphis to the pyramid of Sakhara. The journey continued in spite of sand storms and chilly weather, and on the twentieth they arrived at Beni Hasan, from where they visited the famous city of Akhetaton. After another pause at the site of the city of Thebes (about which Churchill had been reading a great deal) they embarked at Assuan for a two-day journey to Wadi Halfa, arriving at their destination on the sixth of February.[16]

Both of the Churchills found the trip a delight, and the vacationing novelist had time to read Greek and Egyptian history and make long entries in his datebook. His descriptions of land-and-seascapes, especially the descriptions of the trip up the Nile, are unusually vivid and from a strictly literary point of view are as good as anything he ever wrote.

Ending their stay in Egypt on February 23, they made a

quick trip through Greece and Italy, and a month later Churchill was in Paris taking lessons to improve his pronunciation of French. Their arrival in England on April 10 was marked by a dinner with Lord and Lady Northcote, and the following day they visited Parliament. Their time in London was taken up with visits to museums, which Churchill enjoyed, and a constant round of dinners, some of which he did not enjoy. He makes special note of a dinner given for him at the Titmarch Club by Sir Frederick Macmillan, where "there was a lot of twaddle about Thackeray . . . . "[17] The last few days of April they were guests at Lord Dartmouth's estate, where they again faced a spate of dinners and teas. This visit to the vast estate of a man he so much admired led Churchill to speculate on the place of the English nobility in the modern world. Although he believed the English nobility had earned its position through its devoted service to the country, an estate such as Dartmouth's seemed out of harmony with the times. It was an anachronism in the world of Lloyd George's famous budget of 1909. "Our own commercial kings in their palaces," he noted, "don't give one the same reflection."[18]

The visit to England was capped by a pleasant dinner given for Churchill by Colonel Harvey of *Harper's*, and the Churchills set sail aboard the *Mauretania* on the first of May — not, however, before an encounter with the indomitable English suffragette, Emmeline Pankhurst. She had written Churchill some time before that his account of Honora Leffingwell's frustrating life was a good argument for woman suffrage. And on their last day in London she cornered the novelist who informed her that he was not a woman suffragist but that he might become one if he were left alone. She was determined, however, that he should have all of her literature on the subject, and he had to accept it to escape. The incident annoyed him, though his account shows that he saw the humor in the situation.[19]

It was a memorable trip and a necessary break for the novelist-politician. Six months before, Churchill had been exhausted; he returned with the energy to fight the victorious political war of 1910 and fired with enthusiasm for his next novel.

CHAPTER XIII

A Map of the Kingdom of God on Earth

Winston Churchill, like most Americans of his generation, was a religious man. From his earliest youth he was taught the doctrines of orthodox Christianity; at Annapolis he discovered that these precepts did not answer all the questions which arose in his active mind. Yet until he was nearly forty he went through the motions of being an orthodox Episcopalian. Until about 1910, however, the beliefs of his church had little influence on his view of the phenomenal world. Until that time he believed that the evils of contemporary society were a product of business domination of politics and that the way to cure the evils was, consequently, through political reform. Then, gradually, he came to believe that political and economic reforms were insufficient. What was needed was a religion which would rise above dogma and teach all men to be brothers. From then on Churchill devoted most of his time to preaching the new faith, a faith that would allow mankind to survive in an industrial world by inaugurating a utopia of social cooperation.

A friend once said of Churchill's new-found, activist faith of these years, that while most people had known about religion for a long time, Winston had just discovered it.[1] This may not be strictly correct, but it does indicate the intensity and enthusiasm with which Churchill approached each new solution to the world's

169

problems. Not an original thinker, he encountered, absorbed, and popularized many of the ideas of his age, and he always did so with the zeal of the convert. Under the circumstances, it was almost inevitable that he would enter into the religious battle of the Progressive period, the contest between orthodox Christianity and the new forces of the Social Gospel. It was equally natural that his major contribution would be in the form of a novel.

This does not mean that religious reform totally replaced political reform as a means of saving society. In his famous *Farewell to Reform*, Chamberlain has suggested that "for Churchill . . . the end of the Bull Moose stampede meant the end of worldly hopes; there was nothing left but a retreat to the kingdom of heaven that is within."[2] This is nonsense. Churchill began work on his *The Inside of the Cup*, as early as 1910, and he was to engage actively in two political campaigns after that.

The first indication of his new departure is contained in his 1910 datebook, in which he began to keep notes on church-unity movements and to write down story suggestions for the new novel, at this point entitled "The Greatest of These." On the trip back to New York from England he first began to put his thoughts in order. At this point he was planning to set the scene in a mill town with the mill owner playing the role of villain that was ultimately assigned to a big city financier. The mill owner's daughter was to be a married woman seeking a divorce, and it is obvious that the problem of divorce was still much on his mind.

When he returned from Europe, Churchill communicated his thoughts about the new book to Brett, and the publisher was delighted.

> I am naturally immensely interested in the next novel, seeing that I talked over its possibilities with you several times, and have immense faith in its vitality and interest. I am taking the liberty of sending you Rauschenbusch's book, which I consider to be one of the best of recent books in this field . . . .[3]

Brett, who was well read in a number of fields, constantly sent Churchill suggestions for reading and frequently offered his own ideas about the subject at hand. Throughout the summer (during which Churchill was involved in the Bass campaign, as well as in study for the new book), Brett tried to keep the novelist's enthusiasm alive. He knew that Churchill had a saleable topic and he did not want his friend's interests to turn in some other direction.

Churchill did a great deal of reading during this period, both for the novel itself and for his own pleasure and education. He was reading Eucken on Plato and Aristotle, Mathew Arnold's *Literature and Dogma*, everything he could find by Phillips Brooks, Bucken's *The Problem of Human Life*, the confessions of St. Augustine, Carlyle's *Sir Walter Scott*, Robert Browning's *Man and Woman*, Hawthorn's *The Scarlet Letter*, Mrs. Charles B. Perkins' *A Catholic View of the Bible*, several books by Lyman Abbott, *The New Democracy* by Walter Weyl (which Churchill called "a splendid book"), Royce's *William James and Other Essays*, a number of works by James himself, a book by Simon Patten, and, of course, books by Walter Rauschenbusch, the foremost theologian of the Social Gospel. His datebook also contains extended passages from the Bible, which he was reading carefully. He corresponded and consulted with many ministers, and he also kept a file of press clippings about the difficulties encountered by reform-minded ministers.[4]

Churchill had trouble getting started on this novel until he switched the setting from a small mill town to a large city. By December of 1910 he was writing fluently. Brett highly approved of the change of locale, and Churchill pushed ahead, putting down about 18,000 words by Christmas.[5] This concern about finding the best possible setting for the story is only one indication of Churchill's determination to make this novel as good a book as he was capable of writing. But he still had even more difficulties than usual putting this story together. In December of 1911, he wrote, "I have never encountered a more difficult piece of construction, and I think I may truly say that I have never given more work and thought to anything that I have attempted." And, although he had originally refused to permit serial publication, the major magazines refused to give up. Offers came in from *American Magazine, Century, Harper's, Good Housekeeping, The Saturday Evening Post,* and the Hearst syndicate. The offers were too attractive to ignore, and Churchill's concentration on the novel was constantly interrupted by these financial considerations.

Arrangements were finally completed with *Hearst's Magazine* for $30,000, and the serial began in April of 1912. Churchill's disappointment with their presentation of the story again shows his deep involvement with the message he was trying to present.[6] The editors of the magazine wanted to present an interesting story to their readers and had, consequently, cut out the didactic presentation of theological matters. But Churchill had slipped off the mantle of entertainer and donned that of the social critic and the religious prophet. The transition had been coming for some time; in *The Inside of the Cup* it was complete.

The story takes place in one of the largest cities of the Midwest (undoubtedly St. Louis), where St. John's Episcopal, the church of the old and wealthy families of the city, is left in a slum area by the encroaching industry of the city. The plot of the novel concerns the conversion of the new Rector, John Hodder, from orthodox Episcopalianism to liberal, social Christianity. Hodder was selected by the wealthy members of the vestry because of his absolute belief in the doctrines of the church and his proven orthodoxy. Once in the city, however, a series of events causes Hodder to become uneasy in his faith. Then one night he overhears a conversation among some of the business leaders of his congregation which convinces him that they do not want the world changed, that the aspirations he holds for the church are foreign to their way of thinking. From a prostitute whom he has befriended, Hodder also learns about the protection money that women of her profession are forced to pay to the local political boss — a politician supported by most of the parishioners of St. John's.

Hodder's doubts are intensified by his relationship with Alison Parr, the daughter of an unscrupulous businessman who is the main exponent in the novel of the laissez-faire, survival of the fittest view of society; he is also the main financial supporter of Hodder's church and the ruler of the vestry. Alison maintains that the charity work in which her father and his friends have been engaged is nothing but a sop to their own consciences. Her analysis of her father as one who would have crucified Christ as an agitator because he feared the vital spark that lay at the heart of Christianity, forces the Rector to face the truth. He perceives that the core of the problem is the unnatural alliance between the clergy — who preach the brotherhood of man — and the businessmen, who are unalterably opposed to such ideas. Here, too, is the reason why Hodder is unable to attract the working class to St.

John's; the church of the businessman has nothing to offer them.

During the months that follow, Hodder passes through a crisis. Testing his old beliefs in the light of history and modern criticism, he finds them wanting. But even as he approaches complete skepticism he feels a conviction growing in him that the universe is not empty; he begins to sense a guiding hand on his shoulder. From the writings of James, Royce, and other non-naturalistic modern philosophers and scientists he discovers that faith means not adherence to some creed but personal belief; the will of the spiritual world is revealed to and through the individual. He has found it exemplified in a kindly old man who helps the down-and-out; he himself must stay in the church and reveal it to others.

Hodder's new social gospel beliefs naturally lead to a showdown with Parr, but he refuses the vestry's request for his resignation. His revised ideas do attract the poor people of the neighborhodd back to the church, and the unity between social Christianity and reform politics is symbolized by the union of Hodder and Bedloe Hubbell, the reform leader who is led back to the church by Hodder's stand against the vested interests. During these events Alison and Hodder also finally proclaim their love for each other; together they will fight to establish the cooperative society, the Kingdom of God on earth.

Since the novel appeared in *Hearst's Magazine* more than a year before it was published in May of 1913, public interest had already been aroused, public approval and condemnation had begun. The novel sold better than the previous one by far and was probably as widely reviewed as any book of the period. Considering the theme of the novel, the reviews were surprisingly favorable, but a large number of them did object to the didactic approach which the author had used, calling *The Inside of The Cup* "less a novel than a tract."[7] While the secular critics were concerned about the didactic element in the novel, the more religious reviewers debated Churchill's presentation of the modern church. Many reviewers for the religious journals understandably resented the implication that all churches were like St. John's and all church-going Christians like Eldon Parr.

Some of the critics pointed out that Churchill's ideas were hardly new among thoughtful people and would have agreed

with the comment that *The Inside of The Cup* "is a bit of contemporary life, a work to which future sociologists may turn
when they want to learn of an important aspect of the attitude
toward religion in the opening years of the twentieth century."
Very few reviewers perceived the more revolutionary aspects of
some of Churchill's ideas, although one noted that his position was
"not far from that of a social revolutionist."[8]

There is no doubt that Churchill was hurt by the criticism
that *The Inside of The Cup* was too didactic to be a good novel,
but instead of replying to the criticism publicly, he committed his
thoughts to his datebook.

> To those who object that the Inside of the Cup is
> not art, let them try to construct a novel on such a
> subject and see how many people they can get to
> read it . . . . I am quite aware that it does not harmo-
> nize with the generally accepted canons of realism.
> As well accuse Isaiah of a lack of art when the stiff-
> necked adjured him to "prophesy false things." The
> very artistic tone of such a book is self-determined
> by the subject, and to make it [word smeared] would
> have been to make the book ineffective and futile.[9]

Let the critics write a book on an important subject and see
how many people they can get to read it — not see how many
copies they can sell. This comment is indicative of Churchill's
changing attitude toward his work. Still a professional, he had to
live by his pen, but his major concern was to convey a message to
as many people as possible. From this point he would use the
novel as a vehicle to educate the public. He refused to see the difficulty (perhaps the impossibility) of advocating a definite course
of action in a novel without sacrificing its artistic qualities. This
truth would dawn slowly and then with crushing finality.

Many critics predicted that *The Inside of the Cup* would not
sell because it was too serious for the novel-buying public. They
were wrong. The public was in a mood to consider serious problems, particularly if a solution were offered to the many puzzling
questions facing American society. Dozens upon dozens of letters
poured in to thank Churchill for writing the book, for articulating
ideas which the correspondents themselves felt but could not express. Many came from clergymen who claimed to have had experiences much like Reverend Hodder's. Letters of praise arrived

also from religious scholars like John Wright Buckham and William F. Bade' of Pacific Theological Seminary, and John P. Jockinsen of Union. Croly and Roosevelt were enthusiastic about the book, as was Lord Bryce. Social gospel leaders like Washington Gladden, Charles M. Sheldon, and Walter Rauschenbusch sent their congratulations. Rauschenbusch, who must have recognized much of the theological disputation in the novel, made a typical comment.

> Allow me to thank you personally for the contribution you have made to a task with which my whole working life has been more or less bound up. I feel with you that the emancipation of the individual must come through religion; mere economic changes do not change the personality at the core. Also that the Church contains tremendous reservoirs of power and can approach all classes of men along lines which no other organization can utilize in the same way.[10]

In a letter to Brett, Rauschenbusch said that in Churchill's novel the central problem of the modern church is "given artistic concreteness in the case of John Hodder and his wealthy church, and works out in stirring situations . . . . This book is a symptom of the renewed religious feeling in the upper levels of intellect . . . . "[11]

The Inside of the Cup certainly precipitated a clamorous and widespread debate. Ministers across the nation were giving sermons and having discussions on the novel, while women's organizations, church groups, and other clubs held meetings to discuss the merits of Churchill's indictment of the modern church. The novel also inspired a spate of articles denouncing Churchill's religion. The most widely publicized of these was one by the naval theorist, Alfred T. Mahan, which appeared in the Churchman, along with a reply by Churchill.[12] This novel also called forth the first objections to Churchill's treatment of sexual matters. Burton Rascoe reported the indignation at a Chicago Women's Club meeting in 1913 at which one woman said that with the publication of this novel, "literature in America seems to have struck sex o'clock." Another alleged that "Winston Churchill in his new novel, has fallen into the sex snare, and gives a recital of free love philosophy."[13]

Modern critics agree that the artistic qualities of The Inside of the Cup leave much to be desired. The value of the novel rests on its merits as source material for the important debate about the role of the church which occupied the attention of so many people during the Progressive period. This fact, however, should not obscure the impact which the novel had on the mind and imagination of Churchill's contemporaries. A book which is seriously referred to as being to the church's fight for freedom from their bondage to the "Princes of the World," what *Uncle Tom's Cabin* was to the liberation of the slaves, cannot be dismissed because it is not great literature.[14]

CHAPTER XIV

A Period of Study and Optimistic Enthusiasm

Both Churchill and his wife were relieved when the year 1912 drew to a close. Churchill said, "It has been a great satisfaction to me . . . that I did not by chance become governor." The time when he had aspired to high public office had passed by 1912, and his wife shared his sentiments. "I am glad my husband didn't get the office," she wrote Brett. "He isn't made for that kind of work . . . . "[1] By November the fight had been fought, *The Inside of the Cup* was completed, and the Churchills were ready for a vacation. Partially for Mrs. Churchill's health and partially to escape the constant pressures of state politics, they decided to vacation in California.

Just before their scheduled departure, Brett wired Churchill that a very important matter had arisen which he could discuss with him only in person. The publisher apologized for all the mystery, but said he had been approached in strictest confidence about the proper man to write a certain book. He had recommended Churchill, but the interested parties would not let him give out any further information until the novelist expressed a willingness to undertake the project. When J. P. Morgan died in March of the following year, a number of items appeared in the press suggesting that Churchill had been commissioned to do Morgan's biography.[2] The rumor was vigorously denied by all

177

parties involved, but Churchill's reply to Brett indicates that he knew more about this venture than he could have gotten from Brett's letter and that the project was, indeed, a biography of the famous financier.

> I am sure you will understand that I greatly appreciate the favour you have done me in presenting the proposal to me for consideration. But I do not want to do a biography. I have already begun a scheme for my new novel. I realize all you say, that I should learn a great deal about modern business, but I feel that I cannot undertake it.[3]

It certainly would have been ironic if the author who had lashed out at modern financiers in his portrait of Eldon Parr had been commissioned to do a biography of the most famous financier of them all.

One reason Churchill was not interested in worrying about Morgan's idiosyncrasies was that Churchill conceived of *The Inside of the Cup* as the first in a series of novels depicting various aspects of contemporary society. He had spent three years working out the basic approach and was anxious to proceed with the next novel. The California trip would not be a real vacation for the novelist, just a period of uninterrupted work.

Nor was the trip beneficial to Mrs. Churchill. The birth of their second son, Creighton, in October of 1912, had a debilitating effect on her health, and she was slow to recover. They spent the winter and spring at San Ysidro Ranch near Santa Barbara and the summer on Lake Tahoe. Churchill enjoyed both places and was working well, but Mrs. Churchill's health did not improve. A short stay in Berkeley brought no improvement either; and in October Churchill informed Brett, "My wife has had to go to a sanitorium in San Francisco for a nervous breakdown which apparently has been coming on for years." By November the novelist began to feel the strain. In a letter to Garland, he said, "Mrs. Churchill has had to go to a sanitorium in San Francisco and is very dependent on me. The result is that between my new book and going over there nearly every day, I am at my wits end."[4]

The strain on Churchill's nerves was increased by his other commitments. In spite of his dissatisfaction with the way the Hearst syndicate had handled *The Inside of the Cup*, he had agreed to give them the serial rights to the new novel. The result was constant bickering over illustrations, publication dates, and other matters. He also gave a large number of religious talks and lectures, including one at the University of California. That address led to an invitation to give the Earl Foundation Lectures the following year, an opportunity that he found especially flattering since his predecessors included Roosevelt and Bryce. Despite his commitments, he managed to take a course in philosophy and was reading "with the most intense interest" the neo-Hegelian works of Bernard Bosanquet.[5] Bosanquet's theory that the individual achieves self-realization through willed involvement in the cosmic drama gave Churchill philosophical justification for the ideas which he himself was trying to communicate.

Because Mrs. Churchill did not want to remain so far from her daughter (who was attending a boarding school in Baltimore), the family returned to the East in December of 1913. Churchill, the two boys, and Mrs. Gazzam took a small house in Aiken, South Carolina, while Mrs. Churchill was under the care of doctors in Baltimore. From there she traveled to Washington and, accompanied by Senator Hollis, went to hear Wilson address Congress. Wilson impressed her but Secretary of State William Jennings Bryan did not. "Bryan sat in the next box, and if I were placing him in life, I should say he belonged in P. T. Barnum's circus ring. With cap and bells on, he would look exactly like a court jester or a mummer."[6]

Although his concern with the problem of divorce during this period suggested to some that Churchill and his wife were having difficulties themselves, this suspicion is not born out in their letters. The only real domestic friction during these years was the result of Churchill's preoccupation with religion. Mrs. Churchill had been very much interested in his historical, political, and social novels, and he had relied heavily on her criticism; but discussions about religion did not interest her, and she felt that her husband was becoming too involved with his subject matter. "Winston goes off to Canada for a two week fishing trip next week," she wrote Brett. "He is very well but needs a change and a new point of view. I think fifteen months of religion and very little else is, to say the least, a narrowing life." Some months later she wrote from Harlakenden House, "We find ourselves happy and contented up here. Winston is always happy if the book goes to suit him, and he lives in a world all of his own."[7]

By 1913 Mrs. Churchill also had grown tired of the work involved in the upkeep of Harlakenden House, and they decided to sell it. The house had been depicted in several magazines, but a dwelling of such size was not in great demand. Consequently, when they received word from Guy Murchie that he thought President Wilson might rent Harlakenden as the summer White House and that this publicity would help in finding a buyer, they quickly agreed. The arrangement was completed and the resulting publicity was all one could ask. Newspaper accounts of Wilson's life there and of his daily trips to Hanover to play golf, were carried everywhere. The state even managed to pave the road, an improvement that Churchill had been trying to get for years.[8]

During the following winter, Murchie (who was handling all negotiations about the house) wrote that the Wilsons would take the house again but wanted many improvements, especially in the water supply. Mrs. Churchill opposed this and Churchill himself was not happy about the President's demands. He was losing money on the deal, but since Wilson was the President he agreed to make the changes. Arrangements were agreed upon, but Mrs. Wilson became critically ill in the spring of 1914 and died that August. The President spent only a short while at Harlakenden House after his wife's funeral. The following summer Miss Helen Woodrow Bones, the President's cousin and his hostess after his first wife's death, and Mrs. Edith Bolling Galt, Wilson's wife-to-be, opened Harlakenden House in June of 1915. The President followed them a few days later; and, except for a brief period when he returned to Washington, he remained there until the middle of August.[9]

Although the Churchills were living nearby for two of the summers Wilson was in Cornish, there was little intercourse between the two families. The novelist's only surviving comment about his famous tenant is this: "I had a nice little talk with the President the other day. At close range his personality is very pleasing."[10]

At this point in his career, Churchill had nearly everything a man could ask — a fine family, a lovely house, a national reputation, a substantial income, a wide range of friends and acquaintances, and unusually good health. He had the physical presence and personal dynamism that make a spontaneous impression upon those who come in contact with it. Few men who met Winston Churchill (perhaps even fewer women) went away unimpressed. The excellent health he enjoyed was partly due to the time he set aside for relaxation and physical activity. An enthusiastic hunter and fisherman, he also played golf and tennis. The approach he brought to a sport was the same as he brought to a new subject for a novel. The datebooks contain many excerpts from treatises on golf and fishing, and he wrote instructions to himself on how he could improve his skill at these sports. Like the writing of novels, sports were to be approached systematically and worked on for constant improvement.

Churchill continued to be active in many things other than work and sport. There was a continual demand on his time and energy for varied activities, pleasant and otherwise. In 1913, at the urging of Rex Beach, Percy Mackaye, and G. B. McCutcheon (among others), Churchill agreed to accept the presidency of the Authors' League. The reasons why they wanted him and the nature of the job are set forth in Beach's telegram.

> Authors League elects officers for 1913 in April. Nominating committee want you as President. Roosevelt agrees to accept vice-presidency if you will be president. So it is important to purposes of League that you take the office. It now has three hundred members best working men in the profession. More joining daily. Is already accomplishing important work and will do big things for all authors. You will not be called on for more effort than you are willing to put in.[11]

Unless he could address himself to his favorite topic — the intimate relationship between religious and political reform — the novelist still tried to avoid the public platform during these years. He did speak at Colonel Harvey's famous dinner for William Dean Howells, he was the toastmaster at an Authors' League luncheon for the English poet John Masefield, and he was a featured speaker at an Independence Day banquet given by the state of Pennsylvania in Philadelphia. Among the dozens of addresses that were religious in nature or combined religion and politics, the most important were delivered at Groton, Union Theological Seminary, Barnard College, the Institute of Arts and Science at Columbia, the Harvard Union, and the Congregation of the Free Synagogue in Carnegie Hall. He was unable to accept invitations to deliver commencement addresses at Oberlin, Ohio University, and the University of Missouri, even though Missouri's offer included the bestowal of an LL.D. Tufts University did honor him with an LL.D. in 1914.[12]

The reading that Churchill was doing is indicative of his broadening interests during the years that he was formulating his new approach to society. His datebooks from 1913 to 1915 show an extensive though unsystematic survey of philosophy, religion, and literature. He was fascinated by philosophical idealism — especially as formulated by Hegel and Royce — and read a great many books and articles on the subject. Notes on Bosanquet's *Philosophical Theory of the State* and *The Principle of Individuality and Value*, and on the works of Bergson cover many pages, and lead to considerable speculation on the problems of man and the state. Wilhelm Windelband's monumental *History of Philosophy* appears to have been his major guide, from which he moved to more detailed studies and to works of Plato, Comte, Santayana, and the men mentioned above. In the area of social and religious thought he was reading Symond's *Age of the Despots*, Graham Walles' *The Great Society*, Watson's *The Interpretation of Religious Experience*, Preserved Smith's Freudian analysis of Martin Luther, E. A. Ross's *Social Psychology*, and everything he could find by the British socialist, J. A. Hobson. And, although he is not prominently mentioned in the datebooks, Churchill's articles are full of references to John Dewey and he was strongly influenced by William James' *Varieties of Religious Experience*. Many of his ideas about religion came from the writings of Rauschenbusch and Washington Gladden, but the most important scholarly influence on his religious thought was William F. Bade', Professor of Semitic Languages at Pacific Theological Seminary in Berkeley. The two men corresponded regularly and met while Churchill was in California. Bade' was an Old Testament scholar who laid great stress on the evolutionary nature of Hebrew theology, and his ideas were undoubtedly a strong influence in the development of Churchill's evolutionary theism.[13]

Churchill's religious writings (and the speculations he put down in his datebooks) reveal an evolutionary approach to the subject that was firmly grounded in a sense of religion as a part of the changing historical milieu. The original biblical expression of Christianity, Churchill contended, had naturally used the imagery of its Middle-Eastern origins and had taken on the neo-Platonism of its Greek expositors.[14] Under the guidance of the Roman Catholic Church, this Greco-Hebraic religion assimilated much of the superstition and paganism of Latin mythology, but it was returned to a semblance of its original purity by the Protestant Reformation. These developments, however, had taken place in a pre-scientific world; by 1900 orthodox religious doctrines seemed contrary to modern science, and consequently many people had drifted away from the religion of their childhood. This was because people confused religious faith (which is a feeling) with theological interpretations of religion. Religion is "the stream or tendency through which man grows toward his God. Step by step the <u>interpretation</u> of it has risen higher and higher."[15] Modern development in religious beliefs were a supplement rather than a reversal of the older interpretation which was incomplete rather than untrue.

> We must get into our minds, I think, that religion is an experience, not a creed. The creed comes later. Religion is a personal experience with God, although we do not always consciously recognize him in it. We are stirred, gently at first, as a rule, by a cause or a personality who represents that cause . . . .
>
> When we do become conscious that our experience has been a religious one, we try to make a creed of it. And although we can never adequately convey to others what we have felt, we do our best to put it into words; to give it intellectual expression in terms of the learning, of the science and philosophy of our time, with which we are familiar. We try to translate our feeling in order that others may experience it — may be galvanized as we are. This is what the ancients did; and their creed unchanged, has come down to us in the churches.[16]

One important difference between the old religion and the new was the assumption of the former that the world was inherently bad; the watchword had been to shun the world, not to reform it. Since poverty and vice were considered to be natural and incurable phenomena, the convert to orthodox Christianity was given no important work to do in this life. This divorcing of Christianity from the social order was one of the causes for the drift of the workingman away from the churches. "Unless and until the Church becomes identified with the cause for which they are suffering alienation will continue."[17] In the meantime many laborers were finding a substitute for religion in socialism, which espoused the enthusiasm, service, and self-denial that had characterized the early church. Modern churches did not provide that enthusiasm.

The new religion would include a broad spectrum of belief, and the new church would be composed of those "who hold nothing in unthinking acquiescence that is not true for them." The notion that it is the mission of the church to turn out men and women like bricks from a kiln, all alike, would be replaced by a conviction that it is not what one believes but what he is that counts. Churchill's new religion was basically a rational system of ethics, but it rested upon a faith that could be achieved only through the traditional religious experience.

An unlimited faith in God, but a reliance on oneself — this was the core of the new religion. The world would be transformed through the efforts of the individual human being. "Not only religion, but science and common sense teach us that the assumption of individual responsibility, and that alone, leads to growth. If we try to shift that responsibility to the church, our development ceases. The keys of heaven and hell are within us, and nowhere else in the world."[18]

The individual would see the light and understand his role through a process of rebirth similar to that experienced by Reverend Hodder, a process which "means precisely to enter into a hitherto unimagined relationship with God, to comprehend with certainty the existence of other spheres of which our intellect can give us no information."[19] The reborn would then assume a true "Personality," would faithfully perform his work in the world, conscious that his strength arose from mysterious currents springing from within him. These reborn individuals would lead others to an awareness of God and the new religion. They would be the moving force in the realization of the kingdom of God.

It is not surprising that Churchill's new religion contains an implicit acceptance of the Great Man Theory which runs like a leitmotif through all of his writings. "Great men are the torch-bearers on the mountain," he noted on one occasion. "The history of a nation is the record of its great men. Men are events."[20]

As a corollary of his reliance upon leadership from the re-born, Churchill placed a similar emphasis on the old Calvinist doctrine of service in a worldly calling. This idea in a more secular framework was presented as early as *A Modern Chronicle*, in which Honora finally discovered that she could achieve self-integration only by abandoning selfish interests. As Churchill turned more and more to a religious framework, he integrated this idea with the idea of rebirth. "We see," he wrote in 1914, "that all morality is to be finally construed in terms of service — of its acceptance or rejection."[21] Here he was willing to go so far as to define sin, not as a breaking of the commandments, but as a rejection of service.

This service in a Christian calling need not be channeled into the traditional mold of such things as settlement work; it need not tear the individual out of his natural surroundings. Each individual must find out what he does best and develop his personality through service to society in that pursuit. In fact, he maintained that "the most effective reformers are the men who write the text books which construe the new philosophy and the writers who translate religion into terms of modern thought, whose serious books fill the publishers lists, and are read by hundreds of thousands."[22] This certainly indicates that Churchill understood his own role in the development of the new society.

He handled the problem of traditional Christian doctrines by declaring invalid those he considered dispensable (like the virgin birth), and by suspending judgment on those that were central. The existence of God and the divinity of Jesus clearly had to be accepted on faith or not at all, but the resurrection was a troublesome hurdle for his basically rationalistic religion. The contradictions in the Bible itself he dispensed with by accepting the book as the work of inspired, but fallible men; "the music of eternal truth is transmitted but imperfectly through human instruments."

In his early work Churchill had accepted the traditional American belief that man is free and creative, basically good, rational and benevolent. The development of his ideas during the years between 1910 and 1914 called some of these concepts into question. One problem that bothered him was the reconciliation of man's free will with the submission of the individual to the will of God. This he resolved by an appeal to the dual nature of man.

> . . . in obeying God, we do not bend our will and weaken it, as so many seem to fear. By such obedience we develop our will. By putting our will more and more at the disposal of that part of us which is God, we become more godlike, and grow in power. And that part of us which is God is our true self. Will here is the overcoming of the desires of the flesh, and in proportion as we overcome these we grow more godlike.[24]

Within himself man has the power to become more godlike, and those who denied that human beings and human conditions could be changed for the better were not true Christians.

Churchill developed considerably more sophistication on the question of free will through his reading of Bergson. He was impressed with Bergson's image of the musical phrase to present evolving consciousness and by the idea of liberty in duration — action arising from its antecedents by an evolution sui generis. Churchill described it in these terms. "The phrase once started, preserves its individuality; proceeds in harmony through the notes; and by the inherent impulse in itself determines itself. Each note in a sense completes the last and determines the following . . . . The determination of each note is free, but free because it is the proper expression of the ego, which determines to strike that note." A free act is one which arises from the expression of the total personality. When we do not act from the whole personality we strike false notes; "we are played upon by habit, which is not original, and hence we are not free."[25] Churchill was not completely satisfied with this explanation. There still seemed to be some logical contradiction between the fact that each note is determined by the preceding one, and the notion that the melody (if it proceeds from the whole personality) is new and is a creative act.

Churchill's ideas about reforming society also had undergone a considerable change since that first campaign in 1906. This increase in depth and breadth was characteristic of the reform movement as a whole, and Churchill's own account of this change, looking back from the vantage point of 1914, is interesting.

All that we saw at first was political domination by corporations. But it dawned on us that we had mistaken the symptom for the disease. Little by little we perceived that democracy had an humanitarian aspect, and that democracy, somehow, had gotten out of gear. Those who had enlisted began to realize that the war — for it was war — was a struggle for freedom, freedom from a kind of tyranny, industrial and economic. We became aware of the great misery which this tyranny was causing in the world, and that political domination was but one expression of it.

Thus the scope of the reform movement was gradually broadened until it now has incorporated into its platform a "social programme" which embraces the modern sciences of sociology, social psychology, and the new economics now beginning to be taught in our universities. The new economics lays emphasis, not on the dollar, but on the contribution of the individual to society. And therefore on service . . . .

It is difficult to realize how much the point of view of the majority of our citizens has been changed within a few years. This new philosophy of service, like an electric current, is passing through the individual cells of our state organism, transforming them. And they awake to a life with a new significance. These are discovering their "index of personal efficiency." Scientists, lawyers, literary men, business men and physicians are gradually taking a new attitude towards their occupations, are looking at them more in the light of contributions to humanity; not as the mere means of making a living, of getting rich.[26]

These statements contain a rather curious contradiction that seems to be present in much of Progressive thought. Here, as in his other writings of the period, Churchill confuses the state and society by picturing them as one and the same thing; he also refers, somewhat casually, to the organic nature of society. Yet Churchill and most Progressives continued to picture the individual as the prime reality and to direct much of their thought to preserving man's individuality in a complex industrial society.

Another aspect of the ambiguous political and social philosophy that developed in later Progressive thought involves the role of the government in the creation of the new society. In much that he wrote Churchill emphasized that strengthening the national government was a prime goal. Yet he speaks at the same time, as do other Progressive thinkers, of the small role which the government will play in the newly developing cooperative society. "The Christian ideal is the least possible government," he wrote in 1912, "a government wherein neither you nor I nor any other man or woman will labor and obey because we have to, but because we have learned the lesson which Christ taught, that happiness lies in service, in giving to the world that which God gave us." Freedom from oppressive government, Churchill insisted, is an American heritage. Society had paid a price for this freedom through the years and until "individual responsibility begins to be felt, excesses are the inevitable result of liberty."[27] Since it was impossible to return to the power of mere authority and tradition, society had no choice but to encourage the development of this individual responsibility.

The place of Churchill's powerful government is not made clear at this point. The obvious answer is that the government must act in a positive way to curb individual "excesses" until the individual could be educated in the new ideals of service and responsibility; then it should fade into the background. But this is not made clear in any of his writings during this period. The connection he does make is with the establishment of the kingdom of God on earth and the life everlasting. The implication of *The Inside of the Cup* was that when all men were reborn or achieved the transformation of their material self-interest into spiritual self-interest (which would express itself in service to mankind), the kingdom of God on earth would be achieved. Traditional Christianity had emphasized a life after death in an ethereal heaven that would compensate for the misery in this life. "Modern Protestantism, however, recognizes that the Kingdom of Heaven is here on earth."[28]

Churchill's religious articles were widely reviewed around the country (especially "Modern Government and Christianity"), excerpts were reprinted from them, and his views on all religious issues were widely discussed. Most of the comments were favorable, except in the Catholic papers and journals which objected to his insistence that church doctrines should be submitted to the conscience of the individual Christian.[29] Churchill received many letters concerning these articles and his religious addresses. Some of those who wrote agreed with his position, while others tried to show him the error of his ways — but all were attuned to the subject and seemed to consider his views important.

One man who did not consider them important was the evangelist, Billy Sunday, who preached a fundamentalist religion that stressed conversion and emphasized personal vices, but ignored the problems of society. In an address before the Twentieth Century Club in Boston, Churchill used the evangelist as an example of the fact that orthodox Christianity gave the convert no important work to do in modern society. During the course of this address he said that Sunday was sincere but was an obscurantist, all emotion and no intellect. These remarks were widely reported in the newspapers. A clash between two prominent men, especially figures in the world of religion, always makes good copy; and the press seems to have tried to generate a feud between the two men. But the evangelist would have none of it, dismissing Churchill's criticism of him as unimportant.

> Churchill doesn't deserve any notice. When he connects with me in this way, it gives him some publicity, but if he does not know any more about religion than he shows in the "Inside of the Cup," we'll have to excuse him.[30]

As a matter of fact Churchill knew considerably more about religion and theology than the famous evangelist did. Through his writings and speeches he gave his contemporaries a way to retain their Christian faith in an age of science and technology. In so doing he participated with Rauschenbush, Gladden, and a host of others in spreading the message of the Social Gospel — a movement which went a long way toward making the institutional church a relevant part of the twentieth century.

CHAPTER XV

The Peak of Optimism

By 1911, Churchill was thoroughly convinced that a man of letters should do more than sit in his study playing word games. In his earlier advice to literary aspirants he had confined himself to admonishing them to work over their material again and again; now, in good Progressive fashion, he urged them to become activists. A man of letters must know and understand the world around him and he must learn to use the English language correctly and beautifully. And what are the qualifications for being a writer? "I answer, only desire so great that he will never be satisfied until he produces valuable and lasting literature. It is the same in every profession — the holding up of an ideal before his eyes until it grows into action and result."[1]

At this time Churchill was interested in using the novel as an instrument of reform, as a vehicle of the new thought; he was not concerned about the possible conflict between the novel as art and the novel as propaganda. Not until after so many critics agreed that the didacticism of *The Inside of the Cup* spoiled its artistic qualities did he give much thought to this problem. A reading of Theodore Dreiser's *Traveler at Forty* led him to reflect upon his own approach to the novel.

> Aside from my pictures of the life of various
> periods, I began as a romanticist of the old school,
> practically skipped the realistic school, and am now
> writing as a religious idealist. This may account for
> the bitterness toward my writing in certain realistic
> quarters, and the charge that any viewpoint save the
> agnostic viewpoint produces bad art.

He believed that realism as a school of art involved a "lack of
faith."[2] Obviously, he was feeling the need to justify his approach
to literature to himself.

It is interesting that Churchill now readily admitted that his
novels were marred by Victorian morality and didacticism; it is important that he finally realized the difficulty of combining art and
preaching and was going to try to blend the two more effectively;
it is most important that he does not mention abandoning reform
in order to further his reputation as a man of letters. He would
try to subdue the didactic element in order to present his solutions
to contemporary problems more effectively, but if this were not
possible, there was no doubt as to which of the two factors — art
or reform ideas — would be sacrificed. Aware for the first time
that his novels were marred by his attempts to reform the world,
he would approach his form and style more self-consciously, but
he proceeded with the more important task of enlightening the
American public.

It would seem that Brett, too, looked upon his prize novelist
not only as a money maker for Macmillan but also as an important
popularizer of the new thought who would help save the nation
from revolution. He wrote Churchill:

> Croly is proposing to write a book on the aims and
> plans of the Progressives and what they stand for,
> and I have asked Miss Addams to do the same thing
> in a somewhat different way, but neither of these,
> not even Miss Addams' book will touch the people
> widely or largely, because the public, alas, no longer
> reads serious literature.
>
> So that your series of novels, of which you now
> tell me, will be just what is wanted to awaken the
> public to that change which must surely come, and
> which can come without serious disturbance and
> revolution only if some of the aims of the Progres-
> sives succeed with the people.[3]

The novel in question is *A Far Country*, a story in which

Churchill tried to combine the religious ideas of *The Inside of the Cup* with an analysis of the modern business ethic. He had begun the novel in December of 1912 and completed it in late April of 1915. Despite continued difficulties with the Hearst syndicate, he allowed them to retain the serial rights. "My object in letting them have these novels for serial publication," he informed Brett, "was largely to enable me to gradually get into a more comfortable position financially in order that I might have the more leisure for the work ahead of me in the years to come."[4]

Churchill described the novel in another letter to his publisher.

> The story . . . is the intimate study of the mind and experience of a lawyer, who goes through Harvard in the eighties and enters law in a middle western city. He is on the make, becomes a corporation lawyer, and is gradually led from one thing to another. His philosophy of law, the laissez faire philosophy, colours his whole life, until at last he is given a revelation. The book, of course, is primarily the study of the man, not the lawyer.[5]

The trials and tribulations of the lawyer-hero, Hugh Paret, are less interesting than the political philosophy of Hugh's major opponent, Hermann Krebs. The son of a German Forty-eighter, Krebs is an idealist, a social misfit, and a "socialist." It is he who integrates politics with the social and religious ideas Churchill had elaborated in his earlier writings. Through Krebs, Churchill again maintains that social evils are "merely the symptoms of that disease which had come upon the social body through their collective neglect and indifference."[6] Krebs denounced the "people" themselves and told them that they had received the kind of government they deserved. Nor did he have much use for the earlier reformers who, in his opinion, had conducted their campaigns along the lines of Sunday school morality. Kreb's new morality was common sense — a combination of the new science and the new religion. Since God intended man to weigh his beliefs in the light of human reason, the scientific point of view and the religious were really one and the same. "The new education, the new viewpoint was in truth nothing but *Religion Made Practical*," and "socialism, in the proper sense, is merely the application of modern science to government."[7]

The spread of the new viewpoint depends upon the development of leaders, and Krebs repudiates the traditional Jacksonian notion that any man can handle a public office. "Leadership, and the wisdom it implied, did not reside in the people, but in the leaders who sprang from the people and interpreted their needs and longings."[8] Hugh saw a close connection between this leadership principle and the assumptions of the conservative business leaders, like Mr. Watling. But there was an important difference. Watling's leaders, in line with the business ethic and the Gospel of Wealth, were to be the fittest, those who survived the struggle; Krebs' were to be the reborn.

It has been suggested that in espousing this leadership principle, Churchill abandoned his earlier Jeffersonian political slogan of giving the government back to the people in exchange for the aristocratic Hamiltonian principles advocated by his neighbor Herbert Croly. But this apparent shift is only a change in emphasis. If the leadership was to be made responsible, as Churchill stated it was, the people would still have the final word; they would still have to be trusted. Furthermore, the idea of leadership, in the sense that people are attracted to the good man who draws strength from his goodness, had been a part of Churchill's scheme of things from the first, and was exemplified by the mugwump-liberals of his own day. Indeed it was embodied — as far as Churchill was concerned — in his political idol, Theodore Roosevelt.

This novel also demonstrates that as late as 1915 Churchill remained convinced that the new generation was aware of the evils that existed in their society, and that they could and would reconstruct that society in the light of human reason. After his conversion, Hugh Paret issues this declaration of faith in human freedom and creativity.

> "The birthright of the spirit of man was freedom, freedom to experiment, to determine, to create — to create himself, to create society in the image of God!"[9]

If it was not clear from statements such as this (and from Krebs' highly individualistic philosophy) that Churchill was not espousing any known variety of socialism, the novelist made this perfectly clear in an article written in 1916 called, "A Plea for the

American Tradition." [10] In this article he opposes any form of collectivism (indeed, it would almost seem that he opposes any legislation at all) as unAmerican. The American tradition, he asserts, is one of volunteerism — individuals voluntarily cooperating. Salvation and social reform will both be achieved by transforming the materialistic individualism of classical economics into spiritual individualism. Then the pursuit of happiness would become self-realization, and this self-realization of the individual Churchill equates with the good of the whole society. By a kind of spiritual "invisible hand" the self-interest of the individual would be in accord with that of society.

In this same article Churchill makes the point-blank statement, "I believe I am in accord with experience and modern opinion when I say that environment is stronger than heredity . . . ."[11] But this comment should not be taken too literally, for he continued in his novels to imply that nobility of character (or the possibility of developing it) is inherent. Even in *A Far Country* he makes note of the heroine's good breeding, and Hugh comes from an old-line family. This dichotomy between a commitment toward changing the world by improving society, and the ingrained belief that nobility of character is dependent upon heredity, is one that Churchill never resolved (and may not even have been aware of).

Any analysis of the merits and defects of *A Far Country* should take into consideration Churchill's growing awareness of his changing role. When the Hearst people engaged an artist to do the illustrations for the serial of *A Far Country* without getting his approval, Churchill complained bitterly. He objected primarily to the sentimental, romanticized style of the artist in question. "I have been trying for years to get away from the 'best seller' idea of my novels," he wrote Brett, "and I feel that I am succeeding."[12] Such a statement from his prize author may have made the publisher's heart skip a beat, but Churchill certainly did not mean that he hoped the public would stop buying his books. He meant that he wanted to avoid the stereotype of a best seller as a light romance which provides an entertaining diversion on a rainy afternoon. Churchill at this point in his career would have welcomed the stigma by which later critics have dammed him — that his books were sociological documents rather than high art. He thought of his novels as serious social commentary, an amalgamation of the best of modern scholarship in economics, politics, sociology, psychology, and religion.

Nonetheless the comment to Brett is ironic, for his popularity did begin to decline. The reasons for this are by no means so simple as literary historians have tended to believe. Certainly the role of the critics was a minor one. The criticisms leveled against *A Far Country* are almost identical to those made against *The Inside of the Cup*. Although it was praised as an analysis of contemporary problems, few suggested that it was an artistic success. The critic for the *Dial* said that Churchill had become addicted to the lecture habit to such an extent that he was subordinating all artistic demands to the preaching of a sermon.[13] But the same critics had objected to the same things in *The Inside of the Cup* and that novel was a runaway best seller.

Part of the difference in the public's response may have been that the criticisms were more accurate with regard to *A Far Country*. It is not so much that the hero is a stereotype — other heroes of his had been such — but that the supporting cast does not come to life. In spite of his efforts to combine reform and art, Churchill was so intent upon converting his audience that he does not appear to have been vitally concerned about his characters. No one could worry much about the fate of Hugh's banal wife, Maude Hutchins; Nancy Willett has possibilities which never materialize; Hugh's journey into a far country is more of a trip across town; and Krebs, in addition to being too much of a Christ-like (or perhaps Isaiah) figure, was an outlander with whom the book-buying, middle-class audience could not identify. The actual message which Churchill wished to convey was only an elaboration of the one he had delivered in *The Inside of the Cup*, and the narrative of *A Far Country* (in spite of the illicit love affair) was not sufficiently engrossing to carry the novel on its own.

Two other factors may have entered into the picture. By 1915 large segments of the American public had grown weary of the reformers' long crusade. Domestic reform had actually passed its zenith, and the war drums from across the seas distracted their attention from the social and economic evils at home. In addition, Brett had been complaining for some years that the public was acquiring the abominable habit of borrowing books from libraries instead of buying their own copies. In any case, both Churchill and his middle-class audience were soon to turn their attention to new interests.

CHAPTER XVI

A Time of Study and an Unusual Teacher

In 1916, as the war in Europe raged on and America moved ever closer to a total commitment to the Allied cause, Churchill found himself pulled more and more into that conflict. Churchill's interests continued to change and broaden, and were decidedly less political than before. At forty-five, he made a rather serious effort to learn something about music for the first time. Aside from the many notes on technical matters in connection with the new novel, the most frequent references in his datebook concern love, marriage, and divorce. There are many notes on the nature of love, and he cites at considerable length (and with apparent approval) several of George Bernard Shaw's famous diatribes against the bonds of marriage.

Churchill also continued to devote time to the Authors' League. In April of 1916 he chaired the third annual dinner at the Plaza Hotel, with French editor and author Jules Bois as guest of honor. The keynote of Churchill's address on this occasion was his plea to the authors to instill more democratic ideals in their work. He felt the League was occupied far too much with "matters of commerce."[1] Perhaps for this reason (among others) he opposed the projected affiliation of the League with the American Federation of Labor. This issue arose in the summer of 1916; and Churchill joined with Brander Matthews, Garland, Ida

Tarbell and a number of others to protest against this action. Churchill notified the council of the League that he would resign from the organization if the affiliation went through.[2] Part of his opposition to affiliation also stemmed from his opposition to labor unions in general. In 1913 he had written that "labor unions [are] abnormal, a sign of economic disease, as every powerful organization is which is arrayed against the state."[3] He shared the paternalistic attitude toward labor that was a characteristic of many middle class progressive leaders. It said in effect that it was all right for the government to pass laws protecting the individual workingman, but it was something else entirely for the laborers to band together to protect themselves and to further their own interests.

After 1913, in addition to the problems of serialization and the incredible difficulties that arose from the dramatization of his novels, Churchill was also faced with the question of movie rights. There was no problem over the rights to the books themselves; Brett wrote Churchill that Macmillan had no claim to any of the profits and that he should go ahead with the contracts. The negotiations with the film companies themselves, however, were not quite so simple. The difficulty centered upon the dramatic rights for The Crisis. This was the story which most of the film companies wanted, and Churchill's agent, Miss Alice Kauser, felt certain that Churchill did not have the right to sell the movie rights to the novel since these were considered as part of a previously awarded play contract. Her advice was to wait until the option on the dramatic rights lapsed so that he could offer the movie companies the rights to the novel as such. Churchill contended that the play and movie rights had nothing to do with each other. An arrangement was finally worked out with Selig Polyscope Company to produce The Crisis.[4]

The movie was completed by the fall of 1916 and was advertised as the biggest and greatest ever made. That fall it played at private showings for which the individual theatres sent out invitations. At the showing in Orange, New Jersey, in November, Governor Fielder and Thomas Edison were present. Edison, who had had much to do with the early development of motion pictures, was favorably impressed by the film. He said:

> From time immemorial men have expressed their
> tribute to greater men and big achievements in iron
> and stone, in marble and bronze. In "The Crisis" we
> have the titanic figure of Lincoln, his actions, his
> characteristics preserved for posterity in moving
> pictures in a manner so true to life that it recalls to
> my mind the great emancipator as I knew him.[5]

The publicity department did its job well, and the movie got rave
advance notices in newspapers all over the country. The reviews
of the movie were also quite favorable, many of them emphasizing the film's educational value. In Pittsburgh it was shown on
several Saturday mornings at special prices for school children, to
enable them, wrote the Pittsburgh *Leader*, "to see the greatest
period in our national life portrayed before their very eyes."[6] The
popularity of the picture led to the filming of movies based on
Richard Carvel and *The Dwelling Place of Light*, neither of which
was particularly successful.

These material concerns were pushed to the rear of Churchill's mind as his energies and attention were increasingly absorbed
by the question of America's entrance into the stalemated war of
attrition in Europe. From the beginning of the conflict he had
been a supporter of the Allied cause; his military education and
his own inclinations led him also to support Wilson's preparedness
campaign. With five hundred others, he signed the "Address to the
People of the Allied Nations," in March of 1915, supporting them
in their fight against the Central Powers. He also signed an open
letter to the people of the United States, sponsored by fifty prominent prelates and laymen, protesting what they considered to be
premature peace efforts that would do nothing to solve the basic
problems involved in the war.[7]

If the United States entered the war, Churchill intended to
offer his services. In the meantime he accepted an appointment
from Governor Keyes to the New Hampshire Committee on Public
Safety, a group of one hundred citizens who were to cooperate
with the civil and military authorities in the work of preparedness.[8]

By March, 1917, Churchill was convinced that the conflict
was a holy war and was certain that it would have many beneficial
results. These thoughts were expressed in his speech to the
Authors' Club in Boston on March 25. This speech is the best

summation of his thought during these years, a plateau in the evolution of his social and religious ideas.[9] The real nature of the conflict was obscure in the first years, he admits, but by 1916 Americans saw that this was "a war for democracy, and, in a far greater sense than any conflict that has gone before it, it is a religious war."

But if this was a war for democracy and a religious crusade, Churchill was quick to point out that he was using these terms in a Darwinian sense. Democracy, he says, is an evolving concept, not a static entity. At the time of the Revolution and the writing of the Constitution, the United States was the most revolutionary nation in the world, but in 1916 it was the most conservative. "Even Russia is outdistancing us." Our Constitution, "as was quite logical at the end of the eighteenth century, is not a democratic Constitution, but a compromise, an attempt to base government on what were supposed to be fixed eternal principles when the conditions of life had changed. But out of the enormous social unrest engendered by industrialism has come also a different response — especially on the part of many women — a response that has found in war work "a solution of the divided personality." This would have come by "democratic evolution if the war had not taken place, but it would have come more slowly."

Whether people liked it or not, certain basic changes in institutions and attitudes were going to follow from the new outlook. Among these would be the end of the Church as it existed at the time, an abolition of supernaturalism and mysticism, and the end of "all static and absolute conceptions of God and of right and wrong." Many people have regarded the teachings of Jesus as impractical, but his insistence on a brotherhood of man that transcends national borders was finding expression, according to Churchill, in the present war. "He taught us that human nature was worthy of trust, yet our society has been built upon the opposing principle of <u>caveat emptor</u>." "In short, we are on the verge of making the remarkable discovery that the practice of Christianity in the social order may not be merely practical, but profitable!"

Churchill felt that preparation for the new world was dependent upon education, and he viewed John Dewey as the modern prophet. The new education would be in harmony with democracy, psychology, religion, and scientific methods, developing the special gift that is in every child and helping him realize himself as an individual. But he insisted that he was not advocating a complete break with tradition. Even the old religious doctrines contain precious grains of truth. "In his <u>natural</u> state man was an animal, involved with the rest of the organic world in a bitter struggle for survival. And we may conceive of the Spirit through the ages working in man, transforming and energizing him, until we begin to perceive that its object may be to change that cruel competition for existence into what may be called emulation." This emulation is a spiritual competition, a competition that "animates the artist in his attempt to paint the best picture; or the writer, to write the best book; or the scientist or the physician or surgeon to spend their lives competing with others of their profession for the good of mankind without much thought of material reward." This spiritual struggle rather than material competition "is the theory that underlies both Christianity and Anglo-Saxon democracy."

In this speech one can see the massive changes which Churchill, and many others like him, felt could be brought about by a change in attitude alone. Here is no great program of legislation, no institutional revolution, but a change in the mind of man himself. This is a characteristic of Progressive intellectuals, and is an aspect of their thought that too many authorities on the period have ignored. By 1916 or 1917 many Progressives had moved byyond governmental action to a much broader field of activity. The war did not kill Progressivism as a political movement, for it was already dead. The modest amount of legislation that was necessary had been enacted; now, through education and (for some) religion, they would work for a society of cooperation outside the realm of coercive governmental action. The new world was on its way, the Kingdom of God would be achieved, the end of history as the story of human error and misery was about to be realized. And it would be realized through a heightening of traditional American individualism, not through legislation. It was the later realization of what the war really meant that destroyed this dream. Churchill and many of his contemporaries looked for a millenium and could find only the gray ashes of a civilization that was destroying itself.

But they did not know this in 1917. In the spring of that

year, as he viewed the social possibilities of the current conflict, Churchill was riding the crest of a wave of optimism. In the year immediately preceding that, however, he had fallen into the first phase of disillusionment about the possibility of massive social change. This is the only possible explanation for the strange dichotomy between his public pronouncements in 1917 and 1918 and the peculiar pessimism that is evidenced in *The Dwelling Place of Light*. His faith in social reform through a spiritual change began to diminish after the writing of *A Far Country*, was temporarily revived by the changes he thought were being brought about by the war, and hurtled downward at an increasing rate in the years that followed it. Before his next novel is analyzed, however, it is essential to examine the peculiar relationship which had developed between the socially prominent novelist and the socially unacceptable Upton Sinclair — a relationship that reached fruition in *The Dwelling Place of Light*.

Sinclair's connection with Churchill is interesting, in part, because the muckraker was one of the few famous figures who retained his interest in Churchill after the novelist withdrew from public life. He looked upon himself as Churchill's tutor in the ways of the world and naturally wondered what had happened to an old student who refused to become a disciple. Some years after Churchill's death Sinclair wrote to the editor of *The Saturday Review*, inquiring about Churchill's mysterious retirement.

> In the days when I was beginning as a writer our most popular novelist was the American Winston Churchill. Today he seems to be entirely forgotten . . . .
> Some years before his death Mr. Churchill ceased entirely to write, and having corresponded with him in the past, I was interested to write him and ask why he had quit. I do not have his reply by me; it was rather cryptic, and the substance of it was that he had found some kind of mystical interest or satisfaction in life which had caused him to retire entirely from worldly contacts. I have never seen anything published about this, and it seems to me that it would be of interest to the public nowadays.[10]

In 1955 Sinclair stated his view of Churchill when he said, "His novels were propaganda, like most of mine, but he had great influence in his time."[11] And in the 1920's Sinclair indicated that this influence had been for the good. At that time he stated, "The last writer I can recall who was able to publish in a big popular magazine any hint that there might be something wrong with the American plutocracy, was Winston Churchill."[12] Sinclair went on to indicate that although Churchill's novels were headed in the right direction, they never quite made it because the novelist did not understand the workings of a bourgeois society.

If Churchill did not understand American society, it was not the fault of the outspoken muckraker. As early as 1907, after reading an interview with Churchill, Sinclair was moved to send him a copy of his *Industrial Republic*. Churchill read at least part of the book and sent its author a complimentary reply. A year later Sinclair had read *Mr. Crewe's Career* and was able to return the compliment.[13] The next contact between the two critics of American society was Sinclair's review of *A Modern Chronicle*, in which he contended that Churchill was a key to the mind of his own times. He further suggests that the most striking feature of Churchill's work is "its peculiar intellectual and spiritual immaturity. His characters are convincing as far as they go, he says, "but they never seem to me to go beyond the age of seventeen." He had been fascinated to learn that Churchill was doing a novel about divorce, "because I knew that I would find out in Mr. Churchill's novel just exactly how far the mind of the American people has progressed on the subject."[14]

The muckraker evidently felt that by educating Churchill he could educate the American people, and he began sending him books, mostly on the subject of socialism. On his recommendation Churchill read William English Walling's *Larger Aspect of Socialism, Social Problems* by the famous British socialist J. A. Hobson, and Bruce Wyman's *Control of the Market*, in addition to a number of other books, magazine articles, and pamphlets.[15] Churchill did nodify some of his ideas, and these changes have confused students of his work. One wrote that in *A Far Country* Churchill "seems to skirt close to Marxian socialism as an answer to the nation's problems," and that "he shows a sympathy for the organized labor movement as such for the first time."[16] Actually, Churchill presented a variety of socialism in the novel that is about as far from the Marxian version as it is possible to get, and he never had any sympathy for organized labor as such.

It is true, however, that his ideas were becoming more radical, and as early as *The Inside of the Cup* there are indications that he was moving beyond such sympathetic spirits as Roosevelt. In that novel he has the hero make a casual comment about private property that shocked many of his readers.

> The Christian government we are approaching will not recognize property, because it is gradually becoming clear that the holding of property delays the Kingdom at which you scoff . . . . The possession of property, or of sufficient property to give one individual an advantage over his fellows is inconsistent with Christianity.[17]

Roosevelt wrote to say how much he enjoyed the novel, stating that he had been "profoundly stirred and impressed by it," but he had a serious reservation.

> There is but one criticism I have to make. I wish you had not in a sudden sentence spoken as if you regarded the abolition of all property as an ultimate end of Christian civilization. You have worked out your other theories very carefully. You have shown the great abuses and laxities; you have given the remedy. But in this case, if I understand you aright, I do not agree with you.[18]

In his reply, Churchill indicates the way in which his novels were connected with the political movement of 1912 and tries to explain his position.

> I am inclined to agree with you as to the wisdom of having spoken about the ultimate abolition of property, — rather of the inadvisability of it . . . . It seems to me that evolution is slowly but surely tending that way; but, if it comes it will not be, I think until a far-distant future . . . . However, I meant it as a prediction, and not as advocating the immediate adoption of it in government. I cannot but think that property is one of the larger roots of selfishness, and that it forms a barrier against the spiritual.[19]

By the fall of 1914 Churchill had considered the problem more thoroughly. Sinclair had written for permission to include something from Churchill's published works in a book he was editing, a request which Macmillan ultimately vetoed. The novelist told him to go ahead, but he asked Sinclair not to use the excerpt dealing with the abolition of private property, because he had come more and more to accept "the modern view that a certain amount of property fills a human need." Four days later he wrote again.

> For the past year or so I have been much interested in Hobson's work, I have also read Walling and other men on the modern socialism, and it was for this reason, because I am more and more inclined to endorse their views, that I did not wish by any chance to have myself quoted as predicting the total abolition of property . . . . Hobson's phrase, "Property which we can personalize", strikes me as a very happy one. I am spending what spare time I have to brush up on my economic education, and I think I fully realize the importance which you put on it.[20]

The most significant phase of the Churchill-Sinclair relationship had actually transpired earlier than this. It came in the summer of 1913 after Sinclair read *The Inside of the Cup*. He wrote that he had read the book with deep interest and had even believed in the hero until the very end of the story when the hero insists that the financier, Eldon Parr, to become a true Christian, would have to make restitution of the money lost by the small investor because of his stock manipulations. This display of economic naiveté shocked Sinclair, but he refused to abandon the educational program.

> Now Brother Churchill, you have done all our American traditions, and you have done politics, marriage, and the Church. There is only one thing left, and you can no longer dodge me. You simply must do Economics. And you will have to do some studying, for it is your weak line at present — else you could never penned that awful paragraph. You have got to the point where other people abuse your hero by calling him a Socialist, but you don't tell us what he is. But the subject beckons you![21]

After this reprimand he recommended some more books for Churchill to read and then made the suggestion which would ultimately lead Churchill to the theme of his last novel.

> Let me suggest a book for Winston Churchill to write. Take Lawrence, or Paterson, and go and study one of those big strikes. I don't care what side you take — all you have to do is to understand it thoroughly, as it

> seems to all parties involved. Tell the story of a young
> man whose father owns the mill; and let him meet an
> I.W.W. girl — I'll introduce you to some, if that will
> help. I'm giving you one of my themes — or offering
> it; the reason being that you could do it better than
> I.

In later years Sinclair realized that *The Dwelling Place of Light*
was the book he had requested, but he disliked it because he felt
that Churchill had reduced the anguish of the strike to a pictures-
que background.[22] Actually Churchill also received a request to
do a study of industrial labor from his publisher who felt that the
public would never understand the labor problem "unless it can be
put into the form of a story such as you gave them in 'The Inside
of the Cup.'"[23] At the time Sinclair introduced the idea, Churchill, hard at work on *A Far Country*, said that he would be happy
to take him up on the offer to introduce him to some of those
engaged in the I.W.W. movement, but as for taking one of
Sinclair's themes, "an offer which has touched me very much — I
could not think of it."[24]

In this same letter Churchill tried to outline his own economic ideas. Readily admitting his lack of knowledge in matters of economics, he wrote that he had spent all of his time during the past
few years trying to compensate for the deficiencies in his education.

> In my talks with men who are Socialists, in the polit-
> ical sense, I have thought that they laid a little too
> much stress on the economic side of the matter. This
> does not mean that I do not think it of vital impor-
> tance. A book I have just been reading by Henry
> Jones on idealism expresses my attitude better than
> I can. "It is not seen that a socialized State brought
> upon a people morally unprepared would be the
> deepest calamity any nation may be called upon to
> meet." But I repeat, I am open minded and anxious
> to know more and more. I believe that that which
> the Socialists advocate, (such main contentions as I
> am familiar with,) is coming by evolution, and that
> quite rapidly. But that a change in the point of view
> of the average citizen, an awakening and adjustment,
> must precede it.

If Churchill was open minded and willing to learn, Sinclair
was ready and willing to educate. He fired back a multi-page letter

that chronicles his own path to socialism. He agreed with Churchill that a general awakening must precede the socialist state, and
contended that this was why he wanted to break in on the
novelist's "mountain solitude, and interfere with your meditations
on the subject of Idealism."[25] As for taking one of his book
themes from him, Sinclair said this would be an act of mercy.
Sinclair then relates that he, too, started out in life as an idealist.

> But I kept a wife and child for three years on thirty
> dollars a month earned by hack-work, and when I had
> got through, there were some things that I knew
> about economics. I knew the relationship between
> poverty and disease, suicide, insanity, and crime, and
> I knew it so well that never after could any book-
> writer be able to unteach it to me. I made a vow
> then that I would spend the rest of my life slaying
> the demon of poverty; and that's why I've been such
> a nuisance ever since.

He goes on to describe the curious place Churchill had come to
occupy in his scheme of things — feelings that other writers of
the period may well have shared.

> For twelve or fourteen years I have envied you more
> than I have any other man in America. I've envied
> you so much that I've almost hated you. And this is
> the reason: Because you've put yourself into a novel
> once every two years, and you haven't said anything
> in between. And each novel has been better than the
> last. It's what I ought to have done, and didn't, and
> never can or will . . . . So you can imagine with what
> wrath I break in upon your olympian calm!

The socialist Sinclair then proceeds to point out to Churchill
the only course open to him as a religious man.

> We hold these things to be self-evident, Mr.
> Churchill; that no man created the land and the sea,
> the coal and the oil and the iron. Every man must
> have them to live; and so long as a few are allowed to
> own them, the non-owners must be slaves to the
> owners. Once admit that, and if you are a religious
> man, in the true sense of the word, you must become
> a Socialist . . . . I don't care what sort of a Socialist
> you become. You'd hardly be a bureaucrat, I think.
> You might prefer the way I have been travelling in
> the last year or two — in the direction of Syndicalism.

In a footnote written at the bottom of the last page in longhand, Sinclair perhaps characterizes his own place, both as a man of letters and in the development of Churchill's thought. "Reading over this epistle I observe a certain rhetorical note, but you won't mind smiling over that. It comes from stump-speaking with one's pen."

Churchill replied to Sinclair's confession and admonition quickly and at some length. He felt that he understood Sinclair's position as well as anyone could who had not been through the bitter experience of his earlier days, but he did not believe that the socialist had correctly interpreted his own position. He did not, he said, regard the kind of competition which involves the acquisition of property as either a permanent or a desirable thing. Evolution clearly points out that the competitive system is passing away, but he felt that idealism and modern social theory were compatible.

> Personally I do not find Idealism, especially as set forth in such modern books as Bosanquet's latest Gifford lectures, in conflict with the great social movement. On the contrary. And I am indeed interested that a new social system shall replace this, one in which there shall be a far greater measure of justice. But I am interested in it for this reason: it is not that those who are now oppressed and starved shall have merely enough food and clothing and fuel, but that they may be given the leisure and the opportunity to <u>live!</u> . . . It is the business of the state to make such ideal citizens, and when we get enough of them we shall have the socialism so ably sketched by the authors and economists of whom you speak. It is all coming and the leaven is at work.[26]

Churchill described his interpretation of his own role and suggested that he already considered himself a socialist.

> For some years I have believed myself to be a Socialist, as you put it, in the vital sense; and I tried to set this forth in the book, — that is, the difference between political and what I may call religious Socialism.

The final significant exchange of letters between the two men came some two years later when Sinclair wanted Churchill to write an introduction to a tract he had edited called *The Cry for*

Justice. The reason that he wanted Churchill to write the introduction — and in effect to endorse the book — is obvious.

> I feel the need of having the book sponsored by
> someone less terrible to the general reading public
> than myself; for it is really an interesting book, one
> which the general public ought to get . . . . I want
> somebody who is not entirely of the literary cast; and
> I cannot think of anyone, not an out and out re-
> volter, who has done more than you to make the
> great public think of justice.[27]

Churchill in declining this request was obviously troubled and
wrote a five-page explanation. "But my real reason for not wishing
to write an introduction to the book," Churchill confessed, "is
that I have not gone as yet as far as you."[28]

Sinclair had taken the novelist as far as he was capable of
going at that point in his career. His education had begun. Churchill was reading the books that Sinclair recommended and he would
continue to study them in preparation for his study of a syndicalist strike, but in 1915 the novelist was not yet ready to endorse
Sinclair's solution to the evils of society; indeed, he was never to
accept the syndicalist position.

In a postscript to one of his letters to Sinclair, trying to explain why he had had his hero confront Parr with a choice between restitution and damnation, Churchill writes, "Of course
in Eldon Parr's case, I am thinking of a solution for <u>him,</u> and not
suggesting an economic solution."[29] This tendency to see individual solutions that did not fully epitomize the social problem is
one of the features of Churchill's new thought that has struck
later critics as unrealistic. The following by one such critic is
typical and attempts at the same time to suggest why Churchill
was so tremendously popular with the novel-reading public.

> Churchill did not care for the Darwinian theories of
> laissez-faire and unbridled competition in a material-
> istic America, but instead of coping with them
> directly and honestly as a later generation had to do,
> he took the typically progressive road of high-sound-
> ing morality and individual regeneration. Truth and
> goodness were positive, identifiable things; falsehood
> and evil were also easily marked. Like Roosevelt,
> his mentor, he was out of step with the true intellec-
> tuals, the minority of his time, men like Lippman,

> Bourne, Laski, and Brooks, but he was impressively in step with the overwhelming bulk of the American people who clung to the old truths about politics and morals . . . . They found him stimulating and worthwhile, because he challenged the prevailing economic winds but did not offer any radical, dangerous alternatives. To read him was to salve the conscience, but not to upset society. [30]

This criticism is justified and demonstrates an insight into human psychology that was perhaps even more true of the Progressive generation than of most others. Nonetheless, given the tendency of Progressive Americans to moralize about problems rather than making revolutionary efforts to solve them, Churchill's approach may have been more significant than his critics have been willing to admit. Whereas the American people were unwilling to accept the more radical solutions of an Upton Sinclair or even the youthful Walter Lippman, they were willing to listen to Churchill. Strangely enough, this aspect of Churchill's value to his society was mentioned as early as 1908 in a newspaper review.

> As a matter of fact Mr. Churchill's novel of present day politics will do a world of good. It will carry conviction where the ravings of the sensation monger would be held as light as air. Men who read "Mr. Crewe's Career" know that its author is no demagogue. He is an earnest and serious man, one who desires to help in the American regeneration. But he is calm, dispassionate, admirable. It is the Winston Churchill, rather than the Upton Sinclair, who does something worth doing, who leaves a work that is of permanent value. [31]

The matter of permanent value is certainly open to question; Churchill never left a document so valuable to later generations as Sinclair's *The Jungle*. Nonetheless it is probably true that society needs the man who can lead from the top of the nearest knoll as well as the voice crying in the wilderness or the prophet beckoning from a distant mountain. The alienated social critic who sees a new way, a radical departure, may receive the plaudits of future generations; but in the immediate instance society will look to the man who travels just in front of the majority, who is learning with them, the man who can show them the path because he himself is just discovering it.

Some of the reviewers saw this just about the time when Churchill's view of his own role was changing. Hildegarde Hawthorne, writing in the New York *Times* in 1915, said, "The important thing in Mr. Churchill's books is himself: his point of view, his observation of conditions, his conclusions and explanations. As a literary artist he may be said not to exist; as a voice on matters that are vitally important to us as Americans he is immensely important." Francis Hackett felt that, whatever Churchill's limitations, his value lay in his ability to show his fellow countrymen how to survive in a changing world. "Every novel that Mr. Churchill writes shows his skill at adaptation, his power of accommodating himself and his tradition to new and awkward facts." By 1915 some people were aware that Churchill had abandoned the role of story-teller for the more significant role of social critic. As a prelude to a review of *A Far Country* the reviewer for the *Nation* noted that Churchill was born with the knack of story-telling and had made steady advances in making story-telling an art. "But his real desire is not to be an entertainer, or even an artist; he aspires to become a lay preacher, even a minor prophet."[32] The reviewer went on to note, as did many others, that the role of prophet interfered with the art of novel writing. And perhaps Churchill's real failure lies here. It is not so important that he did not scale the mountain peak to lead the American people from the vantage point of genius; it is important that he failed to bring his audience with him as he sought the torturous path through the jungle of ideas at the base of the mountain. The American people looked to him as an entertainer who could point out the evils of their own society and give them hope that those evils could be overcome. When he began to allow the preachments to override the entertainment, he lost not only the critics but his large audience as well. This disenchantment was clear by 1917.

CHAPTER XVII

A Temporary Loss of Faith

A Dwelling Place of Light, Churchill's last published novel, appeared in the fall of 1917. He had been working on it for nearly two years, and again his date-books are filled with character sketches, scenes for the novel, and long descriptions of the technical matters involved. Interspersed with these technical matters are notes on realism in fiction. Churchill was concerned about the disparity between the critics' taste and that of the novel-reading public; was it possible to write a novel that would be entertaining enough to get his message across to a mass audience, meet the artistic demands of the critics, and still remain true to his own ideals. He would try.

Churchill called *The Dwelling Place of Light* "the story of modern events strained through the passion of a woman's soul."[1] The woman is Janet Bumpus, the elder daughter of an old and respected New England family which has failed to keep pace with changing conditions and, consequently, has slowly sunk to the bottom of the economic ladder. Janet works as a stenographer in the Chippering Mills until Claude Ditmar, manager of the mills, is attracted to her and makes her his private secretary. The "modern events" concern a strike at the mills that is led by syndicalist organizers.

Churchill's main theme in this novel is the difference between the contemporary industrial society and the older social tradition of a simpler age. The tension in the novel results from the fact that a representative of this older tradition — Janet Bumpus — finds herself trapped by modern society.

In the earlier problem novels, Churchill had indicated that his society was a basically healthy one which simply needed to open its eyes to its own problems. In *A Modern Chronicle, The Inside of the Cup,* and *A Far Country* the problems are more deeply rooted but still susceptible to reform through moral regeneration. *The Dwelling Place of Light*, on the other hand, pictures modern society as an amoral world in which the individual seeks only his own self-interest. One such individual is Claude Ditmar, whom Churchill describes as "a creature rather wonderfully adapted to his environment . . . . "[2] He takes over the management of the Chippering Mills, does away with the old-fashioned but human methods of operation, and makes the company a paying proposition. When confronted about the wretched living conditions of his workers, he replies:

> Isn't it because these people want to live that way?
> . . . They actually like it, they wouldn't be happy in anything but a pig'sty — they had 'em in Europe. And what do you expect us to do? Buy land and build flats for them?[3]

Ditmar is the modern man who accepts the conditions and the dog-eat-dog morality of an industrial society. He knows what he wants, goes after it, and gets it.

Another type of individual produced by modern society is the Syndicalist leader; he becomes the example of those whom modern society has formed yet passed by, and who seek vengence in a doctrine of violence. His ideals and moral standards are exactly the same as those of the new industrialist — to take what one can get. In rejecting Rolfe and all that he stands for — violence and the lack of personal restraint — Churchill blackened the Syndicalist with the brush of free love. "For Rolfe there had been a woman in every strike — sometimes two."[4] He needs feminine stimulus for his genius to flower, and in this strike he settles on Janet through whom Churchill repudiates Syndicalism. Neither Marxian socialism, nor Syndicalism, nor the efforts of organized labor to work out its own problems impressed Churchill as meaningful solutions to the situation confronting American society.

What hope remained for the salvation of society did not lie with those individuals who had allowed their lives and their philosophies to be formed by the values of that society. The only hope was in the other force that Churchill saw at work, the older social tradition which was symbolized by Silliston Academy and personified by Brooks Insall, a famous author, and his friend Mrs. Maturin. Silliston itself is presented as a sheltered spot in "a chaotic world of smoke and struggle," and through it Churchill enshrined the old stability.

> Silliston, indifferent to cults and cataclysms, undisturbed by the dark tides flung westward to gather in deposits in other parts of the land, had held fast to the old tradition, stood ready to do her share to transform it into something even nobler when the time should come. Simplicity and worth and beauty — these elements at least of the older Republic should not perish, but in the end prevail.[5]

Almost the same terms used to describe Silliston could be used to characterize Mrs. Maturin and Insall. Strong, vital, and dependable, they are almost wholly apart from the turmoil of the modern world. Their social attitude is exemplified by Insall's answer to Janet when she asks if he is on the side of the capitalists in the strike. "I?" he replies. "I'm a spectator — an innocent bystander." The key to the approach of these two individuals is their belief that "to understand is to pardon." In this light (and perhaps in Churchill's mind as well) the strike is not the fault of the employers. "Not in a large sense . . . . When people grow up to look at life in a certain way, from a certain viewpoint, it is difficult, almost impossible to change them. It's — It's their religion."[6]

These, then, are the forces at work upon the character of Janet Bumpus, inheritor of the old tradition, inhabitant of a modern chaotic society.

> She was one of the unfortunate who love beauty, who are condemned to dwell in exile, unacquainted with what they love. Desire was incandescent within her breast. Desire for what? It would have been some relief to know.[7]

Unlike her sister, Lise, she cannot find joy and forgetfulness in dance halls, Sunday supplements, and movie houses; if she desires wealth it is only because it would provide a means of escape from her sordid surroundings, from the mills, where she sees herself as a slave in a fortress. When she walks to Silliston the architectural beauty of the academy electrifies her and she feels that at last she has come to the home which she has unconsciously sought.

> For the first time in her adult life she stood in the presence of tradition, of a tradition inherently if unconsciously the innermost reality of her being: a tradition that miraculously was not dead, since after all these years it had begun to put forth these vigorous shoots.[8]

Janet knows that she was given the position as Ditmar's secretary because of her sex appeal, and in his presence she experiences alternate waves of antagonism and attraction, "revealing to her depths and possibilities of her nature that frightened while they fascinated." She is thrilled that he desires her, but her pride revolts because he wants her clandestinely. Marriage, however, does not occur to her in this situation, for "she was not so commonplace."[9] She shrinks from Ditmar's embrace not because she believes — in the usual sense — that it is wrong, but because it involves a surrender of her own personality.

As she works with Ditmar, Janet begins to accept his "modern" point of view about life. She sees men striving for prominence and power and is intoxicated by her own power over her boss. In this mood she becomes pregnant with Ditmar's child. This feeling of power is destroyed when she learns of her sister's planned abortion, and "the scorching revelation of life's injustice lighted within her the fires of anarchy and revenge."[10] It does not take long, however, for her to discover that the philosophy of Snydicalism is really no different from that of capitalism, and that Rolfe's attitude toward her is the same as Ditmar's. The lust of the two men for her body symbolizes the lust of both philosophies for material wealth.

It is at this point that Janet begins to frequent Insall's soup kitchen. There she learns to admire the tolerance of Insall and Mrs. Maturin, and to sense a wider culture of which they are a part — a culture not harnessed to a "Cause." Janet wonders at the friendship which these two cultured people offer her, but to them she typifies the strike, "The protest, the revolt, the struggle for self-realization, that is beginning to be felt all over the nation . . . that is not yet focussed and self-conscious, but groping its way, clothing itself in any philosophy that seems to fit it." Churchill characterizes Janet as typical of the individual in the modern world. "Janet's problems," he states, "was in truth . . . the supreme problem of our time: what is the path of self-realization?"[11] Mrs. Maturin put it another way in her reply to Janet's question on whether or not she believed in God.

> I like to think of Him as light, Janet, and we are plants seeking to grow toward him — no matter from what dark crevice we may spring. Even in our mistakes and sins we are seeking Him, for these are ignorances, and as the world learns more we shall know Him better and better. It is natural to long for happiness, and happiness is self-realization, and self-realization is knowledge and light.[12]

Churchill raised several questions in this passage, not the least of which is the notion that sin is ignorance. This is an idea that is central to his later work, but even here it is apparent that he was attempting to cast traditional morality to the winds in favor of what he felt was a scientific morality based upon the individual, the time, and the circumstance. In his 1914 datebook, Churchill notes that "we have no fixed standards of right and wrong today. We must face this fact, and all it implies for 'the masses'." In this novel he makes a similar assertion. "For Janet had been born in an age which is rapidly discarding blanket morality and taboos, which has as yet to achieve the morality of scientific knowledge, of the individual instance."[13] Sin is ignorance; and as the individual achieves self-realization, which is knowledge and light, he will achieve both goodness and happiness.

Before her death, Janet achieves this self-realization, and she has Mrs. Maturin's word that her daughter will be brought up "in the light." If Janet is a true example of the individual in the modern world — as Churchill indicated she was — it would seem that he was still holding to the notion that social salvation can be achieved. But it surely must have been obvious to him that Janet was not typical. Where was the average modern man to get the social tradition into which Janet was fortunate enough to be born and which Churchill implied was crucial to her self-integration?

One might maintain that while the average individual could not get it, he could be led by those who had it. This would certainly have been in line with Churchill's leadership principle. But Brooks Insall is no leader, he is "an innocent bystander" who deplores all forms of organization. The whole tone of this novel is different from anything Churchill had written previously; it is more somber, less optimistic, and (for the first time) the heroine has to die within its pages. The possibility for general salvation is still present in *The Dwelling Place of Light*, but it is a far more remote and dubious concept than in the previous novels.

Brett, who was always enthusiastic about Churchill's novels, was even more pleased than usual with *The Dwelling Place of Light*.[14] Some critics have agreed with Brett that *The Dwelling Place of Light* was Churchill's best novel, but most of the contemporary critics, the public, and Churchill's self-appointed teacher, Upton Sinclair, disagreed.

Many reviewers suggested that Churchill was moving in the direction of lurid naturalism, and several of these compared the book with the work of Theodore Dreiser. Some of the reviews, especially in the Catholic journals (whose favor Churchill had lost with *The Inside of the Cup*), went even further. In essence their criticism was that Churchill had been a good author when he was writing historical novels, that he had been going downhill ever since, and had finally sunk so low as to espouse the Syndicalist philosophy — including the idea of free love. They managed to garble his ideas even further by bringing in the wartime hysteria against any criticism of "Americanism." The following quotation from the *Catholic World* shows the absurd extent to which such criticisms distorted the meaning of his story.

> Frankly we believe that this novel merits severe condemnation. It can make no appeal whatever to the American Catholic: it is equally bad from the religious standpoint, and as a social document. Any man who, at this stage of our national life, with a war on our hands and many internal dangers and problems to cope with, will publish such a defense of the propaganda of syndicalism and mob-rule, deserves a reprimand.[15]

The novel, of course, does not espouse syndicalism, or mob-rule, or free love. It simply shows what can happen to a plutocratic society when the masses, adhering to the same materialistic standards as their oppressors, decide to strike off their shackles. Churchill's condemnation of their actions is clear. Indeed, many later critics — accepting Churchill's picture of the existing conditions — have criticized him for not accepting the Syndicalist answer. They have suggested that he posed a clear problem, but that having no answers to that problem, he took refuge in a meaningless idealism. And far from espousing free love, he commits the Victorian sin of killing off both participants in the adulterous affair. In other words, Churchill is criticized for not being Theodore Dreiser.

It is true; he was neither a naturalist nor a socialist in the accepted sense of that term. In spite of his attempt to demonstrate that morality varies with time and place, the atmosphere of the novel is Victorian. In spite of his sympathy with the laborers, his portrait of them is typical of the native, Anglo-Saxon Protestant's view of the new immigrants. And the reason so many critics have felt that he did not provide an answer to the problems that faced an industrialized society is because his solution was not an economic one. His solution in *The Dwelling Place of Light* is the same as that which he had presented in his two previous novels — the evolving cooperative society. He did not favor the victory of the laboring classes because the dominance of any class would impede the establishment of this society. The message is not hammered down the reader's throat so hard as it had been in *The Inside of the Cup* and *A Far Country*, but whether this was because he had made a partial success of his attempt to meet the criticism that his novels were didactic tracts or because he was less certain in 1916 that the cooperative society was just around the corner, is not clear.

In one way this novel returns to Churchill's interests of about 1910, when he first presented in Honora Leffingwell the pursuit of self-integration. The social concern is still present — the suffering of the workers at the hands of their exploiters, the bitter feelings of a society divided against itself — but all of this is more of a background for the personal story than it had been in *The Inside of the Cup* and *A Far Country*. His primary concern was always with the individual. He had always presented social reform as something which would come about through the moral reformation of individuals, but in the two previous novels he was much more openly concerned about society as a whole than in this one. Here he rarely moves away from the story of Janet Bumpus. The result is, in some ways, a better novel, since he preaches less and demonstrates his indictment of contemporary society through the action of the story. But the implications of this change demonstrate a new departure in his personal outlook on society. It would seem that he was coming to understand (perhaps unconsciously) that the power of the environment to form the individual and hold him prisoner is greater than he had realized. Those who were born to an earlier tradition of self-discipline and moral values, like Janet (and the author himself), might be able to escape; but the chances for the rest of society did not look particularly bright to him in 1916. This novel was the bridge between his earlier optimism and his later withdrawal — a fact temporarily obscured by the revival of his millennialistic ideas during America's participation in the war to end all wars.

CHAPTER XVIII

The Popular Novelist and the War Effort

The period of America's entrance into the war was a time of trouble for Winston Churchill. The aunt who had raised him and who had been part of his own household for eight years, died in April of 1917. Churchill journeyed from Boston to St. Louis for the funeral, and a month later he established residence at the Lafayette Hotel in Washington. In the bustling war capitol, rumor had it that "Mr. Churchill is writing another of his clever novels, mirroring the social and political life of the Capitol." According to the Washington *Star*, Churchill was the hit of the season. "Even in a town filled with princes and potentates, Mr. Churchill is a full-sized lion, and he has been wined and dined so much that, were three-course dinners not in vogue, his digestion might be permanently impaired."[1]

The rumors about Churchill's next novel were well-founded, although in the first weeks of his visit he was still rewriting *The Dwelling Place of Light*. During the weeks that followed he wrote a number of articles on a variety of subjects, did prodigious amounts of research, and became involved in a young Turks' revolt of naval officers against Secretary of the Navy Josephus Daniels. He had earlier indicated that, in the event America entered the fight, he would offer his services to the navy. Just what form this service would take was not clear, but on May 7 he called on Daniels to inform him that he was going to do a book about the navy.[2] The Secretary provided Churchill with a letter of introduction to all naval officers, and with this in hand he left Washington for a trip down the Potomac on May 12. Accompanied by Ernest Poole, Herbert Croly, and several others, he visited the fleet and various naval installations.[3] As the days went by Churchill became more and more immersed in his investigation of the navy and increasingly disillusioned with Wilson's administration. He had opposed Wilson in 1916, not because he disapproved of his policies or his personal beliefs, but because he felt that the President's party did not stand for the same things Wilson did. The stay in Washington caused him to become critical of Wilson himself. He noted the widespread criticism in the Capitol of William Denman, whom Churchill himself felt was totally unsuited for his job as Chairman of the Shipping Board. The fault, he said, was Wilson's. "The secret of all this is that the President insists upon running affairs himself through little, subservient men."[4]

Churchill substantiated his belief that Wilson was surrounded by men of limited capacity for high office through his investigation of the navy. This affair is something of a mystery. Secretary Daniels was the most controversial member of Wilson's cabinet, and his enemies were a variegated group. The second Mrs. Wilson and Colonel House, believing that Daniels and Joe Tumulty were political liabilities, engaged in a sub rosa effort to dump the two men before the 1916 election.[5] Daniels had also alienated many naval officers. He was an ardent exponent of democracy and refused to recognize the difference in kind between officers and enlisted men. Nor did he feel that naval officers were necessarily more intelligent than civilians, and he tended to seek advice from the latter rather than the former. As a strict prohibitionist, he compounded his other offenses against naval tradition by barring alcoholic beverages from ships, naval yards, and stations.[6]

There is no reason to suspect that Churchill's investigations had any connection with the machinations of Colonel House and Mrs. Wilson. Nor is there much likelihood that he realized the deep affection which the President had for his Secretary of the Navy and how upset and irritated Wilson had become about the myriad criticisms of Daniels. Certainly Churchill's connections and his friendship with many of the naval officers, along with his own training, inclined him toward the anti-Daniels camp.

The man who brought Churchill into the matter was Franklin D. Roosevelt, the Assistant Secretary of the Navy. As soon as the United States entered the war, Churchill offered his services to the Bureau of Naval Intelligence and to Roosevelt. The tone of the letters and the fact that he wrote to Roosevelt rather than to Daniels, indicates that the two men had met. They were not, however, well-acquainted; and Senator Hollis wrote a strong letter urging Roosevelt to bring Churchill (whom he describes as "of the caliber of which Cabinet Ministers are made") to Washington. Roosevelt's initial reaction was to have Churchill work with George Creel's Committee on Public Information to popularize the war and explain its meaning. More specifically, he would be the exponent of the American Navy, because, Roosevelt wrote, "you can do more real good along this line than anybody else in the country."[7]

By the time Churchill arrived in the Capitol, Roosevelt had additional plans for him. The energetic Assistant Secretary had become extremely irritated by the dilatory manner in which Daniels was preparing the navy to fight a war. He was anxious to present his more ambitious ideas and plans to Wilson, but it was impossible for him to do this himself without bringing about his dismissal for insubordination. The solution appeared in the person of Winston Churchill. While the author did the research and conducted the interviews for his articles selling the navy to the people, he could also collect concrete data that would prove Daniels was not doing his job.[8]

By the fifth of June, Churchill was in the middle of this hassle. That day he met with the Board of Naval Strategy, where he learned that the English situation was more critical than the public had been led to believe and that the fate of England depended upon the ability of the American navy to increase England's food supply within the next few months. He also learned that Admiral Fletcher had urged Daniels in February to call in all destroyers and get them in shape and that this advice had been ignored. There is some indication that by the end of June, Daniels knew what was in the wind and that the novelist was a party to it. Churchill records that the Secretary sent for him "and wanted to put me on a Board to investigate the seamen's moral conditions in the training camps. I respectfully declined." This may have been a genuine offer (Daniels later issued an order barring houses of prostitution within five miles of a naval installation), but it may also have been an attempt to get rid of an annoying gadfly.[9]

By the third week in July Churchill had boiled down the myriad criticisms of Daniels and was ready to confront Wilson with his report. Churchill doubted that he could get the Secretary to change his ideas; all he could do was submit a plan for a reorganization of the department along the lines suggested by the officers with whom he had consulted. Also he was aware that Wilson would not dismiss the Secretary and that any changes would have to come about through Daniels.[10]

A long draft — highly critical of Daniels — was boiled down to a six-page report which Churchill presented to Wilson. On July 19 Wilson wrote, "Of course, I shall be glad to receive your memorandum and am glad that you have prepared it. I would be pleased to see you next Wednesday, the twenty-fifth, at half-past two, at the White House."[11] According to the story that Churchill told in later years, when he arrived at the White House, he and Wilson went for a long drive — during which they talked of everything except the Navy — and that was the end of the matter. Nonetheless, there must have been some discussion because just after Churchill left Washington, Wilson wrote, "I took up the matters about which we talked the other day with the head of the department and think I have things in course to carry out the essential purpose you had in mind." And the day after Churchill met with Wilson, Roosevelt reported that he had lunched with Churchill, who had seen the President the previous day "and apparently had a pretty satisfactory talk."[12]

Surprisingly, Churchill's work seems to have brought about some changes. Roosevelt noted, "The more I think over the talk with the President, the more I am encouraged to think that he has begun to catch on, but then it will take lots more of the Churchill type of attack."[13] Younger men were called in for consultation, decisions were speeded up, and the campaign against the submarine was made much more aggressive. Churchill had served Roosevelt well, and by that fall the younger man's criticisms of his superior subsided.

Meanwhile Churchill was trying to maintain the difficult position of stirring an admittedly apathetic public to greater effort without appearing to endorse Wilson's administration. This he explained to Bob Bass in reply to a request that he write a letter to the President supporting a New Hampshire man for a government appointment.

> My situation is a little peculiar. I will willingly put my name to an endorsement of Beaton, but I feel that I cannot write a personal letter to the President because I do not want to be under any obligation to this present Government. I am writing articles trying to stir up patriotism and an interest in the Navy, and between ourselves I think they would be glad to have me endorse the Administration, and back up their conduct of the war. I am not prepared to do this, nor am I prepared to oppose it. I feel that I must keep myself free.[14]

The six articles he wrote were syndicated and published in newspapers around the country during the last two weeks in June. The titles are indicative of the content: "A Call for the Marine Corps," "Midshipman Churchill O. K.'s the Navy," "America Must Trap 'Sea Rats' to Curb Victorious Germany," "Destiny of Britain and America Closely Linked," "Winston Churchill Admires the Admiral," and "Winston Churchill Salutes the Navy Gunner."

His work for the war effort was not the only thing that kept the novelist away from Cornish the summer of 1917. His datebook leaves no doubt that he intended to divorce his wife and marry another woman.[15] Churchill had indulged in affairs before 1917, but these did not cause an open break in the family. The evidence indicates that he and Mrs. Churchill had strong feelings for each other and that they got along as well as most married couples. Nonetheless, one reason Churchill remained in Washington during the summer of 1917 was that he was estranged from his wife; by July she knew that he was having an affair and that he wanted a divorce. He went to Europe in 1917 not only to visit the warfront, but also because he expected this woman to meet him there.[16] Some of their acquaintances thought that Mrs. Churchill refused to give her husband a divorce because such things were not done by proper people, but this is not true. Churchill had always considered Mabel to be a prime example of what the writers of the time liked to call an "emancipated woman," one who thought for herself and was not bound by the shackles of Victorian morality. Probably he was right. Letters which have recently come to light show that she viewed his affair as a temporary aberration which would pass away. She conceded that he had done everything in his power to make the marriage a success and that she herself might not have done all that she could. But, if he ever wanted to come back, if he ever needed her, she was willing to try again. If after a period of separation he still loved the other woman, he could go to her; if not, he could return to his family.[17]

Under this obvious emotional strain, Churchill sailed for Europe aboard the *Chicago* on August 28, 1917. He was accompanied by his young friend and protegé, Brooks Henderson, a Princeton Ph.D. for whom the novelist had secured a position with the Macmillan Company. By September 6 they were off the coast of Spain and three days later were safely established in Paris, where Churchill wrote a long and beautifully detailed description of the scenery on the trip. During his two weeks in Paris he had many conversations with Admiral Sims, who was married to Churchill's cousin. By late September he was in London, lunching with the Lloyd Georges, Winston Spencer Churchill, and Sir Edward Carson at Number Ten, Downing Street. During his stay he also lunched or dined with Sir James Barrie, H. G. Wells, John Galsworthy, British Admiral Sir Lewis Bayly, the famous doctor Sir William Osler, and General Jan Smuts, the author of the mandate system; he stayed for a week with the Waldorf Astors at Cliveden and was invited by General Pershing to visit the American training camp.[18] At the invitation of the British government he paid a five-day visit to the British front in France, then spent a few days in Paris before returning to London for a short stay with Wells.

Suffering from ill-health and emotional exhaustion, Churchill returned to the United States in November and began revising the hodgepodge of ideas and accounts which he had put together for *Scribner's*. From December of 1917 through April of the following year he was in New York under a physician's care, but he managed to keep working on the revision and finished an additional essay when he returned to Cornish in May.[19] *A Traveller in War-time With an Essay on the American Contribution and the Demo-*

cratic Idea, a collection of these articles, appeared in July of that year. In this book Churchill combines his concern for contemporary social problems with an attempt to demonstrate the uniqueness of World War I. While he is not uncritical of some aspects of the American social and economic order, the book could be classified as war propaganda.

The travel accounts embrace two major themes — his observations about the condition of the participants in the conflict and comments on the influence of the war. Given the bloody nature of the trench-type warfare that was going on, his comments have an unrealistic sound. His picture of England underestimates the suffering that was taking place there, and his comments about the American troops in France say more about his own idealistic interpretation of the war than about the actual conditions. "It is a curious commentary on this war that one does not think of these young men as soldiers but as citizens engaged in a scientific undertaking of a magnitude unprecedented," he says. And these scientific soldiers "are cared for as no enlisted men have ever been cared for before."[20]

Churchill's most interesting observation on the conduct of the war came with his first sight of the weapon which would make the trench-type warfare of World War I obsolete — the tank. "After some two hours of progress," he writes, "we came . . . to an expanse where many monsters were clumsily cavorting like dinosaurs in primeval slime."[21] He climbed into one of these monsters, and his description of the ride over the trenches is quite humorous but at the same time conveys his sense of horror at the possibilities of mechanized warfare.

Despite his overly rosy description of Allied morale and the conditions of the enlisted man, he was quite aware that "from a military point of view the situation of the Allies at the present writing is far from reassuring." He felt that Americans had not fully measured the magnitude of the task facing them, and he speculated on the possibility that George M. Cohan's bombastic "Send the Word" (which he admitted thrilled him) might be the prelude to tragedy. "We have always been so successful, we Americans. Are we to fail now? I am an American, and I do not believe we are to fail. but I am soberer, somehow a different American than he who sailed away in August."[22]

Churchill's idealistic approach to the war is demonstrated in his comments on its beneficial side effect. On the boat to Europe he saw that all the passengers, in one way or another, had enlisted in the war effort. "Many elements which in a former stratified existence would never have been brought into contact were fusing by the pressure of a purpose . . . . " This was particularly evident among the women of the Red Cross, of whom he remarked that "no sharper proof of the failure of the old social order to provide for human instincts and needs could be found than the conviction they gave of new and vitalizing forces released in them." At last they had something real and useful to do. "Be useful! There she struck the new and aggressive note of emancipation from the restricted self-sacrifice of the old order, of wider service for the unnamed and the unknown; and, above all, for the wider self-realization of which service is but a by-product."[23]

But he went further than this. Not only was the war providing the means for personal integration, it was also opening the way for the spiritualization of the whole of society. The great events of the war were taking place not on the battle lines but behind them. A social revolution was in progress, most particularly in Russia, noticeably in most European countries, and even in his own nation, which had "now become the most conservative in the world!" The only question in his mind was whether this social revolution would lead to unguided anarchy or would be taken over by wise leaders who understood the evolutionary trend. The emphasis upon the necessity for leadership which was characteristic of his fictional writing permeates these essays.

He continued to emphasize the strong ties between England and the United States. The novelist was impressed by the moves England had made toward social justice and by David Lloyd George. Churchill spoke frequently and favorably of the changing order in England, though he wondered still what would happen to the tradition of dignity and leadership which the aristocracy had maintained.

The most important part of the book is the long *Essay on the American Contribution and the Democratic Idea*, which concludes the period of Churchill's optimism and involvement with social reform. In many ways that essay can stand as a symbol, perhaps a monument, to the most hopeful aspects of the Progressive

movement, the swan song of the world that had already disintegrated but was as yet unaware of the fact. To many it looked as
though Western Civilization had passed through its moment of
trial, its battle against itself, and was on the road to ever-better
tomorrows. In this essay Churchill undertook to analyze America's
contributions (past, present, and future) toward the accomplishment of this dream.

The essay begins with an assessment of the American character and the American past. The two greatest interpreters of the
American character, he suggests, were Ralph Waldo Emerson and
William James, who saw that theirs was a nation of idealists, not
of money-grubbers. This had been true in the past, and in 1918
"our inherent characteristic today is a belief in the virtue of ideas,
of a national, indeed, of a universal mission."[25] Churchill admits
that Americans had not always lived up to their beliefs, that in
the past they had yielded to the temptation of imperialistic ventures. A change began, however, with the Spanish-American War
which, he suggests, was fought (at least in part) for an idea, and
this change was exemplified in what he considered to be Wilson's
enlightened policy toward Mexico. Following the arguments of
J. A. Hobson, the British analyst of imperialism, Churchill contends that the opponents of enlightened policies in Mexico and
elsewhere were the commercial classes, which had obtained
profitable investments for their surplus capital from the dictators
of under-developed nations. When these dictatorships bred almost
inevitable revolutions, the capitalists appealed to their own governments to send in troops to protect their property. This imperialistic method "reacts so powerfully on the growth of democracy
at home — and hence on the growth of democracy throughout
the world — as to threaten the very future of civilization."[26]
The essay offers no solutions. Its point is simply to show that
imperialism is the heritage of a misguided past, and that this im-
perialist outlook was being altered by Wilson. In this example as
elsewhere in the essay, Churchill quite objectively assessed American failings in the past, adventures that were frequently carried
out in the name of some ideal, but he failed to perceive that the
current situation might fall into the same pattern. That World
War I might not save the world for democracy does not seem to
have occurred to him.

Consequently, his interpretation of the reason the United States entered the war is distorted. He admits that the war initially appeared to be a typical example of the European balance of power struggle. Dedicated to peace, Americans endured the taunts and insults of Germany as long as it appeared that world peace might best be brought about by our neutrality. Only when it became clear that this could become a war to advance democracy and bring an end to the evil of war itself did America enter into the struggle. "We war only in behalf of, or in defense of, democracy."[27]

Churchill viewed the war in Europe and the Progressive movement at home as two parts of a whole. In a contracting world the point had been reached where democracy's "very existence in every country was threatened, not only by the partisans of reaction from within, but by the menace from without of a militaristic and imperialistic nation determined to crush it . . . . " America entered the war to protect democracy at home and to advance it around the world by defeating Germany and establishing a league of nations which would replace imperialistic exploitation with the democratic principle of self-determination. Implicit in this world crusade was the assumption that "our own household must be swept and cleaned. The injustices and inequalities existing in our own country, the false standards of worth, the materialism, the luxury and waste must be purged from our midst."[28]

Churchill juxtaposed these views about American entrance into the war with some comments on how it might end following the same general lines proposed by Wilson. The German people should not be crushed but should be made to "come to their senses as to the true meaning of the war and their misfortunes," so that they would rise up and take charge of their government. The conquered nations should be restored on the principle of self-determination, and the smaller nations should recover indemnities "as a matter of justice."[29]

Churchill felt that the transcendent issue of the war and of the times was industrial democracy. Just as the French and American revolutions had been struggles for political freedom, so World War I had as its underlying issue economic freedom. "Unless, as the fruit of this appalling bloodshed and suffering, the democracies achieve economic freedom, the war will have been fought in vain." He recognized that there were some conservatives who still insisted that human nature could not be changed from its egotistic paths and that the survival of the fittest was the law of life, but he felt they were a dying breed. Fortunately, he contends, "that element of our population which may be designated as domestic Junkers is capable of being influenced by contemporary currents of thought, is awakening to the realization of social conditions deplorable and dangerous." [30]

Social evil, Churchill contended, was a result of the inability of obsolete economic theories to digest industrialization.

> In America we succeeded in eliminating hereditary power, in obtaining a large measure of political liberty, only to see the rise of an economic power, and the consequent loss of economic liberty. The industrial development of the United States was of course a necessary and desirable thing, but the economic doctrine which formed the basis of American institutions proved to be unsuited to industrialism, and introduced unforeseen evils that were a serious menace to the Republic. An individualistic economic philosophy worked admirably while there was ample land for the pioneer, equality of opportunity to satisfy the individual initiative of the enterprising. But what is known as industrialism brought in its train fear and favour, privilege and poverty, slums, disease, and municipal vice, fostered a too rapid immigration, established in America a tenant system alien to our traditions. [31]

Industrialism also brought with it a division of the American people into laborers and capitalists that resulted in a class conflict that was repugnant to democracy, "which by its very nature depends for its existence on the elimination of the classes." [32]

As can be surmised from the above, Churchill shared his contemporaries' suspicions about the so-called New Immigration from Southern and Eastern Europe. This suspicion is implicit in his handling of the strikers in *The Dwelling Place of Light* and is made explicit in this essay in which he states that "owing to the unprecedented immigration of ignorant Europeans to supply the labour demand, we acquired a sinister proletariat of unskilled economic slaves." This mass migration of unlettered Europeans offended the Anglo-Saxon prejudices of a large percentage of

Churchill's generation, and they attributed to this group many of the evils of the industrial cities.

Almost as large a percentage of that generation were equally uneasy about the labor movement. Although Churchill recognized that most of the unskilled workers were outside of the organized unions, he did feel that labor as a whole had discovered its strength, and he harbored a fear (widely shared both here and abroad) that labor might use its strength to halt the war effort.

To bring about his economic democracy, a new political party was an absolute necessity. Wilson, Churchill felt, had a vision of the new world, but "so far as any party is concerned, Mr. Wilson stands alone." In fact, both the Republicans and the Democrats had offered only token reforms and neither of them truly represented the great issues of the day. The "cleavage between them is wholly artificial." The Socialist Party in the United States was not the answer because it was "relatively small, is divided against itself, and has given no evidence of a leadership of broad sanity and vision." The only answer was the formation of a Liberal Party made up not simply of manual laborers (which would tend to further economic class consciousness) but of all elements of the population. "This would be a distinctly American solution."[33]

His emphasis in this book was more on the positive role of the government and less on the cooperative Christian commonwealth than had been true in his pre-war writings, but the role of religion was still important. The problem as he saw it was that for almost two thousand years orthodox Christianity had ignored the social principles of Jesus' teachings, which "would seem to be the kernel from which has sprung modern democracy, modern science, and modern religion — a trinity and a unity." In the past, these teachings had been regarded (with some justification) as impractical, but in 1917 they were no longer so.

> Physical science, by enormously accelerating the means of transportation and communication, has so contracted the world as to bring into communion peoples and races hitherto far apart; has made possible an intelligent organization of industry which, for the first time in history, can create a surplus ample to maintain in comfort the world's population. But this demands the will to co-operate, which

> is a Christian principle — a recognition of the brother-
> hood of man.[34]

The problem for the social scientist, then, was to organize
society on the ideals of Christianity. But, if commercial competition disappeared, what would be the spur to individual creativity
and productivity in the new society? In the past it had been taken
for granted that "competition of some sort is necessary for self-
realization."

> The answer is that in the theory of democracy, as
> well as in that of Christianity, individualism and co-
> operation are paradoxically blended. For competi-
> tion, Christianity substitutes emulation. And with
> democracy, it declares that mankind can gradually be
> raised towards the level of the choice individual who
> does not labour for gain, but in behalf of society.[35]

None of this is well explained, and his example of the medical profession, in which "the doctor who uses his talents for gain is
frowned upon by those of his fellow practitioners whose opinion
really counts," is unconvincing.

The key to the new society is universal education. "Universal
education is the cornerstone of democracy. And the recognition
of this fact may be called the great American contribution." In a
materialistic, competitive social order, Churchill wrote, one's
success in life depends upon the ability to outwit one's neighbors;
in an "emulative" society, on the other hand, educators will attempt to discover each child's particular aptitude so that the individual may achieve self-realization by using this talent for the
advancement of society. The old system of education failed to
achieve these things because "it inculcates in the future citizen
convictions rather than encourages the habit of openmindedness
so necessary for democratic citizenship." The new system (for
which Churchill gives John Dewey almost complete credit) unites
the search for and cherishing of individual differences, while at
the same time it encourages social cooperation. Each citizen "will
have his choice of the task he is to perform for society, his opportunity for self-realization. For freedom without education is a
myth."[36] Thus education is the key to bringing about the new
emulative social order without coercion and without sacrificing
the individualism of the American tradition. Churchill pointed

out a way — or thought he did — in which the traditional values of an agrarian past could continue to exist in an industrial world.

He strikes one note of caution when he says that the new system of education is experimental and its adoption will be gradual. But this is not a serious problem, for Americans "have arrived at that stage of enlightenment when we realize that the only mundane perfection lies in progress rather than achievement. The millennium is always a lap ahead." But this warning is somewhat out of harmony with the general tone of the book. Much more characteristic is his statement that the war with Germany has "provided the occasion for the socializing of America also; and thus brought about, within a year, a national transformation which in times of peace might scarce in half a century have been accomplished." [37] Nor was this socialization simply a national phenomenon; the emergency created by the war brought home the lesson that international cooperation is superior to international competition. He cites Sydney Webb's contention that following the war a world shortage of food and raw materials would make the free play of economic forces in the old sense an act of international suicide. Nations will realize this; tariffs will become a thing of the past, and international trade will operate on the principle of priority of need rather than on the old law of supply and demand. He concludes:

> We are attempting to turn calamity into good. If this terrible conflict shall result in the inauguration of an emulative society, if it shall bring us the recognition that intelligence and science may be used for the upbuilding of such an order, and for an eventual achievement of world peace, every sacrifice shall have been justified.[38]

The book was an optimistic prediction for the future, but it was also an indictment of American society and of the capitalistic system. It is impossible to read the book without seeing this. For that reason it seems strange that the reviews were so favorable, especially of the essay in which the criticism of the competitive order is most open. Nonetheless, most of the reviews agreed with the *New York Times* that "Mr. Churchill has written a chapter in the history of American thought, and one to be considered faithfully by all true Americans." [39] Perhaps the war had, as Churchill insisted, altered the thinking of many Americans about the virtues of capitalistic competition — a temporary alteration, but one which they would recall and refurbish in the dark days after the fall of 1929.

CHAPTER XIX

A Journey to Hell and Heaven

It seems paradoxical that during the same months when Churchill was writing the optimistic *Essay on the American Contribution*, he was going through a period of extreme anxiety. His troubled personal relationships, along with the pressure of work at a time when his income was reduced by his voluntary participation in the war effort, put a tremendous strain on him. *The Dwelling Place of Light* did not achieve the sustained sale of the earlier novels, and at the usual rate of payment his account with Macmillan soon would be depleted. Consequently, despite the fact that he was suffering from what he referred to as a nervous breakdown, he continued his labors on *A Traveler in War-time*.[1]

It was May of 1918 before Churchill was well enough to leave his New York doctors and join his family in New Hampshire. There he completed the work for *A Traveller in War-time,* but this did little to bolster his financial situation. Published in July, the book sold slightly under eight thousand copies. A second syndication of the travel section of the book was offered to American

235

newspapers; thirteen carried all or part of it with a total profit to the author of $138.60.[2]

The economic failure of *A Traveller in War-time* increased the pressure on the ailing author, and he immediately began to work on a new novel. By July the novel was blocked out, and he felt he would be able to write it quickly, but other events intervened. Despite the incredible difficulties he had encountered in his attempts to dramatize his own novels, Churchill had never given up the idea that he was a dramatist at heart. *Dr. Jonathan,* the three-act play which he wrote at this time, was his last attempt to deal with the meaning of World War I. The play was never staged, but Brett did publish it in October of 1919 and it sold about sixteen hundred copies.

The message of the play is a simple one. "The issue of this war is industrial democracy, without which political democracy is a farce."[3] The position which Churchill takes in this play is actually more radical than any he had taken before, but this probably made little impression upon those who read it since he never reveals what "industrial democracy" means. During the course of three acts a hard-shelled reactionary acknowledges that he is an anachronism in the modern world and he turns over the management of his plant to his son. The youth, who learned his lesson in the trenches of France (after some coaching by the saintly title character), intends to experiment with industrial democracy in the family plants of his small New England town. He unfortunately does not know what the term means either, but he and the leaders of the newly recognized union agree to seek a solution together.

In the play Churchill indicates that in 1918 the alternative was no longer between laissez-faire capitalism and government intervention; it was between total anarchy (again represented by the IWW) and complete cooperation. The capitalists had been wrong in trying to exclude unions from a measure of control; the unions had been wrong in excluding all but members (especially the unskilled) from benefits which they gained. Nor did either labor or management have any plan for fulfilling the promise of the war. The IWW did. In short, Churchill said (for about the only time in his life): I don't know what the solution is; I don't know how industrial democracy can be brought about, but labor and management had better get together and find the solution before it is too late. The forces of freedom had been unleashed by the war. If the laboring classes were not made an integral part of the new world (and he meant by this the amenities of life — education, leisure, culture — as well as a higher standard of living and a share in the decision-making process), world revolution would result. The role of government in the achievement of this cooperative society, a role which had occupied much of Churchill's attention in his books is ignored in the play. Religion, in its noninstitutional form, plays a definite role.

The reviews of the book version of the play usually criticized its technical weaknesses as a drama but were surprisingly enthusiastic about the content. The politically moderate Springfield *Republican* said, "As an exposition of the labor situation and as a plea for industrial democracy the play presents its case in an extremely readable manner." The liberal *Nation* felt that it was not a particularly good play but that it was "a heartening contrast to the insufferable claptrap with which our theatres have resounded." On the left of center, the New York *Call* said, "*Dr. Jonathan* has technical weaknesses and literary lapses. But all these shortcomings are insignificant in the face of the powerful dramatic purpose of the author, his social analysis of modern industrial and political problems, and his wholesome humanity."[4]

The reviewer for the *Nation* felt that the play would not be produced, because of its liberal political and economic position. In the context of the times — the growing disillusionment with Wilson's world crusade, the unrest in the labor movement, and the ruthless suppression of all forms of domestic radicalism — he was probably correct. The dramatic weaknesses were another reason, and beyond this was a third. The heroine of the play, at least by every implication, had indulged in several affairs — including one with the hero. The same agent who was trying to find a producer for the play was handling the movie rights for *The Dwelling Place of Light*, and he made it quite clear that before the novel could be made into a movie it would have to be censored. In particular, the actual adultery between Janet and Ditmar would have to be omitted. It is doubtful that the commercial theater of the day would have been any more receptive to a heroine who was a "fallen woman" than the motion picture people were. This situation was completely changed in the early 1920's, but by then Churchill was no longer interested in producing the play.[5]

Brett, meanwhile, was desperately hoping that the Washington, D. C. novel would be finished quickly. Churchill had completed most of the research for the novel while he was in Washington during the summer of 1917, and when he finished *Dr. Jonathan* in the early summer of 1918 he turned his attention to the new novel, hoping to have it ready for spring publication. The Churchills spent the summer and the fall in Cornish. Then in December they took up residence in Boca Grande, Florida. They had a little cottage there, facing the Gulf of Mexico, and both enjoyed it. The novelist reported that he was getting his strength back and was able to work well there, but about the middle of April he returned to New York for further medical care and remained there until sometime in June.[6] Shortly thereafter an event occurred which was to change his life drastically and which would lead him into a kind of retirement.

Since it is unusual for a successful novelist to retire at the age of forty-eight, it seems curious that the scholars who have concerned themselves with Churchill's seemingly abrupt departure from the literary scene in 1919 have not been more skeptical about the reasons for his actions. The explanations usually offered emphasize that his popularity was declining, in part because of the changing nature of literary styles. Unable or unwilling to follow the change in style, disillusioned by the apparent end of the Progressive movement and by the results of the war, hampered by illness, robbed of his middle-class audience by the "normalcy" of the 1920's, Churchill is presumed to have surrendered his position of prestige and power for a quiet life in the New Hampshire hills. Actually Churchill continued work on his novel until 1921 and he did not stop writing until his heart stopped beating some twenty-five years later. The reasons for his change in genre were not social but were intensely personal. The changing literary styles, the decline of Progressivism, the war, even the "normalcy" of the 1920's had little to do with his actions and decisions.

What happened was that Winston Churchill lived two lives. One life ended around 1918. Up to that time he was a happy and successful American, intimately bound up in all the problems of his day. That Winston Churchill died by his own hand and was

resurrected three years later to live for another twenty-five years
as a happy and contented human being whose interests transcend-
ed those of his own day.

   This dramatic transformation is revealed in the two documents mentioned in Chapter One — the Gideon manuscript written in the early 1920's and the Jonathan manuscript of some ten
years later. They are the confessions of a man born again, and the
comments about his life before his rebirth are scathingly critical.
Churchill had many critics, but none who attacked him with the
fury which he turned on himself. As a description of his travail
in the summer of 1919 and subsequent years the manuscripts are
invaluable documents; as an assessment of the years before 1919
they tend to be undependable and distorted. The ideas and events
related in the manuscripts agree on most of the essential points,
and they are substantiated by the letters and notes which Churchill wrote at the time. Consequently, to avoid the confusion of
the double pseudonymn, the following account is based on the
Jonathan manuscript.[7] The content of his new faith, which con-
stitutes the bulk of the manuscript, will not be discussed at this
point, but some of the discussion of his earlier life has been retained in order to clarify Churchill's state of mind at the time
these events occurred. It should also be noted that from the late
fall of 1918 until about 1921 Churchill suffered from a transient
encephalitis which may have heightened the intensity of his religious experience. Nonetheless, much of what follows sounds like
a case study for William James' *Varieties of Religious Experience*
and is reminiscent of the conversion of Saul of Tarsus, with whom
Churchill, in the early phase of his new life, associated himself.

   The manuscript, narrated by one Jonathan, was not intended
for publication and is a series of notes, not a unified essay. In it
Jonathan explains that up until 1919 he had been one of the
world's great sinners. Not only had he violated the sexual mores
of society, he had even tried to abandon his wife and children. He
had been a social snob, a man without the courage of his convictions, and an artistic failure who had written imitative novels.
Finally his family and friends found out about his double life, and
he stood exposed before them as a sinner. But what impressed him
was that his friends urged him to change his mode of life for
temporal reasons — for his worldly reputation — not because he

had offended God or faced eternal damnation. Further, he saw
that the great sinners of the past, if they had been successful and
charming, were perfectly respectable in later years. Even the "buccaneers" of his own day had achieved respectability. He would,
therefore,

> write a book about a typical buccaneer of today, a
> Richard Lawless, and it would not be very dif-
> ficult to project himself as the hero. He had not
> indeed been a financial magnate, but he had made
> a lot of money out of his books and done a lot of
> swash-buckling, lorded it with a high hand, driven a
> coach and four over the people who got in his way,
> taken the women he wanted. This does not sound
> like the Puritan we have represented one side of him
> to be, but he was a complicated character, and we
> are engaged in unravelling him.

Jonathan saw that his great mistake had been to call attention to
his misdeeds. He had wanted to leave his wife and children for
another woman and had been completely open about it. The
world may wink at sin so long as it is kept quiet, but when he
disturbed the peace his friends acted vigorously to make him stay
with his family. Success in this world, then, Jonathan concluded,
has nothing to do with true virtue. Since there is no penalty for
sin if the sinner refuses to be crushed, there is no reason to obey
the law. It is failure that is punished, not sin.

It was in this state of mind that Churchill began work on his
next book. It was to be, he said, "the history of one Barnabas
Tyce, familiarly called Barney, a modern buccaneer. He intended
to show that nothing happened to the unrighteous provided they
were strong enough, and intelligent enough, and charming."
Barney was the product of a middlewestern farming community.
He avoided work, played hookey from school, and generally went
his own way; the whole community assumed he would end up in
the penitentiary. Instead he became a business tycoon and a
United States Senator who returned to his small community to
dedicate a library which he had donated to the town. His old
minister had told Barney he surely would go to hell, but the new
minister accepted a check for rebuilding his church and called
Barney a benefactor of mankind. Barney's brother, an industrious,
responsible man, had remained on the farm like a dutiful son,

struggling with mortgages until the renegade Barney finally paid them off. Again the evil flourished like the green bay tree and the righteous struggled in vain. This was to be the message of the novel.

The novel was conceived before Churchill went through his religious experience; it reflected his mood of the moment just as the other novels, in spite of his denials, fitted in with his feelings and convictions at the time of their composition. To write a novel openly stating that evil will flourish, he found a refreshing idea, although it was not likely to please his friends among the "good people." Too many Barneys would threaten their social order. "This fear of a social cataclysm, of the weakening and breaking down of law and order as the respect for law weakens, is what grips us all if we have any stake in that society." This fear of social disintegration had motivated the Pharisees throughout history; they had used the threat of eternal damnation to preserve the social stability which enabled them to maintain their position in this world. Chruchill admits that too many Barneys would upset the system, but his concern here was the consequences for the individual. And if audacity triumphs in this world and there is no hereafter, the consequences for the immoral buccaneer as an individual would seem to be non-existent.

But if Churchill managed to suspend moral judgment during the first period of work, and this was his belief in later years — that condemnation of anything is worldly and wrong — he could not rid himself completely of value judgments as he wrote the Jonathan manuscript in the early 1930's. Witness this description of the "buccaneers" who were to provide the fodder for his mount in this novel.

> So he started to write The Green Bay Tree. First he got all his material together from the lives and doings of the financial magnates who were playing marbles for keeps with the railroads, with the light and heat and bread and clothing which humanity used. There was plenty of material about the big boys who were playing this game, written by people who stood on the sidewalks and watched the big boys quarreling and fighting over points, and having such an uproarious time; and indeed, if the truth be told, envying the players, who were the rulers of the world. On the results of these marble games depended how

> much the spectators would have to pay for their
> railroad tickets and food and clothing and electri-
> city and oil. Here was Power spelled with a capital,
> something to make life worth living. Jonathan very
> much envied it himself.

And so Jonathan — sinner and disillusioned moralist — set
out to tell the world of his new philosophy. He began work on
this novel as he had on all those popular best-sellers in the past.
No thought of retirement entered his mind; he was doing the job
he had chosen for himself over twenty years before. A series of
events had altered his view of life but not his desire to express his
views honestly to the world.

Then came the fateful summer of 1919. Perhaps there are no
abrupt changes in the course of a man's life; certainly one can look
back and see elements of his new thought in Churchill's earlier
musings about the course of human events. Nonetheless, the
events of the summer and fall of 1919 form as sharp a turning
point in his life as one is likely to encounter in the life of any man.
The events themselves are related here as Churchill described
them. Whether they actually happened in that way or were simply
hallucinations is perhaps not so important as the effect which
they had upon his life and thought.

In July, Jonathan went from his home to spend a month in
"a place by the sea." It was a place he enjoyed, filled with the
best kind of "Modern Pharisees," one of whom had been a childhood friend. This man, whom he calls Reginald Allerdyce, offered
him a little house on the edge of the ocean. Although Jonathan
was uneasy at the thought of associating with these highly respectable people now that his own life had been exposed, they
received him as if nothing had happened. "So he glided back very
easily into the life he liked and had been long accustomed to. If
these people did not condemn him, his thesis was established. He
worked at making a beginning of The Green Bay Tree."

He was troubled, however, by some unusual events that had
happened the previous spring, when he had visited a medium in
New York. Jonathan did not believe in such things; but he went to
see the show and discovered to his amazement that he was "at
once in direct communion with one who had died some eight
years before, a woman he had loved more than any woman he had

ever known. Her name is Sarah. He had lost her, for he was married, and she could not stay with him." Now his love for her revived, and he felt nearer to her than ever before. Sarah understood his weaknesses and told him that if he could be true to her now, he would be saved.

Sarah had been an artist, as well as a beautiful woman and a member of genteel society. She had tried to live the life of an artist, but social pressure proved so great that "she became discouraged and perplexed and made a conventional marriage, and then died." Now she had returned to him in spirit, and Jonathan left the medium's house "emotionally convinced of a life beyond the grave." He turned to spiritualism and tried to communicate with Sarah through automatic writings, but without success; in a month or two the spell wore off.

When he went to the little house by the sea he entered the gay life around him. He worked on "The Green Bay Tree" but was not pleased with what he wrote. Then a series of bizarre events began to take place. One night Jonathan was awakened by the sound of music such as he had never heard before. It was the sound of the tide, "but the voices of angels were singing with it, and in it." Two or three mornings later as Jonathan sat at his desk trying to write about Barney, his hand was seized and he wrote the words, "Be yourself, and let your real self express itself." A day or so later Sarah came to him again and led him to the woods, where he sat down under the spruces and began to write. The words flowed smoothly and rhythmically from his pen in a way they had not done since he had abandoned his natural style early in his career to imitate others.

Whatever the source of inspiration or cause of these happenings, the events themselves evidently did occur. There is in existence a sheaf of unassorted sheets in an envelope marked "odd writing in July and August, 1919."[8] Most of the material on these sheets is completely illegible; the part that can be read (much of which is dialogue between the novelist and the woman called Sarah) corroborates the experiences related in the Jonathan manuscript. There is also a notebook which contains typewritten notes dated July 18, 19, and 20, 1919, telling the same story. The following is from the first of these sheets.

Started my work after breakfast, the same feeling of
inhibition, as if my hand wished to write something
else, as on former occasions, but the impulse was not
strong enough, and when I let my hand go it merely
slid more or less aimlessly about the page or remained still with the sense of some force on it. On these
occasions the name, S— [the actual name and initial have been altered to correspond with the pseudonymn used in the Jonathan manuscript] seemed
indeed to come, the hand making repeated Ss . . . .

Today the impulse was stronger than ever, the
hand sliding over the page, and letters and words
coming into my mind. I tried to refrain from writing
these, but at last let my hand go and found I could
form these words easily, but when I tried to write
others it was difficult. And if I made a wrong start
on a word I got no result except inhibition. At last
came this: —

"Let your real self express itself."[9]

Churchill was by no means in a perpetual trance. At the time the
above was written he was at Islesboro, Maine, and he was writing
perfectly coherent letters to his wife and engaging in normal social
intercourse. He was also capable of handling business affairs. A
few days after writing the above passage, he had lunch with William Dana Gibson, who agreed to do the illustrations for "The
Green Bay Tree."[10]

Naturally he spoke to his friends about his conversion to
spiritualism and his new-found faith. In these early days of his new
life Jonathan felt that he had been chosen as the new Paul.

Jonathan thought, too, in those days, that his religion
would bring him back into the church, and that pres-
ently he would become a prophet, an apostle. An
apostle to the Philistines, even as Paul had been an
apostle to the Gentiles. For Jonathan still loved the
Philistines. They were the first people he invited to
his feast, his friends and his brethren, his kinsmen and
rich neighbors.

Churchill says that Jonathan at this point not only appeared to be
but was "crazy." He came to his friends as a prophet; he struck
them as simply disoriented. They remembered his recent past and
could not see how he could consider himself a religious man,
whereas Jonathan was apt to forget, "in the flush of his ecstacy at
discovering heaven, that he had ever done wrong."

The time came, after perhaps a month, when Jonathan had to leave his little house and go to Boston. He wanted to be alone, for he was bewildered and distracted; but in his hotel room he found his body in the power of the devils. These devils were the stern and righteous people, those who had sat at the trial of Anne Hutchinson and conducted the Salem witchcraft trials, those righteous men who had throughout the Christian era held inquisitions and tortured sinners in the name of God. They flung him to his knees by the bed, and the sins of his lifetime passed before him.

It was September when Jonathan went back to New York to see his doctor. After his stay there (during which time he was writing up to 5000 words a day) he went back to his family in the country. [11] He did not want to go back, for this was no longer home to him. Nonetheless, he felt he had to tell his wife and daughter about Sarah and something of his conversion. They did not believe in his visions, and he did not expect them to do so. In fact his treatment of the way in which his wife accepted the situation shows a continuing tenderness and an appreciation of what she had been through.

> Let us pay tribute to her courage and her strength and her generosity. She thought him deranged, yet perhaps she thought that this state was easier to bear than others she had been through, and less harmful. She was not a person who thought much about religion, and she cared nothing about churches. Nor had she need to. Her life had been one of straightforward dealings. She loved her children passionately, and she accepted this situation as she had accepted others. Jonathan did not realize then how tragic it was, and what added sorrow he brought on her, although he could not help knowing that he had made her suffer, and this troubled him indeed.

Since he no longer cared for the sports or social activities he had enjoyed in his former life, Jonathan spent most of his time at his writing desk or simply roaming through the hills. Again he set to work on "The Green Bay Tree," attempting this time "to show how Barney had been cut off in the midst of his wickedness and great power — by love." Although he was able to get whole sections of it down in language which he felt was strange and wonderful, he had trouble with the structure of the book. And the atmosphere in which family and friends denied the reality of his new-found happiness became more and more oppressive to Jonathan. He was fearful that he would lose his belief and return to the life he had known before. So he decided to run away. The place he chose was a little fishing village on the Massachusetts cape where Anthony Rindge, a close friend from early childhood, had a summer place. The Rindges were a highly conventional, straight-laced family, but they loved Jonathan. In addition to this tie, Anthony (who had died some months before) was the only spirit besides Sarah to whom Jonathan had spoken during the periods when he was in communication with the other world. He went with his secretary to an old hotel across the water from the Rindges, only to find that the crowded hotel did not appeal to him. So Jonathan left his secretary in the hotel and moved into a little cottage.

It was fortunate, Churchill wrote, that Jonathan got the little house by himself, for his actions became more and more peculiar. He carried on long conversations in which his lips moved involuntarily as he spoke with Sarah or Anthony, or sometimes with groups of people. Although the dark presences still came to torment him, they seemed powerless now and he no longer feared them. So many strange little incidents happened during those days that he came almost to accept them as natural. He was not able, however, to make much headway with his novel. Feeling energetic and strong, he wrote reams, but the manuscript took weird and strange directions. It grew even more voluminous, but the story moved forward at a snail's pace. This also is an ascertainable fact. The various manuscript versions run to several thousand pages. [12]

Jonathan frequently crossed the bay to dine with the Rindges, and his discussion of that family shows that Churchill had not lost his mugwump ideas and attitudes. The Rindges, he said, "are survivals. They are the flower of that American culture that never quite got to flower." Their ancestors had been leaders of men since colonial times, and although they were never really rich, they were never poor. They went to Yale, made the football teams, and grew up to be responsible professional people. "They regarded the modern America with well deserved contempt . . . . "

In his defamatory account of his own life, Jonathan compares his conduct to the model provided by the Rindges; he wants to see himself as their kind but feels he had not earned the honor.

> When, as a young man, he had suddenly made a great success as a writer, they were undoubtedly surprised, as all the people who had known Jonathan intimately were surprised . . . . Moreover, after Jonathan had made a success, he behaved like a fool and a spend-thrift and a snob, and lived in an ostentatious manner that the Rindges and his own blood relations deplored, and quite rightly deplored. He had deserted his own and their tradition. And then they knew his weakness for women — and this also was out of the tradition.

After about three weeks on the Cape, Jonathan decided to go home. He still felt estranged from his family but he was charged with power. He wrote, ate, and walked in a certain mystic rhythm. When out walking he consciously chose the direction, "but he apparently had to make no muscular exertion, or very little." Churchill says that he had never before thought about rhythm (which is not true) but that it now became his guide. Beginning by counting, he would sing chants and marches which came to him, giving him new vigor and dispelling unpleasant thoughts.

Again he was aware that these sensations could be dismissed as the symptoms of a disturbed mental state, but "if Jonathan did have a mental disorder, certain manifestations of it are to be highly desired in a condition of sanity. The rhythm in which he began to live gave existence a zest which he had not hitherto imagined, and seemed to him the very beat of the universe itself . . . . " He regained a taste for simple, everyday foods which he chewed in rhythm until they practically swallowed themselves. In eating (as in everything else) he had always, consciously or unconsciously, been in a hurry. His own wording of this carries with it a comment on eternity.

> Life on the former plane was anticipation, never life in the now. He was always going to have a good time, he rarely seemed to be having one now. And we see that life in this anticipatory state may truly be termed a temporal existence, as distinguished from a state in which the full flavor of the now is realized. For eternity is indeed the now, and not the future.

It was the rhythm which had given Jonathan the power to live for the moment, taking no thought of what the next might bring. He was in eternity.

"Whatever happened to Winston Churchill?" Americans asked in the years after World War I. The answer is clear. As late as 1915 he was still the progressive optimist, looking for the moral, economic, and social reforms that would bring about the new world. By 1917 he had lost confidence that the self-integration of the individual would lead to this new world. Then the entrance of the United States into the war rekindled his faith and enthusiasm. Once again it looked as if social cooperation would replace the old competitive order, not just in America but in the whole of western civilization. This widely shared belief was shattered for most people by the debacle of the peace, the resurgence of economic nationalism, and the "normalcy" of the 1920's. These factors seem to have left Churchill relatively untouched, although he was aware of them. In a brief manuscript written as addenda for *The Green Bay Tree*, Churchill made some very savage comments about how America had failed to live up to its Anglo-Saxon heritage and, with the rest of the world, was facing uncontrolled and undirected revolution. The following quotation shows what he thought of the world situation in October, 1919. He is speaking here of the laboring classes.

> These communisms, these socialisms, which are social only in greed, these wandering slaves who come here mildly aghast to fill the sewers of our cities with their babies and their women-concubines from the hovels of autocracy there, are kept, by thousands, in huge pens of steel and brick beside the belching furnaces in such places as Pittsburgh and Gary and Chicago-by-the lake. These men have taken the suggestions of their fellow-serfs across the sea when they left in search of better things, and now they are beating at the subliminal doors under our domed and white-columned capital of Washington; while our senators sit in their fool's paradise and squabble over the division of power of the kingdoms of the earth. When this happens, at a time like this, when a League of Nations is all but gone the way of the defunct kingdoms of the earth themselves, what shall be said

> of the greatness of a country that wished for a tradi-
> tional honour and probity, of truth and justice, and
> an aristocracy of purity in service before God? [13]

This disillusionment with the state of the world may have encouraged the novelist to withdraw from such a hopeless situation,
but his new attitudes and beliefs stemmed primarily from his personal experiences. He had gone to Europe, at least in part, because
he expected his new-found love to meet him there. When she did
not and his habitual good health deserted him, he entered upon a
very trying period of his life. While he fought to regain his health
he continued to write — first the optimistic *Traveller in War-Time,*
then the cynical version of "The Green Bay Tree." He would show
the world that power is the essential element in human life, not
morality.

Then came the strange series of events, beginning in the
spring of 1919 and continuing through that fall, when the novelist
underwent what he considered to be a religious experience. He became convinced that God had forgiven his sins and had shown him
the true path, a path that led to peace and contentment in this
life. Heaven and eternity were not in the future but were experienced by the individual as he walked through life. Churchill had
found his own "dwelling place of light," his own path to self-
realization.

With his new outlook he could no longer write a novel showing that wickedness goes unpunished. "The Green Bay Tree" had
to be rewritten in such a way that his modern buccaneer would
find truth, would turn from his sinful life to an awareness of a
higher power and the meaning of love. As always, he would write a
novel that set forth the way, the truth, and the light as he saw
them at that moment. His primary concern had always been with
the individual and, increasingly after about 1910, with the way in
which the individual could find happiness through self-integration.
This primary interest tended to be obscured during the period up
to and including the war because of his belief that the integrated
personality would devote his life to serving society. This belief
began to change with *The Dwelling Place of Light* where the
real, integrated individuals, while they did serve society in their
own way, remained essentially aloof from its battles. During
the war this transition was temporarily reversed, but immediately

thereafter went on its way again.

The ideas expressed in Churchill's writings after 1918 are not a radical departure. On the contrary, they are the culmination of a change begun as early as 1910 and clearly evident by 1916. The only path to true self-realization was to withdraw from the turmoil of society altogether, to stop trying either to maintain a position of social prestige or to reform society itself. It meant ultimately not even attempting to convince others of the truth.

CHAPTER XX

Ideas in Transition and an Unpublished Novel

Churchill's original conception of "The Green Bay Tree" corresponded to the suspicions of the Washington wags in 1917. This plan he presented to his publisher early in 1919.

> At present my idea is to call it The Capital. The scene opens and is largely laid in Washington, and has to do with the career, social and political, of a rich Senator and his wife and family from one of our corn belt states. The Senator's somewhat dramatic election takes place in 1894. He has made his money in oil, a fascinating, primitive, wilful man with a fascinating, primitive and wilful wife. I depict Washington society, the various political phases from Cleveland, Bryan, McKinley and Roosevelt, etc., and what happens to the children . . . . I want to get at the essence of what America was before the great war.[1]

Since the social milieu of the Capitol was to play a central role in the book, Churchill collected material with his usual thoroughness. The result is a fascinating collection of factual information about Washington in the years between 1890 and 1917. Churchill had made a habit of collecting pictures of actual houses and clothing from the periods in which his novels were to be set, and he did so with a vengeance for this book. In addition, he combed contemporary newspapers for actual topics of table talk at a given time,

251

speeches and debates in Congress; he collected reams of material on the history of the oil industry, popular songs, social events, and information about the historical figures who were in Washington. Along with these items, the notebooks contain some remarkably astute comments on politics and political issues. With the material he had at hand and the increasing depth of his understanding of American politics, this novel could have been a useful and illuminating social history of Washington.

Such was not to be. Instead of finishing the novel that eventful summer of 1919, he completely changed its character. His mystical experience and his growing obsession with personal salvation led his interest increasingly away from the social setting toward complete absorption with his hero's discovery of God. Curiously enough, Brett himself was an accessory in this. The publisher was unaware of what had happened to his novelist in the summer of 1919 and, although they had discussed the novel, Brett did not know the nature of the revisions Churchill was making in it. He did know and understand the interests of the novel-reading public, and he suggested that Churchill

> consider adding to the book, as a corollary interest,
> the general subject of spiritualism, perhaps through
> one of your characters — perhaps through the hero
> himself. The reading public for the last few months,
> yes, even for the last year or two, has been very great-
> ly interested in spiritualism, and the number of
> readers and the amount of interest in spiritualism
> has been increasing countrywide.[2]

Brett may have been right in his estimate of public interest in the subject; he usually was. And despite his later denials, Churchill did find quite a number of psychologists and laymen who were not only willing but eager to listen to his experiences and ideas. His letters to Mrs. Churchill in 1919 and 1920 contain a number of references to doctors and theologians who had read one of his manuscripts or listened to him tell about his experiences.[3] During those same months he was giving informal talks to some of the faculty at General Theological Seminary in New York, and a number of the theologians were sympathetic with his position. The novelist found another ally the winter of 1919-20 when the famous British scientist, Sir Oliver Lodge, came to New York to deliver a series of lectures on spiritualism. Churchill became acquainted with Lodge and his wife, found the latter particularly congenial, and undoubtedly took solace from the fact that one of the most respected scientists in the world believed in many of the same things he did.[4]

By the spring of 1920, Churchill's novel was 180,000 words in length and the end was nowhere in sight. Brett urged him to cut it but expressed his continued confidence in Churchill and his willingness to wait until the book was written to the novelist's satisfaction. In June Churchill returned to Cornish, and for a while he thought that he had solved his problems. He had sent Brett enough manuscript to feel justified in asking the publisher to recommence his payments, and Brett complied. By August, however, Churchill decided that fall publication was out of the question, despite the fact that Brett had publicly announced that the book would be out at that time.[5] For another year the book progressed by starts and stops with long pauses for thought and meditation. In the spring of 1921 it was coming along well. Churchill had been reading parts of it to his wife and a friend, both of whom liked it, and he had decided to make it simply a story. All of the theories that had crept into the narrative, he decided, were detrimental to the novel. Mrs. Churchill probably had some influence on this decision. She had always liked the story of this novel, but she was uneasy about the theoretical aspects. "I feel a little anxious about the spiritualism in it," she wrote Brett, "but hope he will cut out much of it before the final revision. He has taken this subject very seriously and intensely — as he does all ideas when they get hold of him."[6]

Neither Brett nor Mrs. Churchill recognized that this decision to eliminate the theoretical aspects of Churchill's novel was the beginning of the end. The logical progression of Churchill's thinking was not toward a straight narrative; it was toward eliminating the narrative altogether. He had become so interested in his hero's religious conversion that the story itself became superfluous and he realized that the book he wanted to write was not really a novel at all.

This logical conclusion evolved slowly in Churchill's mind. His first inclination was to lay the novel aside while he worked out the theoretical framework in another book. In September, 1921, he informed Brett that he had practically completed a manuscript to be called "Charity Letters," with the subtitle of "Skychology," which would deal with inspiration and give a scientific statement of Christian doctrines. Shortly thereafter he sent Brett the first hundred pages of a book which was to be the first in a series of volumes along the same line. Churchill hoped that the novel would come next, but he could not be certain.[7]

The Skychology manuscript as it exists runs about 330 pages and is written in the "we" form. Churchill here refers to himself as Theseus and his soulmate as Ariadne. It is straight exposition instead of fiction but, unlike the Jonathan and Gideon manuscripts, is more concerned with the pursuit of happiness than with self-recrimination. The essential message which the manuscript conveys is that the individual should be himself and not be concerned about relatives or property. Churchill argues that economic reforms cannot solve the problems of the world and does not even pretend to know what form of government is the best. If social salvation is brought about (and he seems to feel it can be achieved), it will come through religion rather than through economics or politics. Through a process of skychoanalysis, "First one individual will become happy, and then another and then another, finding that they can live peacefully, even in our modern, sentimental hell, until after awhile — we do not say how long — the whole lump will become leavened." The process itself he describes in this way. "Skychoanalysis, successful skychoanalysis is, like successful psychoanalysis, merely the deliverance of the patient from those who give him the haunting and terrifying ideas to those who give him energizing and 'social' ones."[8] This process differs from psychoanalysis in that Churchill denied the existence of the unconscious and objected to the Freudian emphasis on infantile and sexual experiences. He again relies on William James for the scientific proof of his beliefs and says that it was James' work which first opened his eyes, especially to the fact that knowledge of a certain kind comes through the emotions.

Churchill was quite serious about the ideas expressed in this manuscript, but one sign that his time of crisis was passing is the return of his sense of humor. In one passage he complains that the United States is over-organized, too interested in one-hundred-percent Americanism (without knowing what that is) and too obsessed with the suppression of vice. Americans were becoming neurotic, he contended, and there would soon be a sanitarium instead of a saloon on every street corner

> . . . instead of a good, old fashioned road house, such as we saw a picture of the other day; an eighteenth century road house where Dr. Johnson had a buxom lady on his lap, while he ate a hearty meal, not of breakfast food and malted milk. He was doing the lady good, chucking her under the chin. It was a committee meeting, but the other members were not shocked. There was no ethical culture about it. Roast beef and ale and pudding, a good tom tom meal with a delightful lady who knew nothing about birth control, and who wasn't trying to convert the doctor to being 100% Scotch. She wasn't waving a Chatauqua handkerchief at him, nor did she show any signals of distress; nor did she have to leave in five minutes to attend a meeting of her local of the Tory party to discuss the welfare of the poor working girl.[9]

For over twenty years Brett had eagerly accepted every manuscript that Churchill had sent him, but he wanted no part of this one. The reading public which had admired Churchill's work for many years, the publisher contended, would utterly fail to understand this book, and to publish it would do irreparable injury to the novelist's reputation.[10]

Churchill did publish two articles on the theme of the Skychology manuscript, and his wife had hopes that this would satisfy him. "Winston feels he must get his book ready," she wrote Brett, "but is so interested writing articles on his 'hobby' that the book has been rather secondary lately. Now that the Yale Review and the North American have accepted his two articles, I think the book will progress more rapidly. He had to get these ideas out of his system."[11] The publisher was afraid that even this exposure of Churchill's ideas would be detrimental to his reputation, and he urged him to go back to his old genre and style before the public forgot who he was.

Brett and Mrs. Churchill held onto their hopes for another year. In January of 1923 she wrote Brett about her husband. "You will be glad to hear he is coming out of his latest obsession splendidly and is almost normal on the subject these days. I think there is a chance of his writing a novel before long."[12] In December of that same year, however, Churchill closed the door and locked it. He told Brett that he appreciated all the publisher had done for him in the past but that "what I have been going through in the last four years has led me at last to the determination never again to publish a book for money, or to copyright one." He realized how strange this must sound, but "it has brought me peace." Realizing that this was the end of the matter, Brett wrote a reply that is more a final tribute than a plea. He expressed profound regret that Churchill had decided to abandon his novels, which had held up to the young people the highest ideals of life and character, especially in light of the fact that so much current fiction was inculcating a false morality. Churchill's task, he contended, had been a valuable one, and he did it better than anyone else. Brett concluded by expressing the hope that, for the good of the nation, Churchill would one day return to his earlier genre.[13] A working partnership that spanned more than two decades, produced nine best-sellers, and made millions of dollars, was, for all practical purposes, terminated.

This does not mean that Churchill had abandoned the idea of communicating his new faith to the public. As usual, he believed that he had reached the answer, but in 1921 and 1922 his ideas were tumbling over each other, and within a few weeks after he finished "An Uncharted Way" for the *Yale Review* he was working on another approach. The new version of his ideas was to serve a triple purpose. Entitled "The Knowledge of Good and Evil," it was published in the *North American Review*, and it also served as a basis for a lecture Churchill gave in the ball room of the Plaza Hotel, from which excerpts were printed in the *New York Times* under the title "Two Minds for One."[14]

Churchill had discussed the ideas with Lawrence Gilman, a critic for the *North American Review*, and wrote Gilman that he had been over it with "one of our best known neurologists."[14] The article appeared in April, 1922, the last time Churchill was to publish anything (except for a squabble with the New York *Times*) for almost two decades.

CHAPTER XXI

An Active Retirement

Most accounts of Churchill's life dismiss his last twenty-five years with the comment that he retired from public life after World War I and lived a quiet existence in almost complete isolation. It is true that he lived a quiet life and avoided involvement with society whenever possible, but he never stopped working and certainly did not live in isolation. Nor did he fade so quickly from the public mind as one might assume. In 1924 the readers of the *Literary Digest* voted him number four in a list of the ten greatest writers of the century, and the Macmillan Company had sufficient faith in his continued public appeal to issue a complete edition of his novels in 1927.[1]

Churchill also discovered that it is considerably easier for a public figure to decide that he no longer wishes to be such than it is to convince the public that he is serious about the matter. By 1923, Churchill had determined that affiliation with any organization was a violation of his principles, and he resigned from all of his clubs and his honorary appointments. All of these groups except the National Institute of Arts and Letters accepted his decision regretfully but with good grace. Asking him to reconsider, the Institute pointed out that its membership list was a roll of honor and that once a man was on that list he was there for eternity. Churchill's reply states his position in no uncertain terms.

257

My reason for resigning from the Institute is one of
pursuing a principle which of late years I have adopted, and which is now essential to my life. Personally,
I no longer believe in being a member of any organization, society or club. Hence I have resigned from
every one of the many to which I formerly belonged.
This is a matter to which I feel I cannot make any ex-
ceptions, so I must insist that my letter of resignation
stand. Indeed, I do not wish to be on any roll of
honor, and cannot be.[2]

Even the Institute was easier to convince than some of the movie
producers, magazine editors, academicians, and a host of others
who continued to bombard him with requests to write, speak,
supply information, or sell them the rights to do this or that with
one of his books. It took the retired author most of the decade to
persuade them that he wished to do none of these things.

During those years Churchill lived his life as a scientific experiment, testing the ideas of non-resistance which he was developing. It was primarily for this reason that he opposed propagation
of his earlier books. When Brett wanted to put out an inexpensive
edition of the novels "for the good of the country," Churchill explained to the publisher that he did not feel justified in increasing
the circulation of the novels because they were not in accord with
his present beliefs. The novels urged rebellion against the existing
establishment, and this, he had decided, is wrong in principle.[3]

Because his family and friends did not understand Churchill's
strivings, he conducted his experiments without the aid and encouragement that he had always been afforded in the past. But the
comfort and peace which he had achieved impressed the people he
encountered, and many of them wanted to know more about the
ideas which had brought him such apparent tranquility. To these,
to any and all who showed a spark of interest or enthusiasm,
Churchill was willing to give endless amounts of time. He talked
with them, listened to their troubles, showed them fragments of
his continually revised manuscript, and wrote letters by the hundreds. The people who displayed such interest came from the most
diverse of backgrounds, from the top of the economic and social
scale to inmates of various prisons, but they had one thing in
common — each had passed through or was in the midst of a
personal crisis. They met and talked with Churchill, saw the peace

in which he lived, and were attracted to his philosophy. Some tried for months and even years to achieve the same state of mind by living their lives as he suggested. At first some of them made progress and felt that all they had to do was to understand the ideas more completely. During this phase Churchill provided an understanding ear; they could tell him of their difficulties and temptations without fear of being scorned or humiliated. Then, gradually, they seem to have fallen away, usually because they lost interest or were ashamed that they could not measure up to the standards which Churchill set.[4]

One example will demonstrate the symbiotic relationship between the teacher and his followers. A young woman had suffered a double tragedy in the death of her baby and the suicide of her husband. She had no outlet for her despair until a chance meeting with Churchill, during which she saw an "infinite peace" in his eyes and they talked about his beliefs and his way of life. For many months thereafter he sent her manuscripts and advice, while she poured out her troubles to him, seeking, questioning his responses in a highly rational and intelligent way. Churchill needed to feel that someone understood and cared about his new faith; this woman (and dozens like her) needed a sympathetic ear, a Christlike figure (a term frequently used with regard to Churchill after 1919) she could turn to for sympathy. In many ways he really helped these people, and their faith in turn sustained him. The devotion, adoration, and confidence which many of them expressed in him is truly impressive.[5]

After the initial period of adjustment, the Churchills adopted a way of life that was characterized by warmth, simplicity, and sincerity. Their daughter Mabel was married in the summer of 1921, and John was in school at St. Mark's; so Creighton was the only child still regularly living with the family. Mrs. Churchill devoted considerable time to painting (a pastime that Churchill also cultivated at this stage of his life) and did a great deal of traveling. Sometimes Churchill accompanied her and at other times remained at home. In the early months of 1922 he was living by himself in Wilton, Connecticut, while Mrs. Churchill traveled with Creighton in New Mexico and California. He enjoyed immensely the freedom to do as he pleased.

> I am in clover. I cook my own meals and the care-
> taker and his wife clean up, etc. I sit before a large
> fireplace and write and dream, get up when I choose,
> in the middle of the night if I wish to, and turn in
> when I choose. I made my fires at four o'clock this
> morning. It is heaven.[6]

The following year the Churchills spent several months on St.
Simons Island, Georgia, in a cottage belonging to Maxfield Parrish's wife Lydia. The Churchills both loved the island and resided
there many times during the succeeding two decades.

Later in 1923, Mrs. Churchill became seriously ill and had to
undergo a series of operations. While she was in the hospital her
husband used the opportunity to remodel the Inn where they were
living and devoted considerable time to the education of his young
son. "C is going after his music hard, and I am reading good historical novels to him, Dumas and Scott, and teaching him history that
way." In fact, Creighton received little formal schooling until he
entered Groton — a situation that caused the local school board
some concern.[7]

While Mrs. Churchill was in the hospital, Harlakenden House
burned to the ground. Churchill was painting in a field some distance away and by the time he arrived the whole east wing was in
flames. The most colorful account of the scene was written by
Maxfield Parrish in a letter to Mrs. Churchill.

> I blushed simply dreadful at the things you said
> concerning my conduct at the great fire, but morbid
> modesty aside, I wish to go on record with the state-
> ment that I probably made more noise and did less
> work than anybody there. It may be true that I sup-
> plied a small portion of brains where there seemed to
> be none, such as suggesting they give over saving
> kitchen crockery and concentrate on rugs, and
> antique furniture, etc. So many were lost in admira-
> tion: I recall a crowd gaping at the wonderful col-
> lection of genteel books in the library, the thought
> not having occurred to them that they might just as
> well be moved. Taking it all in all, it was an enter-
> taining affair . . . .
>
> The really hard part was trying to convince George
> Austin that it was the spirit and not earthly goods
> that mattered. In fact, the afternoon before Winston
> had preached an hour and a quarter sermon on the
> subject of God and Mammon, a good one too. All

I could remember of it I shouted in George's ear, but
I fear I left out the point for he looked mighty puzzled and inquired about insurance.[8]

Churchill's account of the affair is somewhat more charitable. The chemicals which the fire brigades used for lack of water did not extinguish the fire, but the house burned slowly, giving them about two hours to move things out of the building. Roughly three hundred people from the surrounding countryside and from Windsor labored mightily and, in spite of the lack of direction, managed to save nearly everything — including the bathtubs. A minimum of things were stolen at the time, but Churchill said it was fortunate that they had moved the books and furnishings into storage because the following Sunday a deluge of sightseers arrived, many of whom decided they would like to have momentoes of the occasion.[9]

Friends and old political colleagues wrote to express their sympathy at the loss of the valuable and famous house, but Churchill wrote Hamlin Garland that he was "not sorry the house burned."[10] Unfortunately Churchill was so unconcerned about everyday affairs that he had allowed the major insurance policy to lapse and they collected almost nothing. The former summer White House had become a white elephant, however, and, in spite of the financial loss, they were not particularly disturbed by the fire.[11]

The following year the Churchills made their third trip to Europe, accompanied this time by the two boys. The trip was high lighted by an encounter with the Italian police during which they were held as suspected jewel thieves for several hours.[12] In spite of this misadventure they had a grand time. Churchill's efforts to paint Italian scenery, however, were frequently frustrated by his wife's constant desire to be on the move. Writing from Rome, he said that he was enjoying himself and painting all the time but complained that he never had time to finish anything.[13] This state of affairs stemmed from the contrast between Mrs. Churchill's bubbling energy and his own deliberate exactness. Her paintings are impressionistic, emphasizing a vivid sense of color rather than line or form. She sketched the scenes rapidly and was soon ready to move on. Churchill, on the other hand, was a realist who compulsively painted every leaf of every tree. Max-

field Parrish facetiously accused him of painting not only this
year's grass but last year's and next year's too. [14] His color sense
was less interesting than his wife's, but he was an excellent drafts-
man and his paintings are almost like color photographs. Consequently, by the time he had started on the second tree or the
fourth window, Mrs. Churchill had set down her impression and
was anxious to seek new vistas. [15] Churchill treated the situation
with calm amusement; and his good-natured complaint that on
this trip he saw Europe only through "a square of gingham" (the
side curtain of their open car) became a standing family joke.

During the years following the European trip the Churchills
continued to live in one of the Cornish houses part of the year and
spend the remaining months traveling. The author preferred to
remain in one place as much as possible, either in Cornish or on
St. Simons, where he could write, paint, or pursue his carpentry.
His skill in the latter pursuit is attested to by the beautiful hand-
made paneling of the living room and dining room in the house
where they lived after Harlakenden burned.

Through the 1920's, Mrs. Churchill clung to her hope that
her husband would return to his former genre. Writing to Brett
in 1925 she said that seldom a week passed that some publisher
or magazine editor did not write her husband requesting a book
or story or interview, but that he refused them all. In the same
letter she confessed that she did not think he would ever write
again, although he was so versatile that no one could tell what he
would do next. "He has made such strides in painting that his real
reputation may be that of an artist, rather than a writer." [16]

Churchill had not been a part of the "sad gaiety" of the Jazz
Age; so he was not particularly concerned when that paradoxical
era came to an abrupt end in the fall of 1929. While the nation
moved from boom to bust, he continued to go his own way. And
the advent of the New Deal appears to have moved him no more
than the disastrous years of depression which led up to the enactment of much of the legislation Churchill had worked for under
the banner of the first Roosevelt. He was concerned with more
fundamental things than the planting of General Johnson's Blue
Eagle on the flagpoles of half-empty factories. In this mood he
continued to repudiate the solutions he had earlier espoused.
   What I would then write seemed good to me, and

> new. But I know now that there was very little, if
> anything new in all the books I have published. They
> were at best new combinations of old ideas, things
> which other men had thought and which "I" put
> together and got a thrill out of which I took for
> inspiration. [17]

In reply to a request for personal information from the author of
a book on American writers, Churchill indicated that he felt sure
the reading public in 1933 was no longer interested in him.

> Now some twelve years ago I made a resolution to
> keep out of the public eye, and I have very little dif-
> ficulty in holding to it. While I feel the compliment
> which you would do me in including me in living au-
> thors, I am really a dead author, and never was much
> of a living one. So I know you will excuse me. I had
> great pleasure in what I wrote when I did write, and
> I am grateful for that pleasure. [18]

But Churchill was not quite so dead, in the eyes of the public,
as he thought, for his novels continued to find a small audience in
the depression days. In 1935 the Macmillan Company cut Churchill's royalties to ten percent, but he continued to receive about six
hundred dollars a year from the sale of the novels. This represented a combined sale of about 2400 copies a year, composed mostly
of the historical novels. *Coniston* also sold until the early 1940's,
but the social-problem novels no longer had a market. [19]

Although there were other indications of continuing interest
in his novels, it was Hollywood that dangled the golden ring. Dis-
satisfied with the early productions of his stories and disinclined
to see the novels given publicity, Churchill held out against the
continuing offers that came in during the 1920's and 1930's. The
only time he seems to have wavered from his position on this
matter was in 1930. At that time he wrote Mrs. Churchill, "Now
about that Talkie, as soon as this contract comes I will sign it and
send it back . . . . [20] The contract was not signed, however, and
in 1937 when W. N. Selig (who had made the movie of *The Crisis*)
asked for the rights to *Richard Carvel*, Churchill again refused to
sell. That same year the Twentieth Century studio offered him a
minimum of twenty-five thousand dollars for a production of
Richard Carvel that was to be a real spectacular. They intended
to cast Tyrone Power in the title role and to put the film under

the direct supervision of Darryl Zanuck. Production costs were estimated at one and a half million dollars — a phenomenal figure for that time. They also pointed out that in eighteen years the novel would be in the public domain and could be used by any-one; so he might as well get something out of it while he could and at the same time ensure a good production. Despite the fact that the family had barely enough income to meet expenses, Churchill refused the offer. The studio then tried to change his mind by telling him that Metro-Goldwyn-Mayer (who had the rights to *The Crisis*) intended to refilm that novel as a counter-attraction to *Gone With the Wind*, and a movie of another of his novels could hardly compromise his principles in this case.[21] Churchill, however, stood his ground.

The modest nature of their income did not interfere with the Churchill's many trips, even during the depression. Most of their winters were spent in the South; and it was in Winter Park, Florida that they encountered the dour Vermonter, Calvin Coolidge. Churchill had long since ceased to make public statements on politics; but Mrs. Churchill had publicly opposed Coolidge's election in 1924, and her statements had made the national press. Naturally the taciturn ex-President was less than enthusiastic about meeting his outspoken critic, and the encounter provided Churchill with material for an amusing letter. The tone of this letter is characteristic of most of his correspondence with members of his family during these years.

> Now this is a letter about Cal. Cal is a boy who has been in the White House, and there is a song about sinners, Run to de mountain, Can't Hide! Run to de sea, Can't Hide! Can't hide sinner, can't hide [This was Churchill's favorite spiritual]. Now boys who have been in the White House can't hide. And Cal ran to Mt. Dora, a little hotel in Florida. Can't hide! There we found him. Now when we arrived at Mt. Dora there was Cal standing at the foot of the steps, and Munga [the grand-children's name for Mrs. Churchill] went right up to him just as if she were going to say, "You naughty boy, don't you know you can't hide?" And Cal looked sheepish. And he is like a Dormouse when he is caught, he pretends he is asleep. But that doesn't work with Munga. So Munga was gentle with him — just as if she said to him, "Now, Cal, I am not going to ask you ques-

tions about your Past History, but you ought to
know that you Can't Hide." And as soon as Cal knew
he wasn't going to be made to express anything —
right away at least, he began to show little signs of
life. So Munga began to tell him tales from the
Arabian Nights about a magician named Rublee who
took thought for a great envoy called Morrow and
travelled all the way to Mexico. And Cal was charm-
ed, and couldn't hear enough of this story. And he
said, "Tell me another one just as good as that."
And Munga said, "You go and play now, and after
awhile perhaps I'll tell you another. But I musn't
get you too excited." And Cal said, "I'm not excited — really I'm not. Tell me another." And Munga
said, "Look at your face, its all flushed with excitement. And you ought to play more, because you have
been stuck up in the White House so long." And Cal
said, "I haven't anyone to play with." And that was
the truth. And Munga said, "I have a boy with me
[Churchill], but I don't think he'll play with you.
He won't play with anybody." Now as soon as Cal
knew that the boy didn't want to play with anybody — why he wanted to play with the boy. But
Munga took the boy away next day because she was
afraid he would excite Cal too much. And they came
to Winter Park to a home for the aged, and there
they are now.[22]

In early spring of 1930, Churchill returned to Cornish, which
he found "a refuge in a mad world." There he walked and talked
with Maxfield Parrish, who had come to consider his old friend a
bit queer but who remained a confidante.[23] At that time the
Churchills were living in the third of a trio of houses which they
had constructed in a checkerboard pattern up the eastern slope of
the Connecticut Valley. That spring the author devoted most of
his time to paneling the large living room. The result was a thing of
beauty, but it was created at the cost of three fingers of his left
hand down to the first knuckle. Churchill's reaction to the accident and his general outlook on life are brought out in a letter
from his friend Judge Learned Hand, who was soon to become
the father-in-law of Churchill's elder son. "Your way of suffering
it did not surprise me; I already believed that you have come to
that accomodation with fate which leaves you serene among its
fairer aspects. You are really a philosopher, a person who has

found his own way of truth."[24]

In June of 1931 the Churchills drove from Cornish to Montreal, where they embarked for France aboard the Cunard liner *Aurania*. After a brief stay in Paris they traveled inland to Innsbruck and Berchtesgarden. As usual, Churchill's desire to remain at each place and paint was frustrated by his wife's urge to be on the move. August found them in Salzburg, September in Venice, and October in Florence, where they remained for the winter.

One disappointing feature of the visit was that the winter of 1931-32 was so cold in Italy that Churchill was not able to do much painting outside — the one place he really liked to paint. In January the cold weather chased them south to Capri, but they remained in good spirits. This was due in part to the companionship of Mrs. Churchill's court jester, novelist Robert Herrick. The relationship between Herrick and the Churchills was an interesting one. Three years older than Winston and five years older than Mrs. Churchill, Herrick had begun his writing career at about the same time as Churchill but had never achieved a comparable success with the public. His work was taken seriously by the critics, however, and he continued to publish throughout the 1920's and 1930's.[25] Churchill had become familiar with Herrick's work as early as 1900, when Brett, who published most of Herrick's books, sent him a copy of one of them (probably *The Web of Life*). Churchill liked the novel, but when they first met in 1907 neither of the Churchills was very impressed with Herrick.[26] Twenty-three years later (in 1930), they met again and the response was quite different. Although Churchill and Herrick were not particularly compatible, the three of them formed a natural trio. Churchill, busy with his study of religious philosophy and his painting, liked nothing better than to be left alone; Herrick and Mrs. Churchill enjoyed activity. Consequently, the older man kept Mrs. Churchill amused while her husband thought, worked, and covered innumerable canvasses with the intricate detail of his art. The relationship has been described by Churchill's son Creighton, who was frequently with them during these years.

> Temperamentally he and Herrick did not jibe, and in those days they had nothing in common . . . . My father was always a person with a strictly one-track

> mind — always totally absorbed in what interested
> him at the moment, to the complete exclusion of all
> else . . . . In all fairness it should be said that he was
> not a very companionable person for a live and alert
> woman, and this is where Herrick came in. In general
> my father tolerated Herrick, but occasionally burst
> out at the seams.[27]

Churchill was not only tolerant, he was constantly amused at the way Herrick allowed Mrs. Churchill to run his life.

After a short trip to Greece, the trio returned to the United States in late May of 1932. By the middle of September, Herrick had again joined them in Cornish but left a couple of weeks later (in the pouring rain) when Churchill insulted him. Churchill confessed that his customary tolerance had been sorely tried by the prospect of having to face Herrick at the table all winter.[28] Nonetheless, Herrick rejoined them in November on the SS Oriente bound for Cuba. After a brief stay in Havana, they boarded the SS Siboney and by Thanksgiving were off the coast of Yucatan. Disembarking at Vera Cruz on November 25, they proceeded to Mexico City. Churchill had anticipated spending some time in the mountains; but as he related with some disgust, Herrick could not stand the altitude because of his weak heart, and they proceeded to Cuernavaca, where they occupied the home of former ambassador Dwight Morrow.[29]

The small party (joined this time by the Churchill's daughter) found life in Cuernavaca pleasant and enjoyable. Social pressures were practically nonexistent, and the beautiful countryside offered many opportunities for short excursions. Churchill, caught up again in the composition of his book, loved the place. It was a busy but relaxing existence, quite different from the social whirl of Florence, and Churchill gloried in it.

During these years of national crisis, as the children matured and married, the Churchill family seems to have grown closer together, the parents and the children drawing strength from each other. Mabel was now the mother of three children, whom Churchill and his wife both adored. He wrote them warm, humorous letters which show both a deep affection and an understanding of children. At thirty-three, the elder son, John, was on his way to becoming a successful architect. John was probably less intimate with his father than the other two children were, but Churchill seems to have had a quiet confidence in the young man, a feeling that he knew where he was going. In 1935, when John's marriage to the daughter of his father's friend, Judge Learned Hand, ended in divorce, Churchill took it all calmly, criticizing no one.[30] Indeed, he was inclined to adopt a similar attitude in most family crises. His younger son, Creighton, had arrived at the age of twenty-one in 1933 with no clear idea of what he wanted to do in life. He had done some writing and he was an accomplished pianist. He had always been an intelligent and precocious youth, and his mother frequently found it difficult to cope with him. Perhaps for this very reason, his father found him a kindred soul and sent him the early drafts of his manuscripts for criticism. He added, "There is no reason why you should not have thought of some of these things for yourself, and one reason I am sending it to you is because you are the only person I know that can get hold of it fairly well, since your mind runs that way."[31]

As might be expected, Churchill strongly influenced the lives of his children. This manifested itself in various ways, but the father whose spirit permeates each of their homes is not the wealthy popular novelist and man of affairs; it is Churchill the philosopher. And more than the influence of any specific ideas, it is the personality of the man himself and his approach to life that one senses. Perhaps the best expression of this is evidenced in a fragment of a letter John wrote to Creighton in 1933.

> I have a great faith in Doc; he is a remarkable man. He can turn his hand to anything and succeed. He wrote ten damn good yarns, with no training in writing, and succeeded by sheer work and will power. No one can say that, as far as he went, he failed in politics. He then threw it all up, and painted some pictures which hang on the walls of my house and which are commented upon by every artist that comes in. They say "who in hell painted those pictures, John?" And I say, "my Father did." and then they say, "Why, they are remarkable. Who taught him?" And now he has turned himself to something which can only be called mysticism: for he is really a mystic anyway. Therein lies the great danger of what he is doing now. But don't think for a moment that I think he will fail at it. Somehow and someday he'll turn the thing out of mysticism and religion and apply it to psychology, and people will

> sit up and take notice. The fact that he is a mystic
> will have nothing to do with it. He can apply himself
> to anything. He was not an author until he started,
> and when he was a politician no one would have ever
> thought he would ever be able to paint pictures which
> are praised by . . . . [32]

It would be interesting to know the identity of the unknown admirer, but the faith of the son in his father is there and it is a faith they all shared.

In the spring of 1934, Churchill decided that the time had come for him to break his self-imposed silence. Approximately a year before this, after a hiatus of ten years, he had begun a systematic development of his religious philosophy. In May of 1934, he wrote Brett that he had been working for fourteen years on a book which would prove that there were sound psychological principles underlying the Gospels. He had not intended to publish it, "but the fact is that the suspension in income from many investments of my wife's has changed my mind." Although his ideas were still in flux, he wanted to publish an introduction to the subject, to be called *The Uncharted Way*. Hoping to avoid another "Green Bay Tree" situation, he made it clear that he wanted no money until the manuscript was in the publisher's hands. By this time Brett was in semi-retirement as Chairman of the Board, and George Brett, Jr., was president of the company. He was anxious to see the manuscript but added that Macmillan's desire to publish the book would depend on "just how the mystic aspect of the theme is handled."[33]

Churchill labored over the manuscript throughout the summer and in October submitted a portion to Brett, who passed it on to a reader. Probably the reader had about fifty-five pages of the manuscript, which obviously contained some biographical information. From this information, the reader concluded that Churchill's friends had doubted his sanity during the 1919-21 period and that some of them doubted "the completeness of his restoration." He went on to discuss the manuscript itself.

> It is utterly incoherent and rambling, without indica-
> tion of either trend or conclusion, and working over
> at wearisome length a few pretty far-fetched illustra-

tions some of which are also repeated. Scattered
through it are some shrewd and rather striking observations and comparisons, but they do nothing to
give coherence to the work as a whole. Had I read
this manuscript without knowing the author or anything about him, I should certainly have said that it
was the maunderings of a disordered mind, and I am
unable to see it differently now. I see no possibility
of making anything coherent out of it by rewriting
it (a melancholy factor is that it is, as a whole, sin-
gularly well written), or any indication that what is
to come will be different from what you have now.
It seems, in short, quite hopeless.[34]

It is doubtful that this report was sent on to Churchill, although
some indication of the nature of the criticism was passed on to
him, and he was irritated. The incident convinced him that he
must try to find a publisher who was sympathetic with the subject. Brett said that he quite understood Churchill's position and
would still like to see the completed manuscript. With this exchange the Churchill-Macmillan partnership terminated. [35]

The Churchill's travels followed the established pattern over
the next few years. With the advent of cold weather, they migrated regularly to Winter Park or Nassau. The remainder of the year
they lived a quiet life in Cornish. There were, naturally, both
visits and visitors, but Churchill was having more success than he
had had for years in expressing his ideas and was working with his
usual concentration. Neighbors shook their heads in wonder as
they saw him wandering through the hills, a copy of the Gospels
in his hands while he memorized the already familiar stories contained in them. According to his family, he had taught himself
enough Greek to memorize the Gospels in that language as well
as in English.

Although the writing was going well, Churchill decided that
he needed some outside help. He engaged Nancy Roelker, a young
philosophy major from Radcliffe, and together they poured over
the many versions of the manuscript, attempting to establish the
proper sequence for the discussion of the various ideas. Miss
Roelker was part of the Churchill household for many weeks and
maintained a close relationship with the family afterwards. As
with many people who came into contact with him during these
years, she found herself increasingly attracted to both the man

and his ideas. "In the course of working on it," she wrote, "we argued out many points and I had a thorough exposure to his mind and personality, which has had a marked influence on my own thinking." Some years later, she expressed her feelings in a letter to Creighton. "I wonder if you find, as I do, that as the years go on the way which he suffered so to find is the only one which makes sense? I constantly remember things he said and did when things seemed insoluble and meaningless and shall forever feel the debt I owe him." [36]

Churchill was equally pleased with his young assistant, but he needed someone stronger to force him to part with the manuscript. The natural candidate was his own son, Creighton, who had been his sounding board for a long time. As it happened, Creighton was available in 1938 when his father needed him. He had graduated with honors from the Mozarteum Conservatory in Salzburg and had studied a year under Pierre Monteux and the Orchestre Symphonique de Paris. Returning to the United States, he served as a Regional Director of the Federal Music Project, as well as guest conductor with several of its orchestras. He was not, however, firmly committed to a musical career, and he declined an invitation from the Buffalo Philharmonic to become their permanent conductor because he had decided that this was not the way he wanted to spend his life. At the age of twenty-six he gave up music and went to work for the New York *Daily News*, but the position failed to hold his attention for long; when his father urged him to come to Cornish and work over the manuscript (in August of 1938), he accepted the job.

In the fall Creighton joined forces with his father, and he spent the winter of 1938-39 with his parents at Winter Park and Nassau. His description of the household at that time is interesting in many ways.

> Both our parents (and I too, for that matter,) have been happier and in better health here than I have seen them for a long time. Up until a week ago, when she got a cold, Ma has seemed to have had no heart attacks, few fits of despondency or disposition. She goes around the enclosure singing and working away, eschews art with Smithy, bosses Duke and our little colored maid Lily, paints most of the day and is, in general, calm and loving toward me and Doc and the

> whole of mankind. I myself have never got along with
> her better; and as you know, Doc's spirits are usually
> a reflection of hers.[37]

Mrs. Churchill also had become convinced that her husband had
something to say and that he would finish the manuscript after
all. This is evident in another portion of a letter, which also explains Creighton's role in the composition of the book.

> Thus we began on the final draft, which I hope will
> not be a complete rewriting — though it _is_ the case
> that every time he rewrites it he makes it better, and
> what he is writing now is so _vastly_ better — even Ma
> says so, in no uncertain terms — that perhaps a re-
> writing of most of it may be a good thing. When he
> began the revision I was ready for him, and we had
> what might be expected as a few days of tussle and
> headaches . . . . Now things are going so well that I
> just collect the manuscript at the end of the day, type
> it out and sit on it. Then every night before I go to
> bed I leave him a little note, which we call "today's
> lesson," giving my suggestion for the next day . . . .
> All of which he seems to value; but it requires some-
> thing, I can tell you, to keep a jump ahead of him,
> which you _have_ to do, because the certainty of Doc's
> working in the morning is just like the certainty of
> the sun rising, or a ship sailing, or Christmas, as you
> know.

As the composition of the manuscript began to move more
smoothly, the question of a publisher loomed ever larger — a problem Churchill had not faced for over forty years. Charles Scribner had been interested in publishing it in 1935, but after reading
an early version of the manuscript he decided that "it would be
over the head of the average reader and would require a steady
mental effort that few are capable of making." In 1939, Mrs.
Alfred A. Knopf wrote Churchill that she was "enormously interested" in anything he might write, and she asked if he would
submit the new book to Knopf.[38] By that time, however, Churchill had found the kind of man he had mentioned to George Brett,
Jr. This man was Gordon Dorrance of Dorrance and Company in
Philadelphia.

The two men had become correspondents for a time many
years before. In 1923 Dorrance wrote several times expressing

his admiration for Churchill's novels and a desire to meet their creator. It was fourteen years later, in 1938, when Dorrance once again wrote, reminding the author who he was, inquiring about his activities, and asking if he had something ready for publication. This was in August; sometime between then and December, Dorrance went to see Churchill, received the usual lecture about his new ideas, and indicated his interest in publishing *The Uncharted Way*. They reached an agreement, and the book was finally published in June of 1940.

CHAPTER XXII

A Final Public Statement

The Uncharted Way is not a simple book to understand or to explain. Churchill thought it would be his last formulation of the ideas and beliefs that had brought him peace and contentment; consequently, he tried to pack everything he knew into it. The result is a tightly reasoned treatise which cannot be easily condensed. For this reason the treatment of it here follows his own organization of the material and (in so far as possible) uses his own terminology.

Churchill suggests that in certain portions of the New Testament there is a doctrine of "non-contention, or non-controversial behavior, which appears to have originated with Jewish thinkers known to history as prophets."[1] It was this doctrine, called the gospel — a word meaning good or glad tidings — which was restated by Jesus and by Paul. But Christianity had proven powerless to prevent human violence. This paradox need not continue, however, for the gospel doctrine could provide a scientifically verifiable sanction for non-violent human behavior if it was clearly understood that the problems of human conduct were produced by the contradictory psychological emphases of religion and science. The distinction between the propitiatory-religious impulse and the self-reliant-scientific impulse is basic to Churchill's understanding of human nature.

274

> The derivation of the word religion most favored by etymologists is from the Greek *Alego*, not to neglect, or to pay attention to a god or gods. These latter are conceived of as supernatural beings who are propitiated to control the operation of natural forces in such a way as to bring about good and favorable circumstances, and avert unfavorable ones, for him who propitiates. This method of gaining good circumstances by propitiation and dependence, then, is distinct from the scientific method, whereby man learns to control natural forces himself, through recognition and knowledge of the fixed and determined law or laws by which these forces are said to be governed. The latter method, properly conceived, is a self-reliant method; the control, so to speak, is taken out of the hands of a god, who is no longer paid for the service.[2]

The practice and development of scientific self-reliance is always opposed by the fear impulse (fear of the hostile forces of nature) instilled in the individual by those who are prospering through propitiatory behavior. "Here lies the psychological basis for the age-old conflict between science and religion."[3]

Propitiatory religion was the result of man's tendency to conceive of supernatural beings (gods) who control the forces of nature. Since these gods demand something in return for their favors, one finds the development of "necessitous" performance or social law which is enforced by those who believe themselves to be benefiting by such propitiatory behavior. The social and political order of the state is, consequently, founded upon the propitiatory method of gaining material benefits. Rebellion against the prescribed behavior is "sin." There is in human nature, however, the urge to be free of such dependence on the gods, an urge that may be described as man's creative or evolutionary potential. When this urge is frustrated by the religious authority, men become rebellious. Such rebellion reaches its logical culmination in what Churchill calls communism, "a social order based exclusively on the scientific authority."[4] But no matter how much man may progress, he can never know enough to explain everything in scientific terms; the unknown and the unexplained still frighten him.

From the two human impulses, Churchill constructed a

cyclical theory of history.

> Thus we see the cycles of culture of man begin-
> ning under the autocracy, tyranny and caprice of the
> strong and fortunate, and law slowly developing.
> There comes a halcyon period of law and order,
> comparative stability, content and prosperity under
> the religious and property authority, and then the
> scientific method is discovered. Like a Samson, the
> scientific authority is at length strong enough to pull
> down the pillars of the temple, but not — considered
> as an authority, or something asserted in conten-
> tion — to build a new structure. The religious author-
> ity reappears, tyranny and despotism return . . . . [5]

Churchill turns from this historical analysis to a discussion of
mysticism. He suggests that mysticism is most likely to arise
toward the end of any cycle of culture when science begins to be
extinguished by tyranny and superstition — such as in Greece
during the fifth century B. C. These are periods of renaissance
when the human spirit rebels against a static existence, and they
lead to what he defines as a psychosis. This term implies in some
degree what is called an inspirational or spiritual experience in
which there is the consciousness of a potentiality of becoming
or change, followed by a frustration of the hopes aroused in it.
As an individual experience it would be analogous to his own experiences in 1919-1920, and he explains it as "the conflict between the basic impulse to practice a self-reliant method and the
impulse to propitiate . . . . "[6]

The first evidence of a world-psychosis in the modern era
came in the Reformation, during which "there was a repudiation
of the religious or property authority to compel the individual
to remain in the place or station to which he was born." Here, as
in the earlier Greek states, the revolt ended in a democracy which
provided partial relief of the psychosis, but the relief was limited.

> In economic freedom the hopes and visions are to be
> realized but inadequately, if at all. As democracy de-
> velops there is more and more repudiation of the
> religious and property authority, but no absolute
> freedom is attained and there is a failure to achieve a
> permanent and stable spiritual happiness. The re-
> ligious authority is still in the saddle: exploitation of
> the creative fruits, and of man by man, goes on apace

> . . . and civilization, instead of progressing, appears
> to be disintegrating.[7]

People abandoned the attempt to relieve the psychosis by rebellion and came to believe that the hopes of mankind would be achieved in a life after death.

Churchill had moved beyond the naive reformism of *The Inside of the Cup*, but he was actually trying to solve the same problem that he had faced in 1912. How can the individual realize himself as a free and complete human being and still bring about social welfare?

> The genius of man, meaning his inborn or essential nature, would seem to be to create or evolve. But it is to be noted that he must do so as an individual, and as an individual make contributions to the progress of society. Evolution, or the progressive control of natural forces, is primarily a self-reliant or self-determining affair, and the problem by which man is confronted is to achieve a way of life, or philosophy, which will reconcile individual freedom, individual self-reliance and self-direction, with social welfare. Any philosophy which falls short of this cannot be said to be adequate.[8]

In his own life Churchill had always been concerned with the relationship between himself, as an individual, and the rest of his society; in his writings (both before 1917 and after) he universalized this same question.

In 1940, Churchill believed that the motive power for personal unification and social progress was faith. Faith brings forth new knowledge and fulfills man's evolutionary potential. In his philosophy these gifts of faith are acquired by conformity to the Law of the Gospel (Law in this case is capitalized to distinguish it from the propitiatory moral law of works), which is characterized by non-contentious behavior. A society which follows a propitiatory religion will naturally enforce the dictates of the moral law; it will judge and condemn, and this is not consistent with evolutionary progress. "Judging or condemnation causes conflicts in the body or mind; and it must first be understood by the individual who wishes to achieve his evolutionary potential that the achievement of this is not possible while he is in a state of conflict." Consequently, both rebellion (the way of science) and judging (the way of traditional religion) are contentious and wrong. To follow the gospel law means to obey the law of works, but to have no part in enforcing it or even judging others by it. Churchill's form of religion would not involve any mystic or ritualistic practices; it would be "a recognition of and conformity to a Law by which science or knowledge is gained."[9]

So the artist or scientist begins by believing that his inner visions will be realized. He tends to shy away from activities which force him to compete for money, position or prestige. This tendency to prefer peace and social isolation is an instinctive impulse of the artist and scientist; in gospel terminology, this state of mind "is figuratively referred to as the kingdom of heaven, and is designated as a state of deathlessness or immortality . . . ." It naturally follows that disregarding the Law is death — not physical dissolution, but failure to realize one's evolutionary potential. With obedience to the Law, one figuratively "rises from the dead."[10]

The social aspect of this philosophy is somewhat more obscure. Churchill conceded that the old law of works had a social basis, but he regarded it as nonscientific, "in that propitiatory behavior does not effect the control of natural forces." He felt that his own approach was scientific because it led to new knowledge which could be used for the control of natural forces; it was also social in that it was to be acquired in social intercourse and it provided a guide for human conduct. Part of the process is explained in this quotation.

> It should be clear that what is implied in *Sunesis*, in putting together of knowledge in any mind to make knowledge original with that mind, is the gaining of one's own things. This is the essence of self-reliance. The individualistic aspect is reconciled with the social aspect, because the putting together of knowledge is dependent upon the agreement with members of the species. This agreement is not achieved by my compelling an adversary to agree with my assertion, so subjecting him; or by his compelling me to agree with his assertion, so subjecting me. The result of *Sunesis* is something to which the adversary must perforce agree, but the agreement had been achieved by my initiation in non-contention. It has been gained by an initial submission to conditions or circum-

> stances which the adversary has sought to impose on me.11

This submission to unfavorable circumstances with a view to making them favorable is called the "way of the cross," and it implies a willingness to deal with any and all situations. One does not pray for good circumstances, but accepts tribulations as a necessary element for progress.

The "way of the cross" is difficult to follow because the two opposing forces in all living creatures — fear (propitiatory) and craving (rebellion) — impel one to leave the path in opposing and equally false directions. This is known as *Hamartia*, which is usually translated as sin, but which Churchill for years had insisted meant missing the mark or direction of life. The method of controlling these emotional drives is developed through faith. The faith that characterizes integrated individuals enables them to hold fast to their beliefs when there is no evidence. Obedience to faith involves the recapturing of an instinct or ability to detect when one's behavior is "off the mark"; this feeling precedes knowing. "This is to say that if one do something which satisfied an inner feeling of what is sensed to be the right way or direction, in which no contention or opposition is felt, the obedience to the feeling is succeeded by a knowledge of why the behavior is right."12

The author felt that he was living in a period when science had made such strides that man had developed a faith in objective rather than emotional behavior. Although the sanity or salvation of the gospel doctrine is an individual rather than a social matter, the final and most essential step would be to apply this objective viewpoint to social behavior. The individual should not concern himself with the proper ordering of society or government, but should conform to its law and mores, making himself an asset to society while it is in the process of self-reformation through the evolutionary "salvation" of individuals.

As a background to the second section on "Instinctive Behavior and the Taming Process," Churchill deals with the question of Jesus' crucifixion and resurrection. He suggests that whatever the phenomenological events may have been, the resurrection of the gospel doctrine has nothing to do with returning from a physical death. In the figurative gospel terms, the Greek word *Aion* (usually translated as a day) should be translated as an age, a stage or dispensation of human development. The first *Aion* was the period of man's evolution from his animal origins. The second was when man began to use tools for the control of natural forces and became clearly distinct from other animals. At the start of this second stage, man's behavior was instinctive and the self was undivided, but when individuals began "to contend for the fruits of evolution, and exploit them and his fellow man, there is competition and strife . . . . Instinctive behavior is lost, and the behavior is in either fear or craving." This second stage is man in historical society, whether that society be propitiatory or communistic, or somewhere in between the two. It is the stage of the divided self or death when evolution advances only by fits and starts and seemingly by accident. In the third stage

> the self becomes single again, the behavior one of obedience to innate feeling, instinct, with science, *Conscience*, which is to say that a scientific sanction is attained for instinctive behavior. The first of the three days, that of the animal single self, may be regarded as a thesis. The second, of the world and divided self, as an antithesis. And the third, when supposedly the self is made single or whole again, as the synthesis. [13]

There follows a lengthy analysis of the instinctive behavior of an animal on a "quest" that involves the interrelationship between time and space postulated by modern mathematics. The neurological aspects of this analysis are interesting as an explanation of the contentment of the instinctive or united self as opposed to the fear-tension of the divided self, but they are too detailed for discussion here.

From this, Churchill proceeds to a comparison of the training of children with the domestication of wild animals. The essence of his argument is that a child who learns propitiatory behavior will probably achieve success in worldly terms, but he will remain in a divided, fear-tension state. On the other hand, "Children who have grown up to be what are called geniuses would be they who have been less deflected from instinctive direction, but they may have been the despair of schoolmasters and parents, and set down as dunces in their youth." [14]

Churchill then moves to a discussion of the evolution and nature of "The Law of Works." It was when man began to exploit nature himself that "he conceived of a god or gods who also exploited and thought himself dependent on them. In this sense man made gods in his own image." When a man seizes a section of rich land, he must defend it against natural forces such as drought or flood. In the latter case he feels powerless so he appeals for the aid of the ultimate owner or exploiter — a god. "The relationship of the human owner or exploiter to the god, then, is that of a vanquished to a victor in a contest; and if the possession and the body are to be spared, an obligation to pay is incurred." [15]

This early period would be a time of chaos. "Before a stable and enduring social order under the law of works has been achieved, we may conceive of something like a racketering age of the gods. When there are many gods, and none especially preeminent, they might be expected to be tyrannical, temperamental and capricious." This state of affairs would continue until the evolution of a monotheistic system, under which "every man supposedly has his own guaranteed share of the contract, provided he lives up to the provisions. He knows just what he will have to pay for his benefits, and what are the prescribed forfeits for breach of the contract; for sin in the meaning of debt to the god." [16] Under this system the whole social order — including the clan and family units — centered around property rights. Even sexual intercourse ceases to be an inspirational, creative relationship; it becomes instead simply a means of maintaining the family as a property-holding unit.

It is obviously the duty of individuals in this order, especially high-ranking ones, to keep everyone under them in their proper station. Human behavior will be ritualistic and propitiatory. A man whose crops are threatened by drought will not seek the evolutionary solution to his problem by seeing how water can be brought to his land by irrigation. Instead, he will make a ritualistic appeal to his god, attempting to achieve by propitiation what could have been accomplished by scientific self-reliance.

This state of affairs will continue until a renaissance occurs. Churchill uses the term renaissance here in its broadest possible sense. "In any such creative dawning, art appears to be the precursor of science; and it does not inspire the same antagonism and fear in the minds of the superstitious rulers and priests." [17] This opening up and expansion of the human mind was the beginning of an evolution from feudalism, through various intervening stages, to communism. He traces this evolution in the chapter entitled "The Technical Authority and the End of the World."

The first step was the "development of Protestantism as a prelude to democracy." The Protestant, however, saw only the idea of self-determination. In an expanding world, the Protestant wanted to free himself from the restrictions of a static feudal order. "As his doctrine developed into democracy the Protestant declared that no king or lord or church had the right to dictate his functions, or what he should or should not know." He went back to Paul for his theology, but "he ignored the Pauline warning not to contend, and he gained not spiritual, but only economic freedom." God was still a proprietor who demanded duty and fees in return for possessions. "The Protestant starts out to be free, and ends up by becoming rich."[18]

Most men would feel too weak to cast off the property authority unaided. They would seek the support of others who desired to be free and would rebel, as the Protestants did, against the existing social order. This intrusion of the "technical authority" into the property order creates a hybrid society which Churchill calls democracy.

> In democracy the technical impulse is not strong enough to remain dominant, and must continually surrender and be supplanted by the propitiatory impulse. What has been gained by the collective assertion of the technical right for a time eases the social and the individual psychosis, and we get temporarily a comparatively stable social order composed, on the whole of contented and active individuals. But we are in a world of change, one in which more and more freedom is sought for by rebellion against the necessitous conditions implied in the philia ties.

Economy remains the cardinal virtue in a democracy, "and the self-made man of the democratic order must not only be willing to learn and to work, but to save in order to gain the kind of freedom he envisages, to be his own master or employer."[19]

It is clear at this point that when Churchill uses the word democracy (which technically refers only to a certain kind of political order and has nothing to do with economics) what he really means is laissez-faire economics in the pure sense of Adam Smith and the Manchester School. Thus he describes democracy as basically a game in which, since it implies the self-determination of individual achievement, the players engage only as individuals. This game is disrupted when any combination of individuals pool their resources and the social order changes from a democracy to a plutocracy (the rule by and worship of wealth). "In democracy the property self of the independent proprietor supposedly takes over what has been gained by skill, but the plutocrat takes over what the individual initiative of others achieves. This is an industrial feudalism . . . . "[20] When it becomes apparent that a syndicate is barring the worker from the benefits of evolutionary expansion, labor forms its own collusion. A communistic revolution would simply mean a general strike in which the workers would take over the resources of production. This would come as the labor movement gained strength and cohesion; the worker would become less consciously a "democrat" in that he would renounce his ambition to become a proprietor. In a democracy a man leaves his master or employer to better himself. This involves the acquisition of new knowledge gained through a succession of experiences. In a communistic society there would be no sense of enlarged experience and the social order would be as deterministic as that under the law of works.

In such a society propitiatory religion would disappear and total reliance would be placed on science; since this would be a triumph of the technical aspect of human nature, which "has no property motivation," there would be no private property. By a natural evolution, the same technical impulse which had gained freedom from the law of works and had achieved democracy, pushed man on to a communistic order. But this total victory of the technical impulse would also be transitory since

> it still remains possible that the things which men cannot yet accomplish, or do anything to prevent, such as wars and famines and floods and earthquakes, will shatter this reliance on what he has already done. The scientific plan of communism may be unset by these occurrences of which it cannot take account, causing discontent with the order and a willingness to submit to dictatorship.[21]

The propitiatory impulse would eventually triumph over the impulse toward freedom and rebellion, and a new strongman would appear — this time in the form of a fascist dictator.

In "The Binding of Power" Churchill tries to explain how and why the doctrine of non-contention brings victory instead of defeat. The key to the writings of the prophets, as well as the sayings of Jesus and Paul, is to be found in the concept of the two selves. This key is found in the allegories and parables which had to be used at the time because the true gospel doctrine could not be presented in a society which had not developed a scientific point of view. Any attempt to present the gospel doctrine to the Hebrew people would have been futile and dangerous, since those who benefited by the law of works would persecute those who advocated a doctrine which would set people free from this law. The upholders of the law of works would see the literal meaning of a parable; the inner significance would be grasped "only by those who have come to desire their own spiritual direction, and who are therefore capable of being instructed . . . . "[22] Jesus, Churchill contends, taught this parabolic method of dealing with adversaries. It was a technique of handling energy. The idea of loving one's neighbor was not a sentimental idea, but a means of using their power or energy without losing any of one's own in counter-contention.

It is through art that this non-contentious behavior finds expression.

> Art is achieved by technique, is technique, and hence must have a scientific basis which is concealed, or not in evidence. The artist, who hides his technique (or scientific knowledge) in his handiwork, is not challenged or persecuted unless he be suspected of having agnostic scientific views. He binds the subject or by a charm of which he himself may not know the technical secret — which allows him to put gargoyles on the cathedral to make faces at the saints.

The art of the Renaissance, for example, used subjects from the Christian tradition, but "in the best of these pictures there is suggested a hinterland not discernible to the literal and pious."[23] The artist, like the prophets, revealed his truth in parables to which the upholders of the law of works could not object.

By 1940 Churchill completely shared the view of those critics who had damned his social novels for being didactic. Here he explains the difference between art, which is an expression of the unified self, and propaganda, which is indicative of a divided self.

> The artist is not didactic, in the sense that he tries to teach a moral lesson. No creative personality wants followers or hangers-on, or dependents. The artist wishes to be free, and if he teaches it is in the desire to make himself and others free, or self-determining. Such would be the very essence of art as exemplified in the allegory and the parable, and those who apprehend the esoteric aspect and desire to learn, do so of their own spiritual will.[24]

Art must subsume, not rebel against, the social order in which it is produced. The artistic productions of the Renaissance were of classical inspiration, but they contained more than that. "That something else is represented by tradition, by which we mean the customs, rituals and conventions, the imposed ways of doing or building things in a society which had developed under a law-of-works or propitiatory order." These necessary conditions would be fused with the style or manner of the artist and produce a technique which would be his distinction; it would supplement the source of his inspiration. "Art would be neither a break with, nor a defiance of tradition, but something which, through an adaptive submission, would be reconciled to the tradition and culture of the period; and the expression of it sweeps into a timeless dispensation those who may be inspired by it."[25] Through art man can escape from the evil of the world and from the tragedy of life itself.

The final chapter of the book deals with "The Third Day." It is an attempt to give a rational or scientific sanction for non-contentious behavior which would confer freedom on the individual when his evolutionary potential is being frustrated by the lords of the law of works. In another sense it is an explanation of the experimental method of behavior which he had developed over the previous twenty years.

He first analyzes the individual mind in a divided state with the two selves engaging in a ceaseless struggle to gain control over the organism. Because the individual believes that he has free will or the power (in either self) to determine his own actions, he feels able to decide for himself whether to be a moralist or a rebel. But he does not really have this ability. The self which is in control will depend on the immediate circumstances and external stimuli, so long as the mind is actually divided. The hatred of the two selves for each other is expressed in the moralist's disapproval of what he calls the sinner and the contempt of the rebel for the moralist. It is possible that an individual could establish a fairly stable self, if he could consistently identify himself with one group of influences or the other. But this is difficult, especially in the modern era;

> when the property and religious authority is greatly
> undermined by the growing strength of a collective
> rebellion, we have an increasing tendency toward a
> kaleidoscopic personality, a frequent shifting over
> from one self to the other.[26]

The way out of this apparent morass is through the process of reconciliation. Churchill's position here is based upon two psychological assumptions. First, he assumes that each self will try to repress the knowledge and experiences stored in the archive of the other self. Secondly, he insists that all human knowledge is associated in the mind with those individuals who either taught the ideas or had some connection with them. For example, he notes elsewhere that his early knowledge of religion was associated with his aunt and uncle; his knowledge of political evils with Jim Remick and Ed Niles; mathematics with the Academy; Bergson with those who recommended the philosopher to him. The problem is that one is not apt to accept the ideas of a person one dislikes and, since all new ideas spring from a synthesis of old authorities, this lack of acceptance blocks creativity. If one follows the gospel way, however, and makes reconciliations between individuals and groups, he paves the way for the reconciliation of conflicting ideas — opening the path for new, creative expressions of his own. When these ideological reconciliations are accomplished, one also reconciles in himself the antagonistic individuals with whom he associates the ideas.[27]

The process which takes place in the third stage, then, is not only the synthesizing of the knowledge and experiences of the two selves, but also of the persons associated with that knowledge — again on the assumption that these individuals are now actually a part of the self. A young man, for example, offends his orthodox father by reading Huxley. The father (in the young man's moral self) will continue to hate Huxley (in his rebel self). The way to reconcile the selves is to reconcile the individuals involved.

The first rule of the experiment follows Churchill's own experience. One must cease striving and accept the circumstances in which he finds himself. If he is completely willing to accept the conditions which are imposed upon him, he is no longer subjugated by them. The opportunities for such behavior, Churchill contends, exist in everyday life. A man who is fond of carpentry goes to his shop one day and discovers that it has been damaged by some boys. The moral self becomes indignant at this violation of his property rights. This reaction is a danger signal which informs the experimenter that he must try to sympathize with the boys. This can be done if he can begin to feel the adventurous, emotional tone of the rebel self, if he can recall something he had done that is similar to the boys' actions. When he searches his mind he recalls his father's indignation at having found him reading Huxley, an indignation that had brought about an alienation between them. When the individual achieves this state, he can smile at both his father and the boys.

By refraining from judging others one achieves a self-integration which makes the practictioner, "in Paul's phrase, a law unto themselves, implying an autonomous behavior in which there is not outer complusion." And, if one can take an objective, rather than a condemnatory view of the behavior of those around him, he will take the same view of his own actions. In the divided state the moral self accuses or judges the technical self which reciprocates with its own condemnation of the moral self. But as the mind is unified through non-contention, "there is the chance to make the past right. It is no longer irrevocable, but is merged, as it were, into the present to make the future."[28] As Churchill forgives his father for deserting him, he loses his guilt feelings for having contemplated leaving his own family.

It is obvious that this new religion of Churchill's bore little resemblance to traditional Christianity, except for a reliance on the gospel doctrine attributed to the Hebrew prophets, and to Jesus and Paul. Organized churches, ministers, ritual, and ceremony would seem to have no place. The one carryover was Churchill's use of prayer, and even here the differences are perhaps greater than the similarities. There is a vast difference,

Churchill asserts, between submitting to a supernatural being as payment for favors rendered or requested, and praying as an attempt to identify oneself with an inspirational, spiritual energy. The purpose of the latter kind of prayer is to cut off the impulse to act in fear or craving when the division of the personality asserts itself.

In conclusion Churchill postulates that any doctrine should be regarded as a means of gaining energy or power, but only a few individuals in history could be trusted not to use power for the enslavement of others. When they did not so use it (as in the case of Jesus), people thought they were weak; they mistook non-contention for surrender. But the doctrine of Jesus and the prophets is a means of gaining the life energy. If civilized man could become again one of his animal ancestors he would feel a thrill of power and life. The truth had been revealed to only a few individuals who understood "the manner in which this energy could be generated, or regenerated — for it is assumed that man as an animal and indeed as a child, had it at his disposal, and to these the gospel repeatedly calls attention." The kingdom of god does not come through observing others, or seeking after the mystical god-man; it comes with power; "and this power is to be generated, or regenerated, by every man for himself. Christianity has dwelt much on regeneration, but attained no realistic conception of it . . . . Jesus and Paul, and the Prophets, as well as other spiritual personalities, must have conceived of the spiritual energy as a current which is poured out in them, *Ekcheo*, and of which they felt the thrill." [29]

Death is the divided state of tension and inertia, a penalty for not learning to handle or generate this energy. It would be "a failure to gain the state of becoming called the soul, and furthermore, we might expect a consequence in emotional suffering . . . . The hazard incurred in not being intelligent enough to cut off the impulses of craving or fear is declared to be that of hell fire . . . . "[30] For the literal mind of the superstitious, this hell fire has always existed in an actual location in the future life. In Churchill's opinion, heaven and hell exist in this life; the way to achieve the former and avoid the latter was to follow the gospel doctrine, the way of the cross, the philosophy of non-contention.

A book on religious philosophy, written by a novelist whom

the public had forgotten, and published by a minor house, could not be expected to attract a great deal of attention. Most of the reviewers were more interested in the fact that there was an American named Winston Churchill than in the book itself. The English Churchill's accession to power meant that the press was naturally inclined to devote more space to the parallels in the careers of the two men than to a discussion of non-contention. The religious journals were shocked by the descriptions of Christianity as a misunderstanding of Jesus, while the learned journals that noticed the book at all devoted their attention to disputing Churchill's translations of Greek words. The popular magazines did not know what to make of it. *Time* called it the work of a "stonily independent amateur thinker" and concluded that "the reader who finds in this [the last] chapter cold comfort may perhaps be pardoned. But he who finds it mere idiocy may perhaps be mistaken."[31]

Part of the difficulty in evaluating this book is that it deals with so many fields of knowledge. In it one finds a philosophy of history, an interpretation of actual historical evolution, both a neurological and a psychological examination of human behavior, and a number of other things. Churchill's scholarship seems most sound and his statements most convincing when he is dealing with the neurological reactions of animals to given stimuli. He is least convincing when he contends that the ideas he sets forth were those espoused by the Hebrew prophets, by Jesus and by Paul. This connection with the Christian tradition (which was important to him) makes the book less convincing than it might otherwise have been. Along the same line, while his translations of Greek words may be legitimate in a particular instance, it is straining legitimacy to insist upon that particular translation in every instance. Most etymologists agree that the meaning of Greek words can be determined only by the context in which they are found. Both Churchill and his critics seem to have ignored this fact.

The psychological insights, however, are sound in and of themselves. Churchill had taken an anti-Freudian position as early as 1919, although he did not have the counter-theory worked out until sometime after that. The major difference between the two is that Churchill did not picture the unconscious and the conscious minds in a stable relationship. He preferred the duality of dominant and sub-dominant minds which changed places, largely in response to external stimuli, until the mind could be unified. His process of unification is also different from that of the usual practicing psychiatrist. He agreed with orthodox psychiatry that the way to get an individual to stop performing anti-social acts is to have that individual understand why he does such things. Further, he would agree that one objective would be to convince the individual that he should conform to the mores of his own society. But Churchill did not want to stop there. This, in his opinion, was substituting one psychosis for another. Simply bringing the unconscious mind to the level of the conscious and telling it to behave would thwart creativity. The way of the cross would prevent anti-social behavior but retain the spark of individuality without which man is dead. It had worked for him; he offered it to others.

Some of the contemporary commentators suggested that Churchill had forgotten how to write in the twenty years since his last novel was published; others contended that it is the best book he ever wrote. In fact, the book is neither so lucid as Plato nor so ponderous as Aristotle. It does not even approach the lyric beauty of certain passages in "The Green Bay Tree," but not even William Ellery Channing could make religious philosophy really lyrical. There are occasional glimpses of the wit that enlivened his letters during the 1920s and 1930s — as in the image of the artist who puts "gargoyles on the cathedral to make faces at the saints," but they are not frequent. Perhaps wit is out of place in a book that is intended to be a message of salvation for mankind.

Churchill probably would not have cared if the book had been proclaimed ponderous, difficult to read, and stylistically sloppy; he would have taken immediate umbrage if anyone had questioned the originality of his ideas. Creativity and the acquisition of new knowledge were the goal toward which his whole system pointed. Fortunately, none of the contemporary critics read it carefully enough to discover more than the superficial resemblance between his ideas and those of Tolstoi and Gandhi. A more careful reading reveals that the book contains elements of most major philosophies since the time of Descartes, with Bergson, James, and Royce's version of Hegel most predominant. One can also find similarities with the work of Freud, of a host of Old Testament scholars, and of contemporary medical research —

mostly in the field of neurology. In fact, if one had nothing better to do, it would be possible to prove that every idea in the book could be traced to some other scholar. Nonetheless the book remains a personal expression of his own experience and is basically a product of that experience. The knowledge which he acquired from his broad reading in a variety of fields did not, of course, evaporate from his mind. When he sat in the shade of a garden in Cuernavaca or Winter Park or Cornish and mulled over the problems which he wished to solve, he was not concerned about whether or not some philosopher had once dealt with similar problems in a similar way; he was concerned about how all of the ideas and facts that were in his mind, all the experiences of an active life, had come together. It was certainly original and creative in his own sense — a synthesis of conflicting authorities which brings new knowledge to the mind of the individual.

It is interesting to note in conclusion that many of Churchill's ideas have been embraced by several groups in the United States during the decades since his death. These groups, sharing only a common objection to the dominant life style of contemporary western man, range from the Hippies and the proponents of Eastern philosophies to such critics of orthodox contemporary psychiatry as Norman O. Brown.

CHAPTER XXIII

From Hebrew Prophets to Greek Philosophers

Shortly after the publication of *The Uncharted Way*, Churchill turned to a new formulation of his ideas. This time he hoped to demonstrate that the fundamental ideas of the Hebrew prophets were identical with those of the classical Greek philosophers. While the world engaged in the most devastating war of all time, he set out to reconcile Isaiah and Aristotle. The major problem he encountered was that which any scholar faces when he attempts to prove that there is but one truth and that all the wise men of the past subscribed to it. He had particular difficulty making Plato conform.

> Plato is really as full of inconsistencies as the Gospel material, and has to be ironed out. Many things affirmed in Plato have to be shown as not conforming to the essential doctrine, which is really identical with that of the Prophets; and must be if it conforms to universal law.[1]

The key which Churchill believed he had discovered since writing *The Uncharted Way* was that man does not have free will when he is in a state of contention. For the next three years he played with this idea, tried to fit all the philosophers into his formula, and enjoyed himself immensely in the process. By 1945 he had given up the idea of writing a book on the subject; he simply wanted to resolve the puzzle.[2] At the age of seventy-three he was still looking for the elusive truth he had often felt within his grasp.

Throughout these years the manuscript was titled "The Rational Release." It was never completed, and the fragmented versions which remain all seem to come from the 1942-43 period. In these fragments there are several matters which deserve comment. His style, for example, is considerably less stiff than it was in *The Uncharted Way*, and his natural good humor breaks through the scholarly analysis more frequently. The scholarship is more difficult to assess since he had not yet inserted the documentation. He seems to have leaned more heavily on such Ionian thinkers as Thales, Pythagoras, Heraclitus, and Anaximander (along with the later Greek Stoic, Epictetus) than on the classical philosophers. One classicist who read a forty-page version of the manuscript said that it reminded him of a Unitarian sermon but that it displayed a thorough knowledge of Greek and Greek writings, although not a professional one.[3]

The basic philosophical difference between *The Uncharted Way* and "The Rational Release" is one of emphasis. The emphasis in the latter is that (for all practical purposes) man does not have free will, a position which was also stated in *The Uncharted Way* but which was not of central concern. In 1942 and thereafter, Churchill asserted that the concept of free will is a delusion perpetuated by moralists. As a result of the creative thinking of some Ionian thinkers in the sixth and fifth centuries B. C., man discovered that the movement of nature is a linked chain of causes. The body of man is but a part of this naturalistic scheme of things. Man can do no more than identify himself with the movement of nature (or the stream of power called God), thus becoming part of a process which he cannot alter. The achievement of this state of mind is called immortality, a condition in which the life or death of the body is of no consequence. It was an attitude which Churchill believed both Socrates and Jesus achieved. The individual accepts life or death as he accepts any other event. The remainder of the manuscript elaborates these ideas and connects them with the doctrines of *The Uncharted Way*.

During the war years the Churchills slowed the pace of their migrations but continued to spend the winter months in the South, usually in one of the cottages connected with Andre Smith's art studio in Maitland, Florida. There were visits with Joe Gazzam in St. Louis and with Mrs. Churchill's brother George in Pasadena. Mrs. Churchill suffered a series of heart attacks during these years but evidently rallied quickly from each one. In spite of her infirmity, they continued to have an active social life, which brought occasional grumbles from the industrious author, who was trying to work on his manuscript. He continued to correspond with a few of his old friends, but most of his letters were to his own children and grandchildren. In addition, two new friends that he met in the early 1940s became steady correspondents. William James' son, William, Jr., a fellow artist, became quite involved with Churchill's new philosophy, and the two men wrote and met frequently. His closest associate at this time, however, was Lumen Goodenough, a retired attorney who had been a lawyer for Henry Ford. The Goodenough and Churchill families met in the early 1940s, probably at Winter Park, and spent much time together in succeeding years. Goodenough was fascinated by Churchill's ideas, and the two men were mutually therapeutic. The ex-lawyer found a new interest in life that helped him adjust to retirement; Churchill found an interested listener.[4]

Although his son Creighton was in the service and John had given up his career as an architect to do research for the government at the Oceanographic Institute in Woods Hole, the war never really distracted Churchill from his philosophic preoccupations. His only direct contact with wartime tribulations occurred during a visit to John in Woods Hole in the fall of 1942. While he was painting a scene with his usual concentration, he was reported to the police by an overzealous Civilian Defense worker as "a suspicious character, lurking in the vicinity, making sketches and apparently reeking with subversiveness." The area was under tight security because of the government research being conducted there, and the chief of police quickly appeared on the scene to investigate. According to his family, Churchill rarely carried any identification with him, and he evidently had none on this occasion. Under the circumstances he realized that he was in a mild

predicament which would not be solved by informing the police-
man that he was Winston Churchill. He solved the problem, with
unusual deviousness, by telling the officer simply that he was
visiting with his son, John Churchill. When this was confirmed,
he went his way and the incident was closed. Unfortunately for
the local authorities, Churchill loved a good joke (especially on
himself) and related the story with great glee, causing some em-
barrassment to the officer and the sharp-eyed spy hunter when
the incident was recounted in the newspapers.[5]

The closing months of the war witnessed the termination of
a companionship that had lasted half a century. Mrs. Churchill in-
jured her ankle and one eye in a fall while they were in New York
City in the spring of 1945. For a month she was confined to bed
at her daughter's home in Brookline while her husband and
Creighton's wife prepared the house in Cornish. When Mrs. Churchill arrived in late May, she was cheerful and apparently in good
health, but a week later she suffered another heart attack, slipped
into a coma and died. Churchill described her burial to their
mutual friend, Una Hunt.

> She always wished to be buried on the place, and
> simply, for she had, as you know, very strong feelings
> in regard to religious form. The grave was under the
> trees, facing the mountain, and covered with flowers.
> The three children were here, and the boys' wives,
> of whom I am very fond. I read two Psalms, and a
> portion of the beautiful Fifteenth Chapter of First
> Corinthians. The old friends left in Cornish were
> here, and more than kind.[6]

Mabel Churchill, who had loved the active whirl of people that
had poured in and out of Harlakenden House, was buried up the
hillside from the burned-out site of her first home, in a pasture
field overlooking the Connecticut River and the beautiful mountain she had often sketched. Churchill wrote, "I have had some
difficulty in realizing that Mabel is no longer here."[7]

His sense of loss was perhaps tempered by the dozens of
letters from old friends who shared his grief. Judge Learned Hand
wrote a gracious eulogy to her charm, grace, beauty, and courage
that was typical of the sentiments expressed. Many others, especially those who had not been famous at the time, recalled that
it was Mrs. Churchill who had welcomed them when they first

went to Cornish. For many of them the days in Cornish before World War I were the happy, gay time of their lives, and Mabel Churchill was an intimate part of that scene.

Churchill's income had been negligible for the past twenty-five years, and the family had lived largely on Mrs. Churchill's income from her trust fund. Since Churchill was not interested in financial affairs, his two sons handled the settlement of the trust, which provided him with an income sufficient to meet his modest needs.

After Mrs. Churchill's death, his granddaughter Margaret stayed with Churchill in Cornish for a while, but he was not in one place for long at a time. Perhaps the years of migratory existence had finally conditioned him. His letters from St. Louis, where he visited with Joe Gazzam, are charming, full of humor and contentment. By the time he left to rent one of Lydia Parrish's cottages on St. Simon's he had acquired a faithful (and quite deaf) cook named Selma Clark, who had been with the family in earlier years. She looked after him and made sure he ate on occasion. Churchill loved the "primitive luxury" of St. Simon's and enjoyed having both Mrs. Parrish and Selma fussing over him — at least for awhile. When he had had enough, there were visits with each of his children, with Joe, and with his friends the Goodenoughs. Tragedy struck his life again when Lumen Goodenough died in January of 1947. Churchill flew to Winter Park to conduct the services himself.

He accepted such losses stoically, continued to work and paint, living his life in much the same way as he had lived for twenty-five years. Then, late on the afternoon of March 12 he walked a mile down the road from Mrs. Goodenough's house in Winter Park to visit Mrs. Churchill's lifelong friend, Mary Semple Scott. It was not a long walk for him, and he looked exceptionally healthy, in good spirits, and happy to be with his friends in Winter Park. "He was quite animated," Miss Scott noted later, "and that merrie twinkle was in his eyes."[8] They talked together about a variety of things, and then, as he was telling her of his plans to go to St. Louis, he stopped talking and sank back in his chair. His expression changed very little, and Miss Scott waited for some time before calling a doctor. One moment he was engaged in lively conversation with a friend, the next he was dead.

He was buried beside his wife in the quiet pasture field, their graves marked by simple flat stones.

Winston Churchill lived a long life and a full one. Born during the era of Reconstruction, he lived to see the nation he loved emerge from World War II as the most powerful the world had ever known. As a writer he flashed on the American literary scene at the turn of the century as an overnight success and for two decades he was looked upon as one of America's foremost novelists. His novels sold an average of 500,000 copies each, and a study of book sales for the first quarter of the century proclaimed him the most popular author of the period by far, in spite of the fact that he published only ten novels — far fewer than most of his competitors.[9] The ten novels went into fifty-four editions in the United States, and most of them were translated into a variety of foreign languages. In addition to the novels, Churchill published three original plays, three poems, numerous newspaper and magazine articles, and two non-fiction books. Two of his novels were successfully adapted for the stage; three were made into motion pictures.

What can be said about his success in his major vocation — as a writer of fiction? One fact which stands out clearly is that the public eagerly brought whatever he wrote; all but one of his novels were best sellers in the year of their publication. Yet when the period of popularity is extended, their position is less exalted. One study which surveyed best sellers by decades shows that only two of his novels met this endurance test. *Richard Carvel* made the list for the period 1890-1899 when the required sale was 625,000 copies; *The Crisis* was a best seller in the 1900-1909 period when the figure was raised to 750,000 copies. None of Churchill's novels met the requirement of 900,000 copies for the decade 1910-1919.[10] This demonstrates that his position as the popular novelist of the period rested on the fact that the public accepted every novel he wrote.

Part of the reason for this acceptance is that the novels received favorable treatment by the critics. An analysis of the reviews listed in *The Book Review Digest* reveals that approximately eighty-five percent of them were favorable.[11] The critics who looked upon his work with most favor were those who, like the reading public in general, were more interested in the ideas and issues he presented than in the artistic quality of the presentation. His mind was atuned to that of his age, and he knew it. This allowed him to write about the problems that interested him, without undue concern about whether they would interest the public. At the height of his success he told one reporter that his novels were successful "because his mind is hitched to the turn of events and that ever since 'Coniston,' people have read him because he was writing in the same stride as the public interest of the moment."[12]

Critics, starting from this same basic premise, have assessed the validity of Churchill's work in a variety of ways. One emphasized his idealism.

> It would be difficult to find in the whole range of American literature an author whose work mirrors the current tastes of the reading public as well as does that of Winston Churchill. But it would be a mistake to adjudge him a mere opportunist. His earnestness is left out of account by critics who claim that in times of social and political upheaval he became a novelist on the strength of a few facts and a little indignation. Churchill was an idealist, and his works treat some mounting aspiration opposed to an entreached regime.[13]

Another favorable commentator says that Churchill's books

> deserve to keep a place in literary history because they so well represent our interests from 1900 to 1917 and because they are probably the clearest expression in our literature of the intellectual crusading progressive who intelligently examined American life and found it lacking. Churchill is more intellectual than is William Allen White, and far more cosmopolitan in his background. However, his cosmopolitanism stops short of socialistic implications. He is committed to traditional American individualism, and he supports this commitment with the liberal philosophy of a Jeffersonian democrat.[14]

Carl Van Doren, on the other hand, condemns Churchill because he "did not get his ideas when they were exciting superior minds but just before the general public caught up with him." In the same general pattern, Henry Steele Commager dismisses Churchill by associating him with Rooseveltian Progressivism.

> Not without convictions, Churchill was without pas-
> sion . . . . Churchill subscribed to admirable ideals
> but to nothing that can be called a philosophy, and
> the ideals were sicklied over with sentimentalism.
> His insights were shrewd rather than profound, his
> moral judgments facile rather than conclusive. His
> villains had hearts of gold, he could not forgo the
> happy ending, and — notwithstanding his own ex-
> perience in New Hampshire politics — he retained
> to the end faith in the healing power of the demo-
> cratic dogma. It is precisely because he was so sensi-
> tive a seismograph that his record of the impact of
> Darwinian ethics upon the older morality has more
> than an antiquarian interest. He is the perfect his-
> torian of the Rooseveltian phase of progressivism.
> That so popular a storyteller should abandon his-
> torical romances for muckraking and that his most
> mature work should deal with economic rather than
> with political corruption was itself significant.[15]

The most aesthetic critics had a justifiable criticism in their
contention that his novels were sociological discourses rather than
art. For this reason, some of the more serious critics ignored his
work; others used him as a foil. H. L. Mencken employed his example to demonstrate what happens to a novelist when he is led
astray by political involvement. In 1919 he wrote, "Churchill,
seduced by the uplift, has become an evangelist and a bore — a
worse case, even, than that of H. G. Wells." A later comment
shows that Mencken believed at one time that Churchill had
promise as a novelist.

> Back in 1908 I predicted the destruction of Upton
> Sinclair the artist by Upton Sinclair the visionary
> and reformer. Sinclair's bones now bleach upon the
> beach. Beside them repose those of many another
> man and woman of great promise — for example,
> Winston Churchill.[16]

Even those who found Churchill's novels lacking in aesthetic
qualities were impressed by his sincerity. Percival Pollard suggested that "such large and genuine earnestness has always informed
his novels, that it is impossible not to take him seriously," while
Carl Van Doren believed that "the contagious passion of a recent
convert," of one who believed completely in what he wrote, was
the secret of Churchill's success.[17] Because of this quality in his

writing, many critics and commentators were willing to overlook any aesthetic shortcomings in the novels. The following is a fitting example.

> His works . . . have become great light-houses warning against the shoals and reefs, and showing the way to the safer paths beyond. Of Mr. Churchill, the sociologist, there can be no conflict of opinion as to the value of his works to American moral development and its national growth. It would be difficult to find another writer of our time with such balanced emotions, such ingrained common sense, possessing his freshness and eloquence in discussing moral issues and having the contagion of his patriotism.[18]

Winston Churchill was an intensely patriotic American who thought and acted within the context of the broad consensus which characterized his generation. He was not a radical, nor an internationalist, nor an original thinker. To later, more sophisticated generations, both Churchill and his readers seem unbelievably naive. Could they really have believed that the cure for the evils of democracy was more democracy, that there could be a war to end wars, that man by nature was good, rational, and benevolent? They could and did. They had not, after all, experienced the failure of their efforts at reform, or lived through the madness of Versailles, or witnessed the horrors of Belsen and Hiroshima. Churchill and his generation were trapped by an experience which had not prepared them to deal with the harsh facts of the twentieth century.

Between 1914 and 1920, Churchill became convinced that he had been living in a fool's paradise. The world, he discovered, was not a place where rational individuals cooperated with each other for the greater good of all; it was an arena of strife and contention where moralists maintained order and tranquility by fooling most of the people most of the time. He came to agree with the critics who had contended that art cannot be didactic. To be creative the artist must retire to the ethereal atmosphere of Axel's Castle. So the crusading novelist-politician abandoned his twin vocation for another, as prophet and philosopher. When he was writing novels, a few critics suggested that Churchill's real desire was not to be a novelist but a prophet, and in the early 1920s there is every indication that he saw himself in that role.

He prepared a banquet where the truth would be revealed to his friends and family. When they did not come he literally went into the fields and roadways, even into the prisons, seeking those who would listen to the revealed word. Disciples came, listened, rejoiced, then went their way. He knew then that his was a personal search, a journey into a far country that must be undertaken alone. He took that journey into the recesses of his own mind, returning with a philosophy that was uniquely suited to his own needs and experiences. Yet he discovered that others found elements of it applicable to their lives as well; so (at the age of sixty) he attempted to explain his ideas to the world. His beliefs had brought him peace and contentment; perhaps they could do so for others. He would not argue or contend, but he would offer the world the one path which could lead it out of the cyclical pattern of history in which it had always been entrapped. Although he continued to insist that his solution was for individuals, not for societies, the salvation of society is implicit in his statements. Social salvation was no longer just around the corner — it was not even likely — but it was possible.

A few individuals found their philosophy of life in *The Uncharted Way;* many more found their model in the man himself, in his ability to accept adversity with stoic calm. When the world greeted him and his ideas with indifference or scorn, he put match to his pipe, brush to his canvas, and smiled. When his few intimates proclaimed that *The Uncharted Way* was the final revelation, he shook his head and went to work to refine and improve his ideas. Those who met him may well have wondered whether he was a deluded simpleton or an authentic genius, but they were impressed. He was seldom impressed. All of his adult life had been spent in a search for the truth; and, although there were many times when he believed he had truth within his grasp, the search continued until the inevitable moment for which he long had been prepared.

The value of Churchill's work before 1920 has been dissected and analyzed by critics and historians. The evidence is at hand, the checks are in, and credit has been given where credit is due. For the period after 1920, when he lived an increasingly varied life that was devoted to the same ends but pursued through radically different methods, the evidence is not yet all in. Only time will tell where the true contribution of such a life, paradoxically pin-pointed on its target and yet scattered in its versatility, actually lay. Certainly it is not the novelist or politician or philosopher who lives in the memories of those who knew him; it is the man himself.

NOTES

All documents, manuscripts, letters, clippings, etc., are in the Churchill Collection in Baker Library, Dartmouth College, unless otherwise indicated. Most of the letters from Churchill in this collection are senders copies, so I have not stated this fact in the specific citation unless it has some bearing on the content.

The following abbreviations have been used throughout the notes:

WC	Winston Churchill
MHC	Mabel Hall Churchill
MCB	Mabel Churchill Butler
CC	Creighton Churchill
JBG	James Breading Gazzam
LMG	Louisa M. Gazzam
CC Coll.	Creighton Churchill Collection
Mac. Rec.	Macmillan Records

SPRING, 1940

[1] Max R. Grossman, "America's Winston Churchill Says:" Boston *Sunday Post*, 6-9-40.

CHAPTER I

[1] George M. Bodge (ed.), *The Churchill Family in America* (published by the family of Gardner A. Churchill, n. p., n. d.), p. 1. All information on the Churchill family is based on this work unless otherwise specified.

[2] James Spaulding-WC, 8-14-28, Butler Coll.

[3] Her diary of this trip undoubtedly furnished Churchill with material for the descriptions of that area which appear in his novel, *The Crossing*.

[4] Brooks Henderson, "Winston Churchill's Country," *Bookman*, IX (August, 1915), p. 610.

[5] See Spaulding-WC.

[6] P. 14. MS is in the CC Coll.

[7] (New York: The Macmillan Company, 1910), p. 12.

[8] Gideon MS, p. 13.

[9] Ibid., pp. 9 and 15.

[10] *A Modern Chronicle*, p. 18.

[11] Ibid., pp. 17-18.

[12] Gideon MS, p. 15.

[13] Jonathan MS, p. 40, CC Coll.

[14] P. 16.

[15] See JBG-WC, 11-2-02.

[16] 6-10-84, CC Coll.

[17]MCB-author, 12-3-63.

[18]See letters Herbert Lakin-WC, 1907-16, Butler Coll.

[19]Both interviews in St. Louis *Post-Dispatch*, 11-19-99.

[20]The only interview I have seen which deals directly with this period is one in the St. Louis *Globe-Democrat*, 1-31-08, and even there his comments are vague.

[21]In this novel, in contrast to *A Modern Chronicle*, Churchill places the male-uncle-father figure in the foreground and makes him the dominant influence, while the female-aunt-mother is a shadowy and rather unimportant background character.

[22]*A Far Country* (New York: The Macmillan Company, 1915), p. 54.

[23]Gideon MS, p. 86.

[24]Ibid., p. 88.

[25]See James Morrow interview, Boston *Globe-Democrat*, 1-30-10.

[26]Ibid.

[27]3-28-90, National Archives.

[28]See letters to Gazzams, CC Coll.

[29]Ibid.

[30]WC-LMG, 11-2-90, Ibid.

[31]WC-LMG, 2-7-91, Ibid.

[32]Report of Naval Cadet Winston Churchill, National Archives.

[33]WC-LMG, 3-6-92 and 4-23-92, Ibid.

[34]Richard A. Glendon and Richard J. Glendon, *Rowing* (Philadelphia: J. B. Lippincott, 1932), p. 175.

[35]See Louis H. Bolander, Librarian at the Naval Academy, to Warren I. Titus, 7-25-55, copy in Annapolis Library. See also WC-LMG, 6-6-92, CC Coll.

[36]6-12-92, CC Coll.

[37]Notebooks in Dartmouth Coll.

[38]WC-JBG, 4-1-94, CC Coll.

[39]The Navy report cards list this as between "good" and "very good." Naval Archives.

[40]WC-JBG, 8-2-94, CC Coll.

[41]P. 10.

[42]Phoebe Grace Storms, "Winston Churchill: A Critical Study" (unpublished Master's thesis, English Department, Southern Methodist University, 1941), p. 3.

[43]Peter Clark Macfarlane, "The Evolution of a Novelist: Who is also an Everyday American," *Collier's*, LII (December 27, 1913), p. 5.

[44]St. Louis *Globe-Democrat*, 12-8-99.

CHAPTER II

[1]Interview with James Morrow, Boston *Globe-Democrat*, 1-31-08.

[2]P. 21.

3 WC-Mabel Hall, 1-8-95, Butler Coll.
4 4-24-95, CC Coll.
5 WC-Mabel Hall, 7-6-95, Butler Coll.
6 WC-Mabel Hall, 4-9-95, Butler Coll.
7 WC-Mabel Hall, n.d., probably June, 1894, Butler Coll.

8 There are numerous newspaper accounts of the event in the Dartmouth Coll., and an account in the *Missouri Historical Review*, III (October, 1908), p. 84. Mabel's mother and grandmother had also been married in this same house, and Churchill later used it in his novel, *The Crisis*.

9 WC-Louis M. Hall, 12-24-96.
10 WC-Shaw, 5-19-96, Shaw Coll., New York Public Library.
11 See WC-Shaw, 9-12-97, 9-15-97, and 9-19-97, Ibid.
12 WC-Shaw, 2-14-98, Ibid.
13 (New York: The Macmillan Company, 1897), p. 5.
14 J. Breckenridge Ellis, "Missourians Abroad No. 11: Winston Churchill," *Missouri Historical Review*, XVI (July, 1922), 519; Storms, "Winston Churchill," p. 13; WC-Shaw, 12-13-97, Shaw Coll.
15 *The Celebrity*, pp. 208 and 269.
16 Ibid., pp. 64-65.
17 *On Native Ground* (Garden City, New York: Doubleday and Co., 1956), p. 41.
18 New York *Times*, 10-5-01.

CHAPTER III

1 WC-Shaw, 10-19-97 and 10-28-97, Shaw Coll.
2 4-24-98, Ibid. See other letters to Shaw in April, 1898.
3 *Review of Reviews*, XVII (June, 1898), p. 682.
4 Along this same line it is not surprising to find Churchill supporting the British in the Boer War. See "My Confidence Man," MS, CC Coll., pp. 3-4.
5 See e.g. the long letter from George Whitelock to WC, 1-3-99, relative to the laws of inheritance and primogeniture in Maryland around 1770.
6 2-12-99, Mac. Rec.
7 6-27-99.
8 WC-Shaw, 8-26-99.
9 *My Early Life: A Roving Commission* (New York: Scribners, 1951), p. 217.
10 1-29-00, Mac. Rec.
11 6-9-00.
12 1-24-01.
13 Quoted in E. F. Harkins, *Little Pilgrimages Among The Men Who Have Written Famous Books* (Boston: L. C. Page and Co., 1902), p. 320.
14 Even at this private dinner the irrepressible Major Pond had a trick up his sleeve. He asked Churchill if he could have a picture taken of the

two men at supper. Winston Spencer, he said, did not object, but left it up to the novelist. The picture, Pond assured him, was not to be used for publicity; it was to be a souvenir for Winston Spencer's mother. There is no evidence that the picture was taken. (Pond-WC, 12-17-00).

CHAPTER IV

[1] WC-Shaw, 6-7-99, Shaw Coll.

[2] WC-M. J. Bachelder, 10-22-01. Bachelder was the secretary of the State Board of Agriculture.

[3] 38-26-99. Shaw Coll.; 8-31-99, Mac. Rec.

[4] WC-Brett, 6-21-99 and 6-25-99, Ibid.

[5] WC-F.W. Halsey, 1-17-99. The editor's reply indicates that Churchill's family matters were frequent subjects of his correspondents. Halsey-WC, 1-24-00.

[6] William H. Child, *History of the Town of Cornish New Hampshire* (Concord: Rumford Press, n.d.), I, 221. The section on the "city folks" was written by St. Gaudens.

[7] Story related to me by Churchill's son, Creighton, in an interview.

[8] Joe Mitchell Chapple, "A Day with the Author of 'Richard Carvel'," *National Magazine*, XI (December, 1899), p. 248.

[9] 4-24-98, Shaw Coll.; see also WC-Shaw, 3-8-98.

[10] WC-Brett, 6-5-99, Mac. Rec.

[11] WC-Brett, 7-28-99, 6-5-99, and 7-28-99, Ibid.

[12] Ibid.

[13] See letters Shaw Coll.

[14] On all of this see letters in Dartmouth Coll., CC Coll., the Missouri Historical Society, and Mac. Rec. For example, when he needed accurate information about the activities of the Emmigrant Aid Society, and particularly about the historical accuracy of having a Dr. Cutter appear in St. Louis on his way to Kansas in 1855, he wrote to Thomas Wentworth Higginson, who knew as much as anyone about the subject, to find out. See Higginson-WC, 12-11-00.

[15] *Book Reviews*, IX (June, 1901).

[16] *The Critic*, July, 1901.

[17] 9-4-01.

[18] (New York: The Macmillan Company, 1901), pp. 11-12.

[19] Ibid., p. 123.

[20] Ibid., p. 468.

[21] Ibid., p. 13.

[22] Ibid., pp. 24-25.

[23] Ibid., p. 54.

[24] Ibid., p. 26.

[25] Ibid., pp. 226, 463, and 30.

[26] Ibid., p. 287.

27Ibid., pp. 76 and 246.
28Ibid., p. 16.
29Ibid., p. 181.
30Ibid., pp. 338-39.
31Ibid., p. 36.
32Ibid., p. 312.
33*Independent*, LIII (June 20, 1901), p. 1435.
34Ibid. (September 5, 1901), p. 2097.
35Grant C. Knight, *The Strenuous Age in American Literature, 1900-1910* (Chapel Hill: University of North Carolina Press, 1954), p. 20.

CHAPTER V

1See letters, Dartmouth College Coll.
2Editor-WC, 9-14-01; R. W. Woodsworth-WC, 10-29-01; Elis. B. Kenyon-WC, 5-13-03; Philip Lindsley-WC, 7-29-01.
3WC-George S. Johns, 10-14-03.
410-13-03.
5See George F. Willey (ed.), *State Builders: An Illustrated Historical and Biographical Record of the State of New Hampshire at the Beginning of the Twentieth Century* (Manchester, N.H.: New Hampshire Publishing Co., 1903), p. 211. Henry H. Metcalf (ed.), *One Thousand New Hampshire Notables* (Concord: Rumford Printing Co., 1919), p. 193; *Granite Monthly*, XXXIV, pp. 344-45; additional information supplied by Mrs. Allan Butler.
68-14-01.
7Frank L. Greene-WC, September, 1901.
8TR-WC, 9-30-01 and 11-2-01; Philadelphia *Record*, 11-17-01.
9See letters between Proctor, Churchill, and Roosevelt.
10P. 7.
11Joseph T. Walker-WC, 2-26-01.
12See Gifford Pinchot-WC, 4-30-01; Philip W. Ayres-WC, 9-30-02; Manchester *Mirror and American*, 9-27-02; and clippings.
13The speech is reprinted in the St. Louis *Republican*, 7-7-01.
14See letters in the Dartmouth Coll., the Mac. Rec., Gazzam letters in CC Coll.; and notebook on trip in Ibid.
158-31-01, Mac. Rec.
16WSC-WC, 5-14-02, n.d.
17Notebook, CC Coll.
18Ibid.
196-23-02, Shaw Coll.
206-3-01.
216-29-06.
22Quoted in Manchester *Union*, 12-24-02.
23See letters; also Chouteau Coll. in Mo. Hist. Soc.
24Notebook entries dated 4-6-03, Butler Coll.

[25] Boston *Globe*, 1-8-03.

CHAPTER VI

[1] Brett-WC, 11-7-02.

[2] 7-1-01, Shaw Coll.

[3] WC-Pierre Chouteau, 3-17-04, Mo. Hist. Soc.; all other letters are in the Dartmouth Coll.

[4] (New York: The Macmillan Company, 1904), p. 596.

[5] See E. G. Titus, "Winston Churchill, American," p. 152.

[6] Albert E. Hancock, "The Historical Fiction of Mr. Churchill," *Outlook*, LXXVII (July 30, 1904), p. 753.

[7] Titus, p. 147; Frederic B. Irvin, "The Didacticism of Winston Churchill" (unpublished Ph.D. dissertation, Dept. of English, University of Pittsburgh, 1947), p. 126.

[8] Henry Nash Smith, *Virgin Land: The American West as Symbol and Myth* (New York: Vintage Books, 1957).

[9] *The Crossing*, p. 85.

[10] Ibid., p. 119.

[11] Ibid., p. 196.

[12] Ibid., pp. 165-66.

[13] Ibid., p. 89.

[14] Ibid., p. 338.

[15] Ibid., pp. 456-57. It is interesting that at the time of the events described in *The Crossing*, a Spanish observer, Luis de las Casas, Governor of Havana and Captain General of Louisiana and the Floridas, made similar statements. "This is an object of greatest importance to them [opening the Mississippi River] which they will not give up, nor can they desist . . . . The people of the Western settlements must overcome in time whatever obstacles oppose their departure to the sea and they will absorb Louisiana." (las Casas-Jaudenes and Viar, 4-5-94, quoted in James A. James, *The Life of George Rogers Clark* (Chicago: University of Chicago Press, 1928), p. 428.

[16] *The Crossing*, p. 89 and 111. The Blacks in this novel are the same simple, faithful retainers that were described in *The Crisis*. They are more sympathetically treated than the Indians, probably because they are submissive and accept the superiority of the white man.

[17] *The Crossing*, pp. 180-81.

[18] Ibid., pp. 594.

[19] Ibid., pp. 596-97.

[20] This is part of a draft dated 12-3-97; it evidently was not sent. The letter from him in the Mac. Rec. dated 12-4-97, is only three short paragraphs.

[21] Boston *Daily Advertiser*, 4-1-02. See also Herbert Croly, "Some Really Historical Novels," *The Lamp*, XXVI (July, 1903), 509-13.

[22] Henry Steele Commager, "Creating a New Nation: Based on *The Crossing*," *Scholastic*, LV (November 9, 1949), 13.

[23]*Contemporary American Novelists: 1900-1920* (New York: The Macmillan Company, 1922), p. 48.

[24]Alfred Kazin, "The Realistic Novel," *Paths of American Thought*, ed. Arthur Schlesinger, Jr. and Morton White (Boston: Houghton Mifflin Company, 1963), pp. 238-53.

[25]New Orleans *Daily Picayune*, 4-4-03.

CHAPTER VII

[1]WC-Sam Thorne, Jr., 10-16-02.

[2]See Guy Murchie-WC, 10-18-02.

[3]Rollins-WC, 7-30-02; and Edward N. Pearson-WC, 7-24-02.

[4]G. L. Deming-WC, 9-27-02.

[5]12-5-02.

[6]10-8-02.

[7]Concord *People and Patriot*, 2-5-03. See also *Granite Monthly*, XXXIV, 343; and clippings.

[8]1903 Manuel of the General Court; Concord *People and Patriot*, 1-21-03; Boston *Advertiser*, 2-4-03.

[9]See political letters, 1902.

[10]See clippings, especially those from the Concord *Daily Patriot* and the Manchester *News*.

[11]Undesignated newspaper clipping; Hollis-WC, 4-30-03.

[12]See clippings. The official discharge is dated 4-25-03; A. B. Woodworth-WC, 4-27-03; Hollis-WC, 4-30-03 and 5-22-03.

[13]7-13-04, Mac. Rec. The two articles were "Winston Churchill Says Convention Lacks Fight," Chicago *Examiner*, 6-22-04; and "Convention Inspiring to Winston Churchill," Ibid., 6-24-04.

[14]This account is based on vast numbers of newspaper clippings.

[15]Leon Burr Richardson, *William E. Chandler: Republican* (New York: Dodd, Mead and Co., 1940), p. 677.

[16]Clippings; see especially Manchester *Mirror*, 7-23-04; WC-Chandler, 9-19-04.

[17]The two men had corresponded about the possibility of establishing a Rural Free Delivery route from Windsor to Cornish, and in Currier's letter of August 10, 1904, he states, "I appreciate fully your kindness in supporting me for renomination. I try to remember my friends to return favors and I hope sometime to have an opportunity to reciprocate." See WC-George E. Fairbanks, 8-2-04.

[18]WC-Sisson, 8-9-04; reply, 8-18-04.

[19]12-21-04; see also the other letters between the two men in December, 1904.

[20]See e.g. WC-Sisson, 11-11-05 and 12-9-05; Sisson's letter of support is dated 12-6-05.

[21]Chandler-WC, 10-27-04; Churchill's 1905 pass is pasted on p. 134

of his 1911 datebook.

[22] 11-7-04; see also Chandler-WC, 12-5-04 and 1-8-05.

[23] 1-1-06.

CHAPTER VIII

[1] *Farewell to Reform*, p. 151.

[2] The above is taken from the summary included in WC-Brett, 4-3-06.

[3] See WC-S. L. Powers, 4-16-07; and WC-Harland Vaughn, 3-1-07.

[4] John C. Underwood, *Literature and Insurgency* (New York: Mitchell Kennerlay, 1914), p. 339.

[5] *Some American Story Tellers* (New York: Henry Holt and Company, 1911), pp. 61-62.

[6] *Coniston*, (New York: The Macmillan Company, 1906), p. 393.

[7] Ibid., pp. 427-28.

[8] Ibid., pp. 61, 67, 221, and 515.

[9] Ibid., pp. 542-43.

[10] Irvin, "The Didacticism of Winston Churchill," p. 156.

[11] *Coniston*, p. 98.

[12] Ibid., p. 57.

[13] See David E. Scherman and Rosemarie Redlich, *Literary America* (New York: Dodd, Mead and Co., 1952), p. 102, for a picture of the store; advertisements for the suits are in clippings.

[14] 8-5-06.

[15] 8-18-06.

[16] 9-7-06; see also Rhodes-WC, 9-10-06.

[17] Concord: Rumford Press, 1906.

[18] Bryant-Richardson, 1906; cited in Richardson's *Chandler*, p. 678.

[19] *Penn State Yankee* (State College, Pa.: Penn State Press), p. 40.

[20] See clippings.

[21] Richardson, pp. 73-74.

CHAPTER IX

[1] Justin McGrath-WC, 3-21-06; WC-McGrath, 3-23-06; WC-Leighton, 4-25-06.

[2] 6-7-06.

[3] 9-15-05. According to Pillsbury, Churchill was an enthusiastic supporter and he attacked him after the convention for his betrayal. Churchill, however, contended that his rather unenthusiastic letter endorsing Pillsbury's principles was his only communication with the candidate on this matter. See draft of a letter to be sent for publication to the Boston *Globe*, 9-29-06.

[4] WC-Clara M. Parsons, 12-22-11.

[5] Richardson, *Chandler*, pp. 677-80.

[6] See WC-Norman Hapgood, 7-31-06.

[7] 6-13-06.

[8] 6-14-06.

[9] *The Age of Reform* (New York: Alfred A. Knopf, 1956).

[10] See statement accepting candidacy, 7-4-06. Subsequent material, unless otherwise specified, is taken from this statement.

[11] Moses-Chandler, 7-16-06, Moses Coll., New Hampshire Historical Society; Chandler-Moses, 7-17-06, Ibid. See Moses-Chandler, 2-3-04; and WC-Moses, 4-28-03; and other letters in Ibid.

[12] Interview with J. Frank Davis, Boston *American*, 7-8-06.

[13] Stanley Johnson, Boston *Evening Transcript*, 7-31-06.

[14] See the mass of letters during that summer in boxes 57 and 58.

[15] Financial statement for 1906 campaign, submitted to Churchill by E. S. Cook. See letters, boxes 57 and 58, especially WC-Cook, 8-22-06.

[16] Copies of speeches and newspaper accounts.

[17] See WC-Rev. G. A. Furness, 7-23-06; and WC-Harry M. Cheney, 10-4-06.

[18] Remich-WC, 12-6-05; WC-Remich, 12-23-05; Remich-WC, 12-25-05. See also Remich-WC, 12-18-05; WC-Hollis, 7-13-06; WC-A. J. Miller, 7-14-06.

[19] See letters and clippings, summer 1906, especially Henry F. Hollis-WC, 7-7-06; Remich-WC, 8-13-06; and an eleven page poem by Arthur Pier, dated 1-18-07.

[20] The above is based on hundreds of clippings from newspapers all across the country.

[21] See letters, boxes 57, 58, and 89.

[22] Boston *Advertiser*, 7-25-06; clippings.

[23] The best accounts of the convention are those in the Boston *Herald*, 9-19-06; and in Richardson, *Chandler*.

[24] Boston *Globe*, 9-18-06.

[25] See clippings; Richardson, pp. 684-85.

[26] Boston *Transcript*, 9-9-06; *Outlook* LXXXIV (Sept. 29, 1906), 243.

[27] Quoted in Springfield *Republican*, 9-20-06, and many other papers.

[28] WC-James B. DeLand, 12-4-06, is one of dozens of letters expressing this sentiment.

[29] 9-20-06.

[30] Remick-E. S. Cook, 12-14-06; WC-R. U. Johnson, 1-2-07.

[31] Chandler-WC, 10-2-06; letters, box 57; Chandler-Moses, 12-25-06, Moses Coll.

[32] WC-J. F. Colby, 1-12-07.

[33] See letters box 66; and e.g. Dan Remich-WC, 1-19-07.

[34] First report in New York *Sun*, 1-25-07; second in Boston *American*, 4-6-07.

[35] N.d. The speech was obviously made in late 1906 or early in 1907.

[36] See Secretary to the President-WC, 1-12-07; Loeb-WC, 1-23-07; Washington *Evening Star*, 1-28-07.

[37]See correspondence between Roosevelt and Churchill, political letters, 1907.

[38]5-9-08.

[39]See e.g. Charles C. Walcutt, *The Romantic Compromise of Winston Churchill* (Ann Arbor: University of Michigan Press, 1951), pp. 17 and 30-31; Titus, "Winston Churchill, American," pp. 333-36; Irvin, "The Didacticism of Winston Churchill," p. 178; and Chamberlain, *Farwell to Reform*, pp. 152-57.

[40]Chamberlain, p. 155.

[41]2-8-08.

[42]2-11-08.

[43]See letters, 1908.

[44]WC-Benjamin Carpenter, 7-7-08.

[45]WC-Phoebe Storms, 3-18-41, in Storms, "Winston Churchill," p. 132.

CHAPTER X

[1]WC-Rev. W. S. Ely, 9-11-08.

[2]Reprinted in undesignated newspaper clipping.

[3]Quoted in Lowell, Mass. *Sun*, 12-12-07.

[4]See 1907 datebook, pp. 324-25; and flysheet entitled, "Statement to the Citizens of New Hampshire."

[5]4-24-08.

[6]Richardson, *Chandler*, p. 700.

[7]Copy in CC Coll.

[8]These sentiments are expressed many times in Churchill's letters. See political letters, 1907-08, and especially a lengthy letter to the editor of *Outlook*, 9-24-08.

[9]See political letters, 1908; also clippings.

[10]See clippings.

[11]See Churchill's letters to Roosevelt, which are numerous in 1907-08.

[12]See New York Globe, 1-9-08; and Richardson, pp. 700-01.

[13]Taft-WC, 2-29-08; WC-MHC, 3-4-08, Butler Coll.

[14]Churchill gives his version of the state convention in a letter to Theodore E. Burton, 4-24-08.

[15]WC-MHC, 7-27-08, Butler Coll.

[16]MacVeagh was not an active member but he did contribute to the campaign fund in 1908. See MacVeagh-WC, 10-12-08.

[17]WC-TR, 12-8-07.

[18]Quoted in WC-MHC, 4-3-09, CC Coll.

[19]See correspondence, 1909.

[20]WC-Ed Niles, 12-26-09.

[21]14-19-09.

[22]See letters, box 54; and Bass Coll., Dartmouth College Library.

[23]WC-Bass, 11-9-09, Bass Coll.

[24]WC-Bass, 11-2-09 and 12-19-09; 6-7-09, Bass Coll.

[25]See James Remick-WC, 12-23-09; WC-Bass, 12-26-09.

[26]Cummins-WC, 7-18-10; White letters are in box 77; *American Magazine*, LXIX (March, 1910), 581.

[27]On Bass' activities see Jewel Bellush, "Reform in New Hampshire: Robert Bass Wins the Primary," *New England Quarterly*, XXXV (December, 1962), 469-88. See also WC-MHC, 7-14-10, Butler Coll.; and draft speeches.

[28]See Bellush, p. 486; Bass-WC, 5-11-10, Bass Coll.; letter boxes 77 and 79.

[29]Drafts of speeches and clippings.

[30]5-28-10.

[31]WC-Roosevelt, 5-31-10; Roosevelt-WC, 6-21-10.

[32]WC-Bass, 5-23-10, Bass Coll.

[33]Clipping in 1911 datebook, p. 60.

[34]11-10-10.

[35]See WC-WHC, 7-14-10, Butler Coll.

[36]See Arthur Link, *Wilson the Road to the White House* (Princeton: Princeton University Press, 1947), p. 124.

[37]See newspaper account of meeting and speech in 1910 datebook, p. 182.

[38]WC-William J. Britton, 10-26-10.

[39]See Richardson, pp. 709-10.

[40]11-25-10; other letters in box 77.

[41]12-2-10 and 3-16-11.

[42]See Richardson, pp. 710-13.

CHAPTER XI

[1]1-27-11, Harvard University Library. His thinking on this matter may not have crystalized at this point, or, perhaps, he was not interested in a third party led by LaFollette. With regard to LaFollette's National Progressive Republican League, he wrote Bass, "The more I thought over the matter of joining the Progressive League, the more I believe that your decision was wise to refrain, at the present time at least from participation in it." 1-24-11, Bass Coll.

[2]Dan Remich-WC, 12-5-11.

[3]See Frank Musgrove-WC, 2-17-12; Allen Hollis-WC, 3-1-12. See drafts of speeches and copies of letters.

[4]Roosevelt-WC, 6-11-12; WC-Roosevelt, 6-21-12; see also WC-Roosevelt, 6-25-12.

[5]9-2-12, Chandler Coll., New Hampshire Historical Society, reprinted in Richardson, *Chandler*, p. 717.

[6]See clippings.

[7]See Bass- WC, 8-1-12; and WC-Bass, 8-5-12; and WC-F. P. Rowell, 8-29-12.

[8]WC-R. S. Childs, 10-7-09. See Brett-WC, 6-29-09.

[9]WC-G. H. Duncan, 2-17-11; WC-C. C. Hardy, 1-18-11.

[10]See e.g. Boston *Herald*, 4-29-03; *New Yorker*, 4-29-03; *Woman's Journal*, 4-11-03.

[11]WC-Mary Chase, 12-28-11; in reply to her letter, 12-20-11; WC-Mary Page, 2-28-12.

[12]9-7-12; Robbins letter is 9-3-12.

[13]Titled *To the Men and Women of New Hampshire*, formally addressed to Robert L. Manning, Chairman of the Provisional Executive Committee of the Progressive Party in New Hampshire, published by Ruemely Press. I have used Churchill's own draft of this statement which varies in some particulars from the published version, because I feel that it more closely reflects his own views. The published statement undoubtedly was revised by the other Insurgents.

[14]See e.g. WC-R. J. Mitchell, 9-9-12; WC-John Bishop, 9-9-12.

[15]See letters, Villard Coll., Harvard University Library; and undesignated speech, 1912.

[16]Undesignated speech, 1912.

[17]WC-W. C. Whipple, 3-11-12.

[18]See Richardson on general details; Robert Manning-WC, 3-15-13, on Republican-Progressive position.

[19]Ernest Poole, *Great White Hills of New Hampshire* (Garden City: Doubleday and Co., 1946), p. 249.

[20]Draft of Tremont speech.

[21]Ibid.

[22]Boston *Journal*, 12-6-12 and 4-23-13.

[23]5-17-13.

[24]Felker-WC, 4-8-13.

[25]WC-Bass, 2-20-14, Bass Coll.

[26]San Francisco *Examiner*, 4-13-13. See also Johnson-WC, 3-3-14.

[27]2-19-15.

[28]2-8-16, Bass Coll.

[29]"Roosevelt and His Friends," *Collier's*, LV (July 8, 1916), 15.

[30]WC-Hapgood, 9-15-16. See Sedgwick-WC, 8-15-16; Hapgood-WC, 9-11-16.

[31]Invitation to notification ceremony and reception in box 25. To the best of my knowledge he did not attend either affair. Request to speak is Ralph D. Cole-WC, 8-13-16. See W. Cameron Forbes-WC, 8-22-16; WC-Forbes, 8-28-16.

[32]See WC-Garland, 2-20-16; Garland-WC, 5-3-16 and 10-17-16, Garland Coll.

[33]9-15-16.

[34]10-6-16, Garland Coll.

CHAPTER XII

[1] 1909 datebook; and WC-W. B. Parker, 7-23-06.

[2] 1909 datebook, p. 215.

[3] Most of these letters are in the Dartmouth Coll.

[4] See letters; Amos R. Wells-WC, 6-28-09; John S. Phillips-WC, 9-6-10.

[5] N. C. Magennis-WC, 3-14-07.

[6] This is the impression I have gathered from the many personal letters in the Butler Coll., from members of the family, and from others who knew her. See e.g. WC-MHC, 3-4-08 and 3-9-08, Butler Coll. Mrs. Churchill, according to her daughter, always believed that her husband would be a famous man and, consequently, saved all of his letters.

[7] See WC-Captain Pope, 7-20-97, Butler Coll. Churchill's correspondence with his daughter is in Ibid.

[8] See letters, Garland Coll.; also Dartmouth Coll.

[9] 1909 datebook. See also WC-Joe Gazzam, 12-26-09; undated note, Mrs. Butler-author. The fact that Mrs. Gazzam went to live with Winston, rather than with her own son, although it indicated the depth of the attachment on both sides, was because Joe was a mining engineer whose work took him to South Africa where she would have been less comfortable than at Harlakenden.

[10] (New York: The Macmillan Company, 1910), p. 173.

[11] Brett-WC, 5-13-10.

[12] See e.g. Los Angles *Times*, 4-10-10; *Christian Work*, 4-9-10; and clippings.

[13] R. A. Scott-James, London *Daily News*, 4-18-10; Blackham *Times*, 5-21-10; Mary Semple Scott-WC, 5-20-10; Titus, "Winston Churchill, American," p. 359; Knight, *Strenuous Age*, p. 198.

[14] Knight, Ibid.

[15] WC-Mabel and John, 1-10-10, Butler Coll.

[16] 1910 datebook.

[17] Ibid.

[18] Ibid., p. 122.

[19] Ibid., p. 134.

CHAPTER XIII

[1] Related to the author by Creighton Churchill.

[2] P. 165.

[3] Brett-WC, 5-13-10.

[4] Datebooks 1910 and 1911. Some of the items he mentioned in letters to various acquaintances. He was also receiving a number of books on religion in England. Charles W. Coit-WC, 2-28-11.

[5] Brett-WC, 12-12-10; for progress on novel see 1910 datebook.

[6] WC-Roland Phillips, 6-22-12.

[7] *National*, IVC (June 12, 1913), 599.

[8] Rex Glendening, "Relation of the Novel to Present Social Unrest,"

Bookman, XL (November, 1914), 303; "The 'Latest American Religion' and Its Critics," *Religion and Ethics*, n.d., clipping.

[9]1914 datebook, p. 1.

[10]7-28-13.

[11]7-27-13.

[12]Mahan (August 30, 1913), pp. 277, 289-90; Churchill (October 11, 1913), pp. 479-80; see also editorial, Ibid., p. 478.

[13]*Before I Forget* (New York: Doubleday, Doran and Co., 1937), p. 382. Rascoe notes that these quotations are from articles he wrote in 1913.

[14]Mercer D. Johnson, *Forum*, LVI (August, 1916), 176.

CHAPTER XIV

[1]11-16-12, Mac. Rec.; WHC-Brett, 1-2-13, Ibid.

[2]Clippings and 1913 datebook. Churchill's own denial of these rumors is in the New York *Times*, 4-16-13.

[3]11-12-12, Mac. Rec. Brett made one further try and Churchill again refused; see letters, Ibid.

[4]WC-Brett, 10-27-13, Ibid; 11-1-13, Garland Coll.

[5]The best record of these matters is in the WC-Brett Correspondence, 1913-14, Mac. Rec., esp. 5-8-13.

[6]To Churchill, 1-21-14.

[7]N.d., sometime around 8-16-11, Mac. Rec.; to Brett, 1-10-11, Ibid.

[8]Murchie-WC, 3-22-13; see clippings, 1913.

[9]Murchie-WC, 11-19-13; MHC-WC, 2-16-14; WC-Murchie, 2-7-14; Arthur Link, *Wilson the New Freedom* (Princeton: Princeton University Press, 1956), p. 464; Link, *Wilson Confusion and Crisis* (Princeton: Princeton University Press, 1964), pp. 2-3.

[10]WC-Brett, 7-30-15, Mac. Rec.

[11]3-5-15.

[12]See F. A. Duneka-WC, 2-21-12; WC-Duneka, 2-23-12; also New York *Sun*, 1-21-16; and dinner program for the Independence Day dinner. See manuscripts for speeches; also Henry C. King-WC, 2-12-14; H. J. Dickerson-WC, 4-12-11; and A. Ross Hill-WC, 5-23-16.

[13]See letters in boxes 15 and 91; also pamphlets.

[14]This analysis is a composite of Churchill's religious addresses, his published articles, and material in his datebooks. The same basic ideas are expressed in each and no citations will be given except for direct quotations.

[15]"The University as a Religious Center," MS, p. 10.

[16]Ibid., pp. 11-12.

[17]1914 datebook, p. 245.

[18]Windsor Address, p. 8.

[19]Ibid., pp. 14-15.

[20]Undesignated notebook kept for notes on *The Inside of the Cup*, CC Coll.

[21] "Religion of the Spirit," p. 371.

[22] Speech to League of Political Education, MS, p. 17.

[23] Windsor Address, p. 11.

[24] 1911 datebook, p. 5.

[25] 1913 datebook, p. 8.

[26] "The University as a Religious Center," p. 5.

[27] "Modern Government and Christianity," MS, pp. 18-19.

[28] 1913 datebook, pp. 182-83.

[29] Typical Catholic reaction is that of the Boston *Pilot*, 12-30-16.

[30] Boton *Transcript*, 1-8-17. See also the Boston *Sunday Globe*, 12-17-16.

CHAPTER XV

[1] WC-R. A. Douglas, 1-9-11.

[2] 1913 datebook, pp. 264-65.

[3] 11-18-12.

[4] 11-28-13, Mac. Rec.

[5] 11-5-13, Ibid.

[6] (New York: The Macmillan Company, 1915), pp. 456-57.

[7] Ibid., pp. 458-59.

[8] Ibid., p. 459.

[9] Ibid., p. 496.

[10] *Harper's*, CXXXII (January, 1916), 249-56.

[11] Ibid., p. 250.

[12] 11-5-13, Mac. Rec.

[13] LIX (July, 1915), 63.

CHAPTER XVI

[1] WC-Garland, 12-12-16, Garland Coll.

[2] See letters between Garland, Matthews, and Churchill in the Matthews Coll., Columbia University Library; Garland Coll.; and Dartmouth Coll.

[3] 1913 datebook, p. 275.

[4] See letters; Kauser-WC, 1-12-14; letters, August, 1916.

[5] New York *Evening Mail*, 12-23-16.

[6] *Leader*, 3-2-17.

[7] See Springfield *Republican*, 1-1-17.

[8] Boston *Globe*, 3-27-17.

[9] The following is from the manuscript version of that speech in CC Coll.

[10] XXXIV (June 9, 1951), p. 4

[11] Sinclair-Warren I. Titus, 12-1-55. Quoted in Titus, "Winston Churchill, American," p. 514.

[12]*Money Writes*, (Albert and Charles Boni, 1927), pp. 115 and 44-45.
[13]7-14-08.
[14]*The New Age,* 5-19-10, p. 62
[15]See letters Sinclair Coll.; N. J. Bartlett-WC, 11-30-13; WC-Mr. More-house, 10-22-13.
[16]Titus, p. 431.
[17]P. 498.
[18]6-17-13.
[19]6-24-13, Library of Congress.
[20]WC-Sinclair, 9-1-14 and 9-5-14, Sinclair Coll.
[21]6-15-13.
[22]*Money Writes*, p. 115.
[23]4-10-14; see also Eleanor Baldwin-WC, 8-17-13.
[24]7-5-13, Sinclair Coll.
[25]7-28-13. This letter Sinclair said was being written on a typewriter that had just arrived half-demolished, and I have taken the liberty of correcting the many errors that are obviously typographical.
[26]WC-Sinclair, 8-11-13, Sinclair Coll.
[27]1-23-15. He states in a postscript that some autograph fiend had absconded with Roosevelt's letter, but he did enclose an enthusiastic endorsement by Louis Untermeyer.
[28]2-1-15.
[29]WC-Sinclair, 8-11-13, Sinclair Coll.
[30]Titus, pp. 4-10-11.
[31]Cleveland *Plain Dealer*, 5-19-08.
[32]*Times*, 6-6-15; Clipping from *Horizons; Nation*, C (June 24, 1915), 711.

CHAPTER XVII

[1]1916 datebook, p. 101.
[2](New York: The Macmillan Co., 1917), p. 232.
[3]Ibid., p. 156.
[4]Ibid., p. 398.
[5]Ibid., p. 125.
[6]Ibid., pp. 334, 427, and 386.
[7]Ibid., p. 13.
[8]Ibid., p. 58.
[9]Ibid., p. 102 and 107.
[10]Ibid., p. 278.
[11]Ibid., p. 390 and 162-63.
[12]Ibid., p. 438.
[13]Ibid., p. 162.
[14]Brett-WC, 10-10-17, Mac. Rec.
[15]CVI, 695; clippings.

CHAPTER XVIII

[1]Boston *Courier*, 6-23-17; *Star*, 6-17-17.

[2]David E. Cronon (ed.), *The Cabinet Diaries of Josephus Daniels, 1913-21* (Lincoln: University of Nebraska Press, 1963), p. 148.

[3]1917 datebook, pp. 132-46.

[4]Ibid.

[5]*Wilson the New Freedom*, p. 124.

[6]Ibid., pp. 122-25.

[7]Hollis-FDR, 4-17-17, Franklin D. Roosevelt Library; WC-FDR is 4-7-17, Ibid.; FDR-WC, 4-18-17, Ibid.

[8]See Frank Freidel, *Franklin D. Roosevelt: The Apprenticeship* (Boston: Little, Brown and Co., 1952), pp. 308-09; WC-FDR, 5-25-17, Roosevelt Library.

[9]Datebook, p. 181; see also Ibid., pp. 155-57; and Cronon, p. 223.

[10]WC-FDR, 7-22-17.

[11]CC Coll. The draft is in the CC Coll.; a copy of the memorandum is in the Roosevelt Library.

[12]Wilson-WC, 8-3-17, CC Coll.; FDR-Mrs. Roosevelt, 7-26-17, in Elliott Roosevelt, *F.D.R. His Personal Letters, 1905-28* (New York: Duell, Sloan and Pearce, 1948), p. 354. In his editorial notes, Elliott Roosevelt mistakenly identifies the Winston Churchill mentioned in the letter as the British Minister of Munitions, Winston Spencer Churchill.

[13]FDR-Mrs. Roosevelt, 8-17-17, Ibid., pp. 356-57.

[14]6-12-17, Bass Coll.

[15]See especially pp. 192 and 237.

[16]See datebook, pp. 237-40.

[17]This is taken from the last two pages of a three page letter of which the first page is missing. It is in Mrs. Churchill's handwriting, is obviously to Churchill, and must have been written late in July or early in August, 1917, CC Coll. See also letters in separate folder, prepared by Mrs. Churchill, CC Coll.

[18]The above is contained in letters to John and Mabel, separate folder, CC Coll.

[19]Letters Mac. Rec.; separate folder, CC Coll.

[20](New York: The Macmillan Company, 1918), pp. 19 and 20.

[21]Ibid., p. 84.

[22]Ibid., pp. 31 and 67.

[23]Ibid., pp. 5, 7, and 8.

[24]Ibid., p. 32.

[25]Ibid., pp. 99-100.

[26]Ibid., p. 106.

[27]Ibid., p. 109.

[28]Ibid., pp. 117 and 120.

[29]E. J. Ridgway was collecting the views of twenty distinguished Americans on the peace terms they would like to see brought about, for a

symposium in the March issue of *Everybody's*. I have used the draft of Churchill's reply.

[30]*A Traveler in Wartime*, pp. 121 and 122.

[31]Ibid., pp. 124-25.

[32]Ibid., p. 126.

[33]Ibid., p. 129 and 130.

[34]Ibid., p. 147.

[35]Ibid., p. 150.

[36]Ibid., p. 159, 160 and 167.

[37]Ibid., pp. 167-68 and 170.

[38]Ibid., p. 171.

[39]7-21-18.

CHAPTER XIX

[1]See WC-William Allen White, 4-26-18, Library of Congress; WC-Wilbur Cross, 3-30-18, Cross Coll., Yale University Library; WC-Burgess, 6-4-19, Bancroft Library; also Mac. Rec.

[2]See Blakely Hall-WC, 1-24-19, CC Coll.

[3](New York: The Macmillan Company, 1919), p. 80.

[4]*Republican*, 11-16-19; *Nation*, CX (January 17, 1920), 79; *Call*, 1-26-20.

[5]The censorship problem is discussed in a series of letters, January through April, 1919, B. H. Stern-WC, CC Coll.

[6]Letters, Mac. Rec., especially MHC-Brett, 1-12-19.

[7]All quotations from Jonathan MS unless otherwise indicated.

[8]CC Coll.

[9]Notebook, Butler Coll.

[10]See WC-MHC, 7-25-19, 7-28-19, and 8-19-19, CC Coll.

[11]On writing output see separate notebook, Butler Coll.

[12]In Dartmouth Coll.

[13]MS, in Dartmouth Coll.

CHAPTER XX

[1]12-21-19, Mac. Rec.

[2]9-17-19, CC Coll.

[3]CC Coll.

[4]See WC-MHC, 10-13-19, 12-29-19, and February-March, 1920, Ibid.

[5]Letters, Mac. Rec.

[6]MHC-Brett, 1-6-20, Ibid. See also WC-Brett, 5-14-21, Ibid.

[7]WC-Brett, 9-24-21 and 10-1-21, Ibid.

[8]MS, pp. 232 and 147.

[9]Ibid., pp. 233-34.

[10]Brett-WC, 10-6-21, Mac. Rec.

[11]12-30-21, Ibid.

[12]1-1-23, Ibid.

[13]WC-Brett, 12-27-23; Brett-WC, 1-16-24.

[14]*North American Review*, CCLV (April, 1922), 483-500; New York *Times*, 3-26-22. Hamlin Garland, who attended the lecture, gives a good description of the impression Churchill made on the audience in *My Friendly Contemporaries* (New York: The Macmillan Company, 1932), pp. 399-400.

[15]2-28-22, Yale University Library.

CHAPTER XXI

[1]"Who are the 'Classic Authors' of Today?" *The Literary Digest*, CXXX (March 15, 1924), pp. 46-54. *The Crisis* was listed as the sixth highest in a list of the ten best books published since 1900, Ibid., p. 48.

[2]WC-Mrs. Vanamee, 11-15-23. The other letters referred to are WC-Arnold Brunner, 5-28-23; Mrs. William Vanamee-WC, 11-13-23. All are in the American Academy of Arts and Letters.

[3]Brett-WC, 10-15-24; WC-Brett, 11-18-24, Mac. Rec.

[4]This account is based upon dozens of such letters, CC Coll.

[5]Letters CC Coll. For obvious reasons, I have omitted the names of the individuals involved. On one occasion Churchill also addressed the inmates of the Vermont State Prison (in 1923), offering to speak with any of them individually if they thought he could help them.

[6]WC-Una Hunt, 2-7-22, Butler Coll.

[7]WC-MHC, 11-20-23, CC Coll.; Blanch L. Daniels-WC, 1-29-24, Ibid.

[8]11-1-24, Ibid.

[9]WC-MHC, 10-8-22, Ibid.

[10]10-11-23.

[11]Related to the author by Creighton Churchill.

[12]See WC-MCB, 11-24-24, Butler Coll.

[13]WC-MCB, 2-2-25, Ibid.

[14]Related by Creighton Churchill.

[15]The painting habits of the Churchills were related to me by various members of the family. The paintings themselves, of which there are hundreds, are in the possession of the family.

[16]7-25-25, Mac. Rec.

[17]MS in CC Coll.

[18]Stanley J. Kunitz, *Authors Today and Yesterday: A Companion Volume to Living Authors* (New York: H. W. Wilson Co., 1933), p. 157. Churchill made a similar reply to this kind of request in 1937. See WC-Mr. Millett, 5-3-37, Yale University Library.

[19]For figures see royalty statements and Mac. Rec.

[20]1-2-30, Butler Coll. See Selig-WC, 1-8-37. At the bottom of the letter Churchill wrote, "I am not selling any rights."

[21]See Halsey Malone-WC, 2-10-37 and 2-19-37.

[22]WC-MCB, 1-3-30, Butler Coll.

[23]WC-MHC, 4-4-30, Ibid. Parrish openly contended that Churchill was a man possessed in the years after 1919. Before that time Parrish found Churchill interesting and full of fun; after 1919 he found him something of a bore, a man who could talk on only one topic. These sentiments were conveyed to the author in no uncertain terms in an interview, September, 1962.

[24]4-26-30.

[25]On Herrick see Blake Nevius, *Robert Herrick the Development of a Novelist* (Berkeley: University of California Press, 1962).

[26]See WC-Brett, 9-20-00, Mac. Rec.

[27]Letter to Nevius, n.d., cited in *Robert Herrick*, p. 318.

[28]Notebook marked "Manuscript Diary Notes before Oriente," CC Coll.

[29]See WC-A. B. Lane, 11-27-32, Yale University Library.

[30]See WC-Mr. and Mrs. Butler, 11-20-35, Butler Coll.

[31]12-23-32, CC Coll.

[32]This part of the letter was copied by Creighton in a letter to his mother, 1-27-33, Butler Coll.

[33]WC-Brett, 5-23-34, Mac. Rec.; reply, 5-28-34, Ibid.

[34]William MacDonald-George P. Brett, Jr., 11-2-34, Ibid.

[35]WC-Brett, Jr., 12-10-34, Ibid.; Brett, Jr.-WC, 12-13-34, Ibid.

[36]Roelker-author, 11-13-62; Roelker-Creighton Churchill, 3-19-47, Butler Coll.

[37]CC-Mrs. Butler, 12-19-38, Ibid.

[38]Scribner-WC, 11-14-35; Mrs. Knopf-WC, 1-3-39.

CHAPTER XXII

[1](Philadelphia: Dorrance and Co., 1940), p. 5.

[2]Ibid., p. 6.　　　　　　　　　　[3]Ibid., p. 7.

[4]Ibid., p. 14.　　　　　　　　　　[5]Ibid., pp. 15-16.

[6]Ibid., pp. 17-18.　　　　　　　　[7]Ibid., pp. 18 and 19.

[8]Ibid., p. 25.　　　　　　　　　　[9]Ibid., p. 27.

[10]Ibid., pp. 29-30.　　　　　　　　[11]Ibid., pp. 31 and 32-33.

[12]Ibid., pp. 40-41.　　　　　　　　[13]Ibid., pp. 48 and 49-50.

[14]Ibid., p. 78.　　　　　　　　　　[15]Ibid., pp. 85 and 86.

[16]Ibid., pp. 91 and 93.　　　　　　[17]Ibid., p. 111.

[18]Ibid., pp. 113, 115, and 116.　[19]Ibid., pp. 121 and 122.

[20]Ibid., pp. 131-32.　　　　　　　[21]Ibid., pp. 138-39.

[22]Ibid., pp. 158 and 159.　　　　[23]Ibid., pp. 185-86.

[24]Ibid., p. 188.　　　　　　　　　[25]Ibid., pp. 192-93.

[26]Ibid., p. 204.

[27]See undesignated notebook, 1931, CC Coll.

[28]*The Uncharted Way*, pp. 221, 222, 223, 224.
[29]Ibid., pp. 244-45.   [30]Ibid., p. 248.
[31]XXXV (June 17, 1940), p. 88.

CHAPTER XXIII

[1]WC-Lumen Goodenough, 3-20-42.

[2]WC-Una Hunt, 6-1-45, Butler Coll.

[3]Kiffin Rockwell-author, 12-20-65.

[4]See voluminous correspondence between the two men, Dartmouth Coll., Butler Coll., and CC Coll.

[5]Unidentified newspaper clipping, Butler Coll., see WC-Mrs. Butler, 11-13-42.

[6]WC-Una Hunt, 6-1-45, Butler Coll.

[7]Ibid.

[8]Mary Semple Scott-Joe Gazzam, 3-19-47, Butler Coll.

[9]Irvin H. Hart, "The Most Popular Authors of Fiction between 1900 and 1925," *Publisher's Weekly*, CVII (February 21, 1925), 619-21.

[10]Frank L. Mott, *Golden Multitudes* (New York: The Macmillan Company, 1947), pp. 312-13.

[11]Irvin, p. 57.

[12]Macfarlane, *Collier's,* LII, 24.

[13]Lloyd W. Griffin, "Winston Churchill," *More Books*, XXIII (November, 1948), 338.

[14]Russell Blankenship, *American Literature as an Expression of the National Mind* (New York: Henry Holt and Co., 1931), pp. 563-64.

[15]Carl Van Doren, *The American Novel, 1789-1939* (New York: The Macmillan Company, 1940), p. 261; *The American Mind* (New Haven: Yale University Press, 1950), p. 256.

[16]*Prejudices, First Series* (New York: Alfred A. Knopf, 1924), p. 131; Prejudices, *Fourth Series* (New York: Alfred A. Knopf, 1924), p. 291.

[17]Pollard, *Their Day in Court* (New York: Neale Publishing Co., 1909), p. 194; Van Doren, *Contemporary American Novelists: 1900-1920* (New York: The Macmillan Company, 1922), p. 51.

[18]Morris E. Spear, *The Political Novel* (New York: Oxford University Press, 1924), p. 321.

BIBLIOGRAPHY

I. MANUSCRIPT COLLECTIONS

The largest collection of Churchill papers, some fifty linear feet, is in Baker Library at Dartmouth College. This collection consists of eighty-four boxes of correspondence and thirty-one large scrapbooks. As the latter contain virtually every newspaper story that mentioned Churchill and copies of all the book reviews that appeared before 1915, they constitute a body of material that could not be duplicated in a lifetime. Unfortunately, there are no scrapbooks for the period after 1915 or before 1898. Equally valuable are Churchill's carefully kept datebooks or diaries from 1902 to 1915. The collection also contains the holograph notes and drafts, type-scripts and galleys for most of his novels and the dramatizations of the novels, in addition to miscellaneous notebooks, photographs (including some of the sets used in the plays), honorary degrees, some pamphlets, a number of unpublished stories, and several versions of his unpublished novel, "The Green Bay Tree."

Virtually the only sources of information about Churchill's life during the period after about 1916 are the large number of letters, personal papers, manuscripts, notebooks, photographs, and pictures that remain in the possession of Churchill's surviving son and daughter, Creighton Church-ill and Mrs. Allan Butler. These documents also are crucial for an under-standing of Churchill's private life and his childhood years.

Three other collections are particularly important. These are: the cor-respondence and records of The Macmillan Company, and the Albert Shaw Papers in the New York Public Library; and the Upton Sinclair Papers in Lilly Library, the University of Indiana.

In addition to the above there is Churchill correspondence in the following collections:

Franklin D. Roosevelt Library
Library of Congress
 Hamilton Wright Mabie Papers
 William Allen White Papers
 Benjamin H. Ticknor Papers
 Theodore Roosevelt Papers
National Archives, Navy and Military Service Branch
New York Public Library
 Albert Sterner Papers
 Century Collection
 Anthony Collection
Dartmouth College, Baker Library
 Robert Bass Collection
New Hampshire Historical Society
 William E. Chandler Collection
 George Moses Collection

James Lyford Collection
Missouri Historical Society
American Academy of Arts and Letters
Columbia University Library
    Brander Matthews Papers
    Ripley Hitchcock Papers
    George Rublee Memoirs in the Oral History Collection
University of Southern California Library
    Hamlin Garland Papers
West Virginia University Library
    Barbe Papers
University of California, Bancroft Library
Historical Society of Pennsylvania
Yale University Library
University of Virginia, Alderman Library
    C. W. Kent Collection
    Baker-Wheeler Collection
    Gorges Collection
University of Virginia, Clifton Waller-Barrett Library
Boston University Library
Harvard University, The Houghton Library
Cleveland Public Library
Haverford College Library
    Charles Roberts Autograph Collection
Pennsylvania State University Library
    Fred Lewis Pattee Collection

A number of people have been kind enough to send me letters that they received from Churchill, and I conducted interviews with: Professor Nancy Roelker (who worked with Churchill on *The Uncharted Way*), Maxfield Parrish, and the late Mr. and Mrs. John Churchill. My discussions and correspondence with Creighton Churchill, Mrs. Allan Butler and Dr. Allan Butler have been an invaluable source of information.

II. PRIMARY SOURCES, PUBLISHED

A. Novels

Churchill, Winston. *The Celebrity*. New York: The Macmillan Company, 1898.
_____. *Coniston*. New York: The Macmillan Company, 1906.
_____. *The Crisis*. New York: The Macmillan Company, 1901.
_____. *The Crossing*. New York: The Macmillan Company, 1904.
_____. *The Dwelling Place of Light*. New York: The Macmillan Company, 1917.

————. *A Far Country.* New York: The Macmillan Company, 1915.

————. *The Inside of the Cup.* New York: The Macmillan Company, 1913.

————. *A Modern Chronicle.* New York: The Macmillan Company, 1910.

————. *Mr. Crewe's Career.* New York: The Macmillan Company, 1908.

————. *Mr. Keegan's Elopement.* New York: The Macmillan Company, 1903.

————. *Richard Carvel.* New York: The Macmillan Company, 1899.

B. Non-Fiction Books

Churchill, Winston. *A Traveller in War-time; With an Essay on the American Contribution and the Democratic Idea.* New York: The Macmillan Company, 1918.

————. *The Uncharted Way.* Philadelphia: Dorrance and Company, 1940.

C. Poems and Plays

Churchill, Winston. *The Crisis: A Play in Four Acts.* New York: Samuel French, 1927.

————. *Dr. Jonathan.* New York: The Macmillan Company, 1919.

————. *The Faith of Frances Craniford.* No place or publisher listed, 1917.

————. "The Rose Light Lingered on the Hill," *The Century,* LXIII (March, 1902), 738.

————. "A Sonnet," *Collier's,* XLIV (January 1, 1908), 8.

————. *The Title-Mart; A Comedy in Three Acts.* New York: The Macmillan Company, 1905.

————. "A Tryst," *Scribner's,* XXXI (February, 1902), 144.

D. Magazine and Journal Articles; Short Stories

Churchill, Winston. "Admiral Dewey: A Character Sketch." *Review of Reviews,* XVII (June, 1898), 676-88.

————. "The Author and His Critic," *Bookman,* IX (July, 1899), 403-04.

————. "The Battle with Cervera's Fleet off Santiago," *Review of Reviews,* XVIII (August, 1898), 153-67.

————. "Glory of the States: New Hampshire," see "Something Hard is Disolving."

————. "Interesting People: George P. Brett," *American Magazine,* LXXI (March, 1911), 601-02.

————. "Ireland and World Democracy, Evolved from a Talk with T. P. O'Connor," *Collier's,* LIX (August 11, 1917), 8-9.

————. "The Knowledge of Good and Evil," *The North American Review*, CCXV (April, 1922), 483-500.

————. "A Matter for the Individual to Settle," *Hearst's Magazine*, XXI (June, 1912), 2395.

————. "Modern Government and Christianity," *Atlantic Monthly*, CIX (January, 1912)), 12-22.

————. "The Modern Quest for Religion," *The Century*, LXXXVII (December, 1913), 169-74.

————. "Mr. Keegan's Elopement," *The Century*, LII (June, 1896), 215-27.

————. "Naval Organization, American and British," *Atlantic Monthly*, CXX (August, 1917), 277-84.

————. "By Order of the Admiral," *The Century*, LVI (July, 1898), 323-41.

————. "Our Common-Sense Marriages," *Good Housekeeping*, LVII (July, 1913), 53-59.

————. "A Plea for the American Tradition," *Harper's*, CXXXII (January, 1916), 249-56.

————. "The Progressives' Creed," *The Progressive Bulleting*, I (September 16, 1912), 4.

————. "Religion in Government," *The Living Church*, XLVIII (November 16, 1912), 86-87.

————. "The Religion of the Spirit," *The Christian Work and Evangelist* (March 21, 1914).

————. "A Reply to Admiral Mahan," *The Churchman*, (October 1, 1913).

————. "Roosevelt and His Friends," *Collier's*, LV (July 8, 1916), 15.

————. "Something Hard is Dissolving," *American Magazine*, LXXXII (September, 1916), 37.

————. "The Supreme Question Facing Our City and Country Today," *The American City*, CCI (January, 1919), 1-5. Also published as the introduction to *St. Louis After the War* (ed.), Harland Bartholomew (St. Louis: Nixon-Jones Printing Company, 1918).

————. "An Uncharted Way," *Yale Review*, XI (April, 1922), 526-45.

————. "On the Wilderness Trail," *Current Literature*, XXXVII (July, 1904), 38-41.

E. Newspaper Articles and Miscellaneous

Churchill, Winston, "America Must Trap 'Sea Rats' to Curb Victorious Germany," Philadelphia *Public Ledger*, 6-16-17.

————. "An Appreciation of Crater Lake National Park," Pamphlet published by the United States Railroad Administration, National Park Series, July, 1919.

————. Introduction to Richard Harding Davis, *The Bar Sinister*. New York: Scribner's, 1916.

_____. "Books I Should Like to Have Written," Washington *Star*, 11-11-06.

_____. "A Call for the Marine Corp," New York *Times*, 6-14-17.

_____. "Free Passes as Retaining Fees," Boston Herald Company, 1906.

_____. " 'Hugh Wynne' in Court Dress," *Book Buyer*, XIX (December, 1899), 369-72.

_____. "To the Men and Women of New Hampshire: An Open Letter," Concord, New Hampshire: Ruemely Press, 1912.

_____. "Midshipman Churchill OK's the Navy," Boston *Transcript*, 6-12-17.

_____. "The Political Situation in New Hampshire," Boston *Herald*, 8-23-08.

_____. "Proportion of Fiction and History in My New Novel," New York *Journal*, 5-25-01.

_____. "Situation Unique Says Churchill," Boston *Herald*, 9-9-06.

_____. "Threat of Hell Sunday's Weapon," Boston *American*, 12-19-16.

_____. "Two Minds for One," New York *Times*, 3-26-22.

_____. "University Congratulated Upon Prompt Response," Harvard *Crimson*, 2-21-17.

_____. "Unrest Behind Lines," New York *Times*, 12-2-17.

_____. "Winston Churchill Exposes Lobby of Railroads in New Hampshire," Boston *Herald*, 8-25-08.

_____. "Winston Churchill on Man's True Nature," Baltimore *News*, 1-3-14.

INDEX